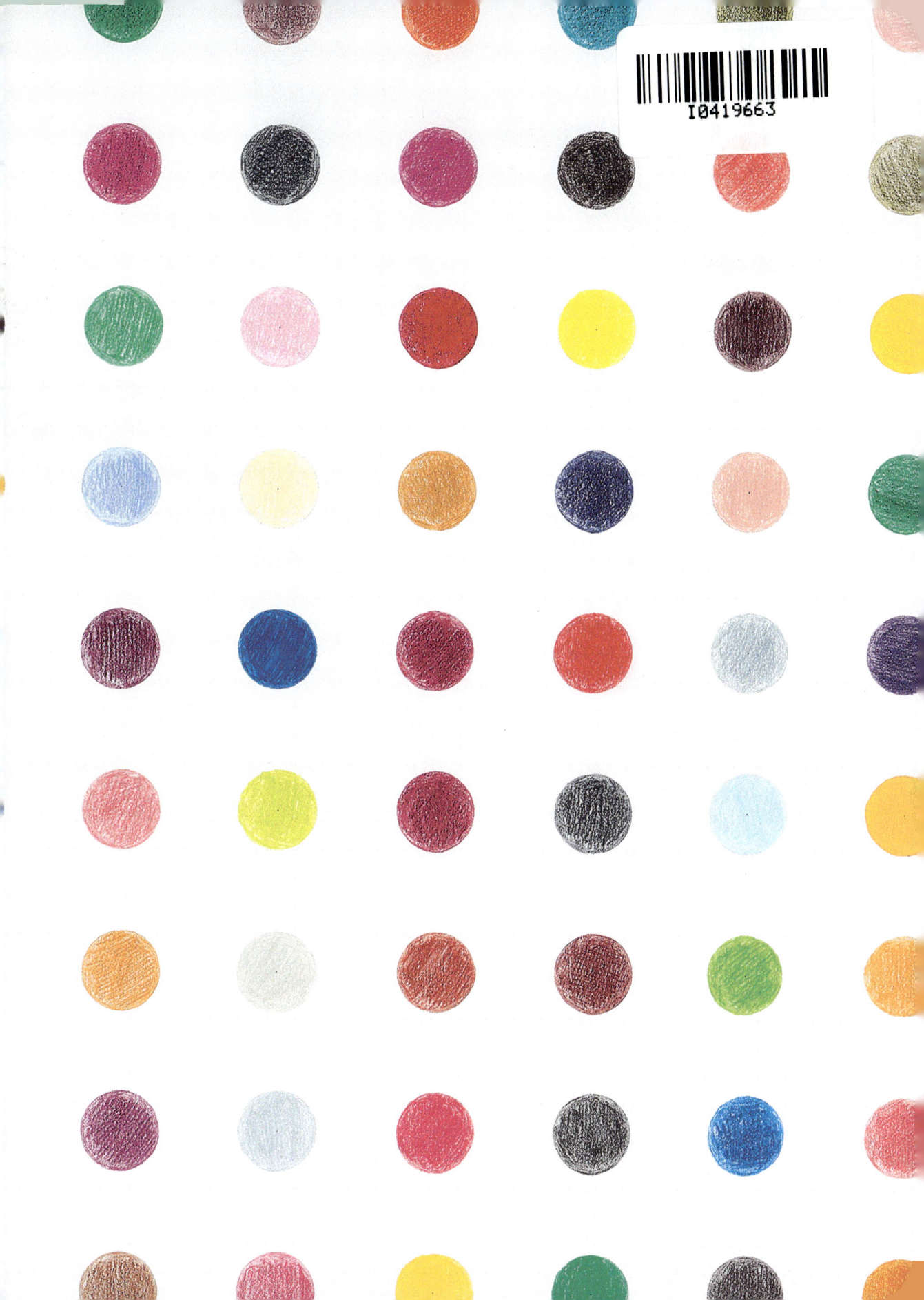

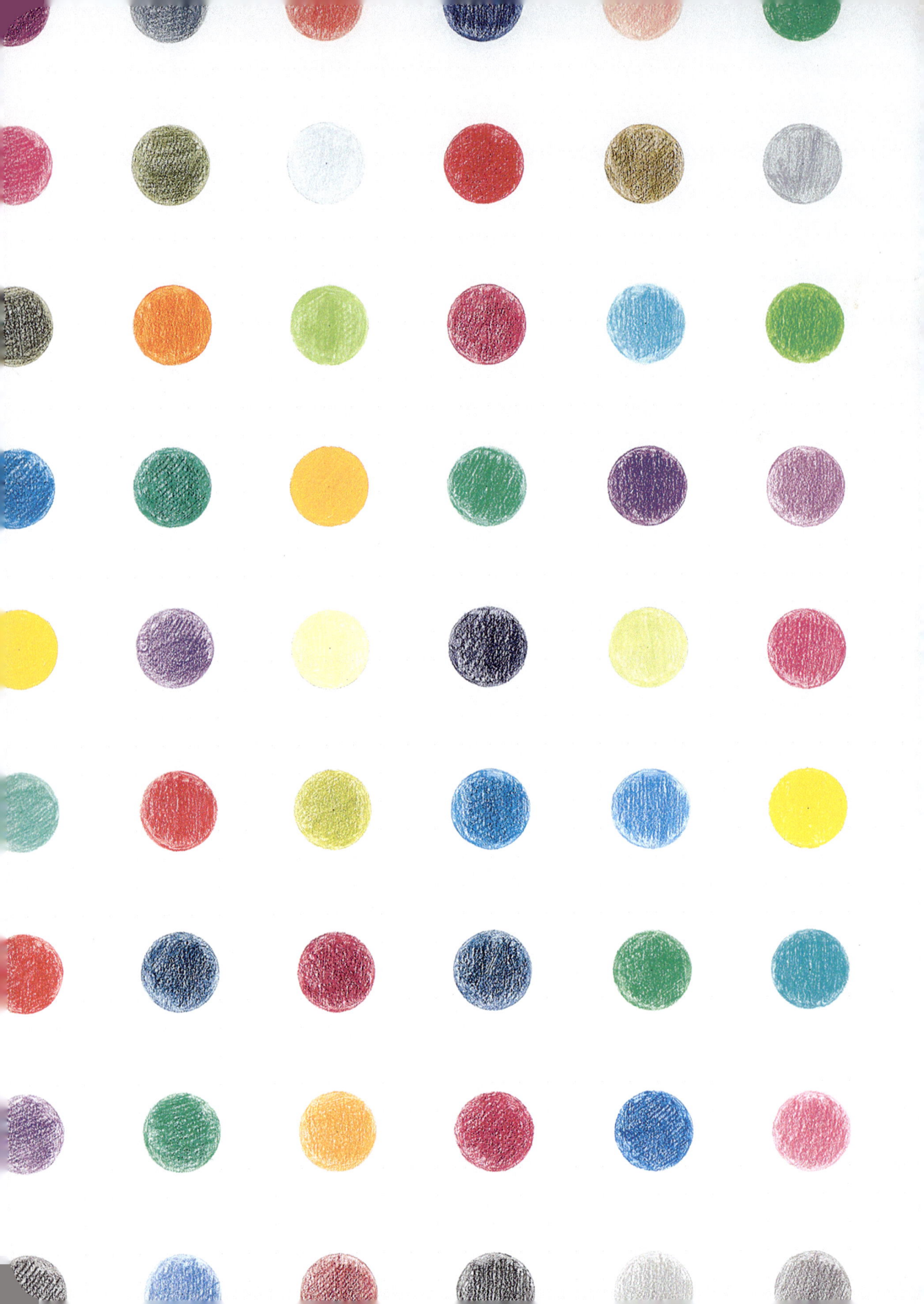

Damien Hirst

DRAWINGS

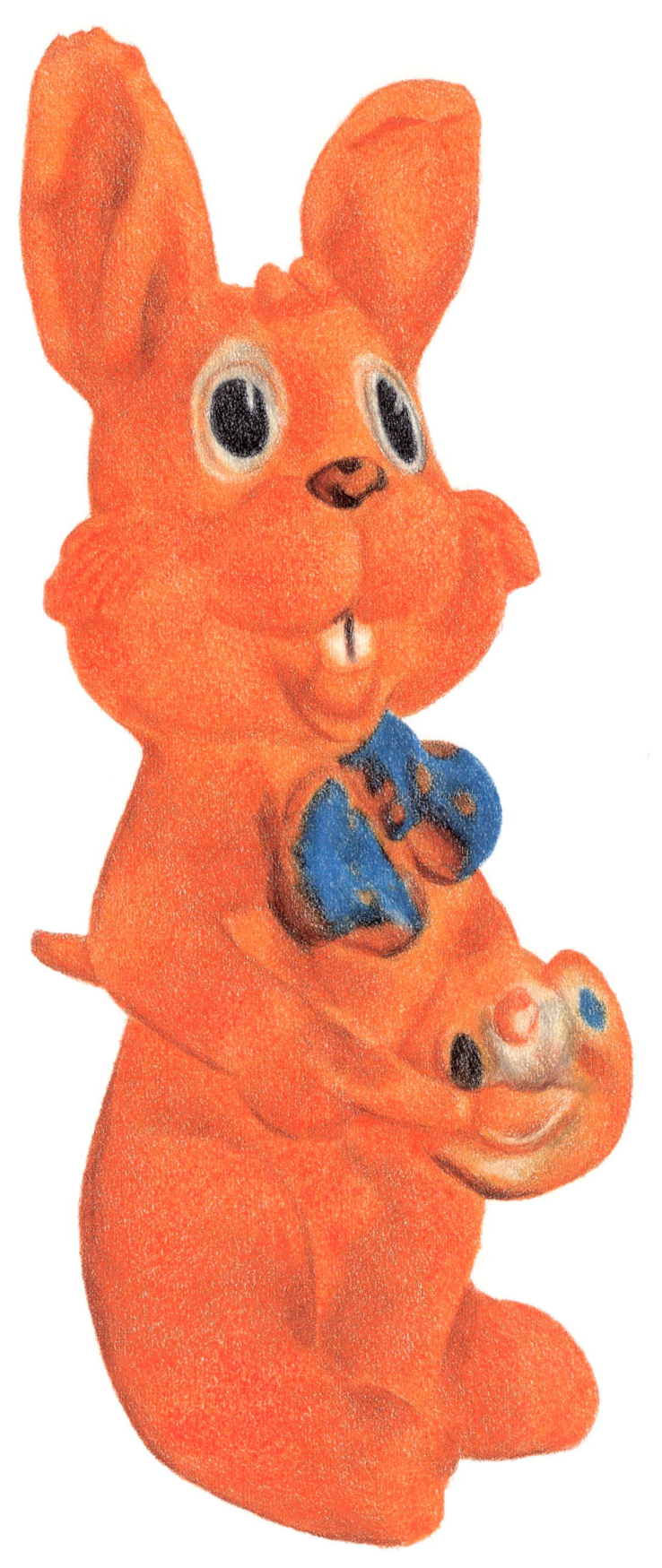

Damien Hirst

DRAWINGS

Herausgegeben von | Edited by
Ralph Gleis und | and Elsy Lahner

Mit einem Vorwort von Ralph Gleis, einem
Essay von Elsy Lahner, einem Gespräch
zwischen Damien Hirst und Ralph Gleis
sowie Zitaten des Künstlers
With a foreword by Ralph Gleis, an essay
by Elsy Lahner, a conversation between
Damien Hirst and Ralph Gleis, and quotes
from the artist

ALBERTINA   HIRMER

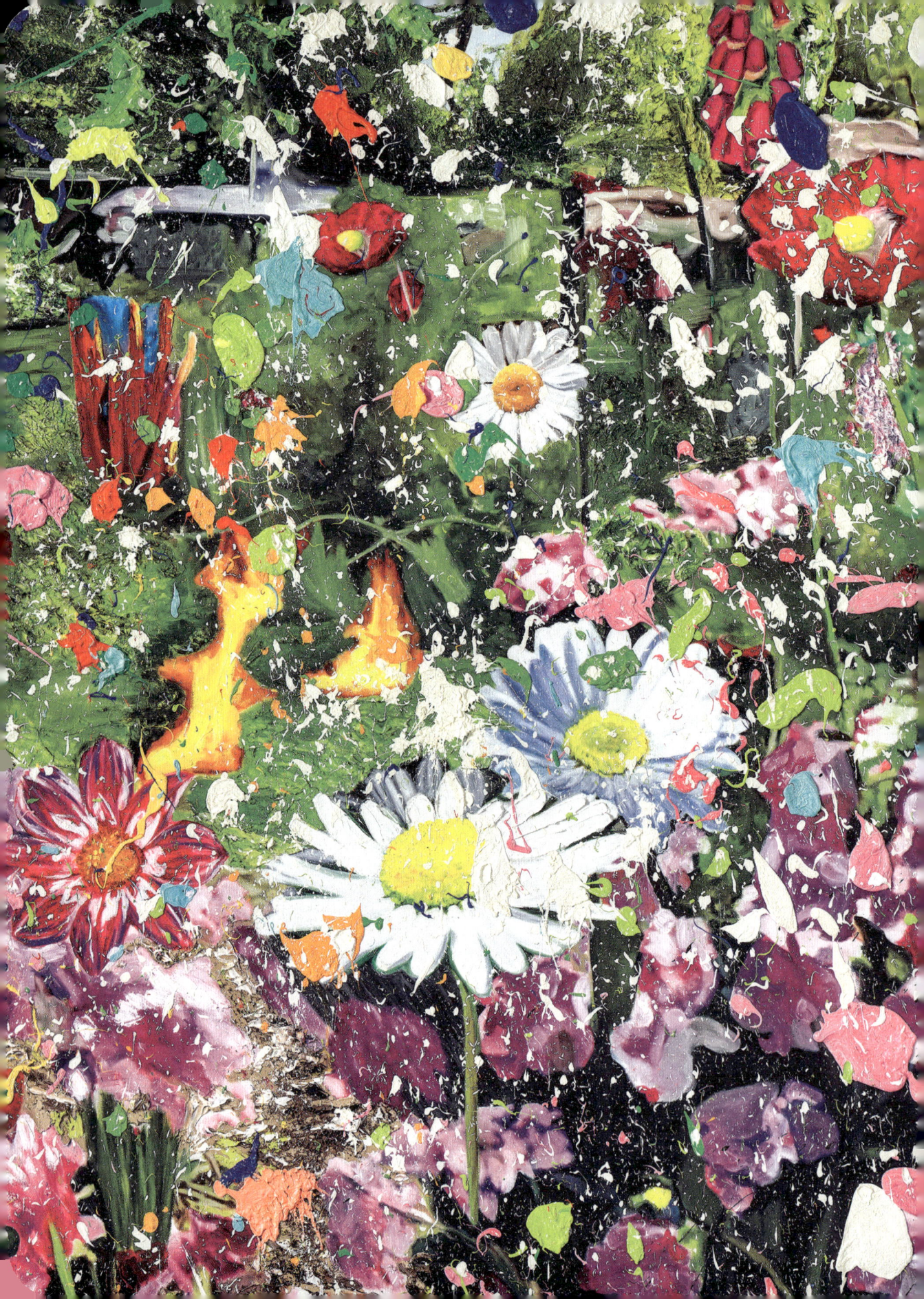

Vorwort

Damien Hirst zählt zu den einflussreichsten Künstlern unserer Zeit. Mit seinen ikonischen Werken – von in Formaldehyd konservierten Tieren bis hin zu mit Diamanten besetzten Totenköpfen – hat er die Kunstwelt nachhaltig beeinflusst. Weniger bekannt ist, dass viele seiner Werke auf eine erste Skizze mit Bleistift auf Papier zurückgehen. Einige seiner berühmtesten Werke wurden zuerst als Zeichnungen entworfen, bevor sie als Gemälde, Skulpturen und Installationen Gestalt annahmen. Die Albertina widmet diesem Aspekt seines Schaffens nun zum ersten Mal eine eigene Museumsausstellung.
Die Schau bietet einen faszinierenden Einblick in Hirsts Arbeitsweise und beleuchtet die Rolle der Zeichnung innerhalb seines künstlerischen Prozesses. Zeichnungen und Skizzen, die ab den 1980er-Jahren in Vorbereitung seiner bahnbrechenden Werke entstanden sind, werden einer Auswahl damit in Zusammenhang stehender Objekte und Gemälde gegenübergestellt. Bemerkenswert ist Hirsts konzeptuelle Herangehensweise an das Medium Zeichnung. Er verwendet Zeichnung in unterschiedlichen Modi – als Gedankenskizze am Beginn des Werkprozesses, als autonomes Werk neben anderen in einer Serie oder im Nachhinein, um die zugrunde liegende Idee zu betonen, die Hirst ebenso wichtig ist wie die physische Ausführung. Dabei beschreitet er auch verschiedene Wege, von der eigenhändigen Zeichnung über die automatisch erstellte Zeichnung, die vom Zufall gesteuert wird, bis hin zur Arbeit, die er nach seinen Anweisungen von seinem Studio anfertigen lässt.
Ein Kapitel der Ausstellung ist seinem monumentalen Projekt *Treasures from the Wreck of the Unbelievable* gewidmet. Mit diesem hinterfragt Hirst die Grenzen zwischen Realität und Fiktion sowie die Glaubwürdigkeit von Kunst und Geschichtsschreibung. Teil seiner Erzählung um ein mythisches Schiffswrack und dessen geborgene Kunstsammlung ist ein umfang-

Foreword

Damien Hirst is one of the most influential artists of our time. From animals preserved in formaldehyde to diamond-encrusted skulls, his iconic works have had a lasting impact on the art world. Less well known is that many of his works can be traced back to an initial sketch on paper. Some of his most famous works began as drawings before taking shape as paintings, sculptures, or installations. Now, for the first time, the Albertina is dedicating a museum exhibition to this aspect of his creative process. The exhibition offers a fascinating insight into Hirst's working methods and sheds light on the role of drawing in his artistic process. Drawings and sketches dating back to the 1980s, made in preparation for groundbreaking works, are juxtaposed with a selection of related objects and paintings. Hirst's conceptual approach to the medium of drawing is remarkable, engaging with it in a variety of ways: as a sketch of ideas at the beginning of the working process, as an autonomous work alongside others in a series, or after a piece has been completed to emphasise the underlying idea, which is as important to Hirst as the physical execution. In doing so, he also takes different approaches, from drawing by hand, to the automatic creation of drawings controlled by chance, to having them done under Hirst's instruction by his studio. One section of the exhibition is dedicated to his monumental *Treasures from the Wreck of the Unbelievable*. With this project, Hirst questions the boundaries between reality and fiction, as well as the credibility of art and historiography. Part of his narrative about a mythical shipwreck and the art collection salvaged from it is an extensive collection of drawings documenting the individual works. By adopting the aesthetic of old master studies or archaeological illustrations, these drawings reinforce the fictional story of the supposedly lost art treasures. At the same time, they combine realistic

reiches Konvolut an Zeichnungen, die die einzelnen Werke dokumentieren. Indem diese Grafiken die Ästhetik von altmeisterlichen Studien oder archäologischen Illustrationen aufgreifen, untermauern sie die fiktive Geschichte der vermeintlich einst verloren gegangenen Kunstschätze. Gleichzeitig verbinden sie realistische Darstellungen mit surrealen und fantastischen Elementen und verstärken so die Spannung zwischen Authentizität und Inszenierung.

Mit *Making Beautiful Drawings* präsentieren wir eine Zeichnungsmaschine, die Hirst 1994 für eine Ausstellung in Berlin entwickelte und die mithilfe einer rotierenden Scheibe, auf die Farben aufgetragen werden, Zeichnungen produziert. Als uns Hirst bei unserem ersten Besuch in seinem Studio davon erzählte, kam sofort die Idee auf, dieses Werk nicht nur auszustellen, sondern es auch für unser Publikum erlebbar zu machen. Ganz im Sinne der ursprünglichen Präsentation kann die Maschine von unseren Besucherinnen und Besuchern bedient werden und es können so eigene Zeichnungen erzeugt werden. Daher freue ich mich außerordentlich, dass wir in dieser ersten musealen Ausstellung von Hirsts Zeichnungen, die ein Highlight in unserem Programm 2025 darstellt, auch eine Anregung zur eigenen Kreativität bieten können.

Ein Projekt wie dieses ist nur durch die großartige Zusammenarbeit vieler realisierbar. Daher möchte ich all jenen meinen tiefen Dank aussprechen, die zu seiner Realisierung beigetragen haben. An erster Stelle gilt mein größter Dank dem Künstler selbst! Seine spontane Einwilligung, einen Blick auf einen „anderen" Hirst zu wagen und an die Anfänge seiner künstlerischen Ideen in der Zeichnung zurückzugehen, hat unser Denken über die Ausstellung erst ausgelöst. Ohne die intensive Unterstützung durch Damien Hirst und sein Team, namentlich Jack Addis, Adrianna Liedtke, Susie Moger, Katherine Nisbet und Rachel Wiseman, wäre diese Ausstellung so nicht möglich gewesen. Ebenso danke ich von Herzen den Leihgeberinnen und Leihgebern für die Bereitschaft,

depictions with surreal and fantastical elements, thus intensifying the tension between authenticity and staging.

With *Making Beautiful Drawings*, we are presenting a drawing machine that Hirst developed in 1994 for an exhibition in Berlin. The machine produces drawings with the help of a rotating disc on which colours are applied. When Hirst told us about it during our first visit to his studio, the idea arose not only to exhibit this work, but also to make it tangible for our audience. In the spirit of the original presentation, our visitors will be able to operate the machine themselves and thus create their own drawings. I am therefore delighted that we are able to offer visitors the opportunity to express their own creativity in this first museum exhibition of Hirst's drawings—a highlight of our 2025 programme.

A project like this is only possible through the collaboration of many individuals. I would therefore like to express my deepest gratitude to all those who have contributed to its realisation. First and foremost, I would like to thank the artist himself! It was his spontaneous agreement to dare to take a look at a 'different' Hirst, going back to the beginnings of his artistic ideas in drawings, that triggered our thinking about the exhibition in the first place. Without the intensive support of Damien Hirst and his team, namely Jack Addis, Adrianna Liedtke, Susie Moger, Katherine Nisbet, and Rachel Wiseman, this exhibition would not have been possible in this form. I would also like to express my sincere gratitude to the lenders for their willingness to share their works for the duration of the exhibition, thus placing a great deal of trust in our institution.

Special thanks also go to the outstanding curator Elsy Lahner, who, together with assistant curator Lorenz Ecker, organised the catalogue and exhibition with great dedication. I would also like to thank Christiane Steinbichler-Schranz of the exhibition management department, who was responsible for the project; Sandra Maria Rust, head of publications,

uns ihre Werke für den Ausstellungszeitraum zu überlassen und damit unserem Haus großes Vertrauen entgegenzubringen.

Mein besonderer Dank gilt auch Elsy Lahner, die Katalog und Ausstellung als hervorragende Kuratorin gemeinsam mit Assistenzkurator Lorenz Ecker mit viel Engagement umgesetzt hat. Darüber hinaus danke ich Christiane Steinbichler-Schranz, die das Projekt im Ausstellungsmanagement mit hohem Einsatz verantwortet hat, Sandra Maria Rust als Leiterin der Publikationsabteilung für das umsichtige Katalogmanagement sowie dem Team der Restaurierung für die gewissenhafte Betreuung der Werke. Gedankt sei auch all den anderen zahlreichen Mitarbeiterinnen und Mitarbeitern in den Abteilungen Restaurierung, Ausstellungsaufbau, Presse, Marketing, Aufsicht und Kunstvermittlung. Zudem danke ich dem Grafiker des Katalogs, Klaus E. Göltz, für die gelungene Gestaltung, dem Team des Hirmer Verlags sowie dem Lektorat und der Übersetzung für die angenehme und produktive Zusammenarbeit.

Ich wünsche Ihnen einen inspirierenden Ausstellungsbesuch und viel Freude bei der weiterführenden Lektüre dieses Katalogs.

Ralph Gleis
Generaldirektor der Albertina

for her prudent catalogue management; and the conservation team for their conscientious care of the works. Thanks are also due to the many other staff members in the conservation, exhibition installation, press, marketing, supervisory, and art education departments. I would also like to thank Klaus E. Göltz, the catalogue's graphic designer, and the team at Hirmer Verlag, as well as the editorial team and the translators, for the pleasant and productive collaboration.

I wish you an inspiring visit to the exhibition and much pleasure reading about the works in this catalogue.

Ralph Gleis
Director General of the Albertina Museum

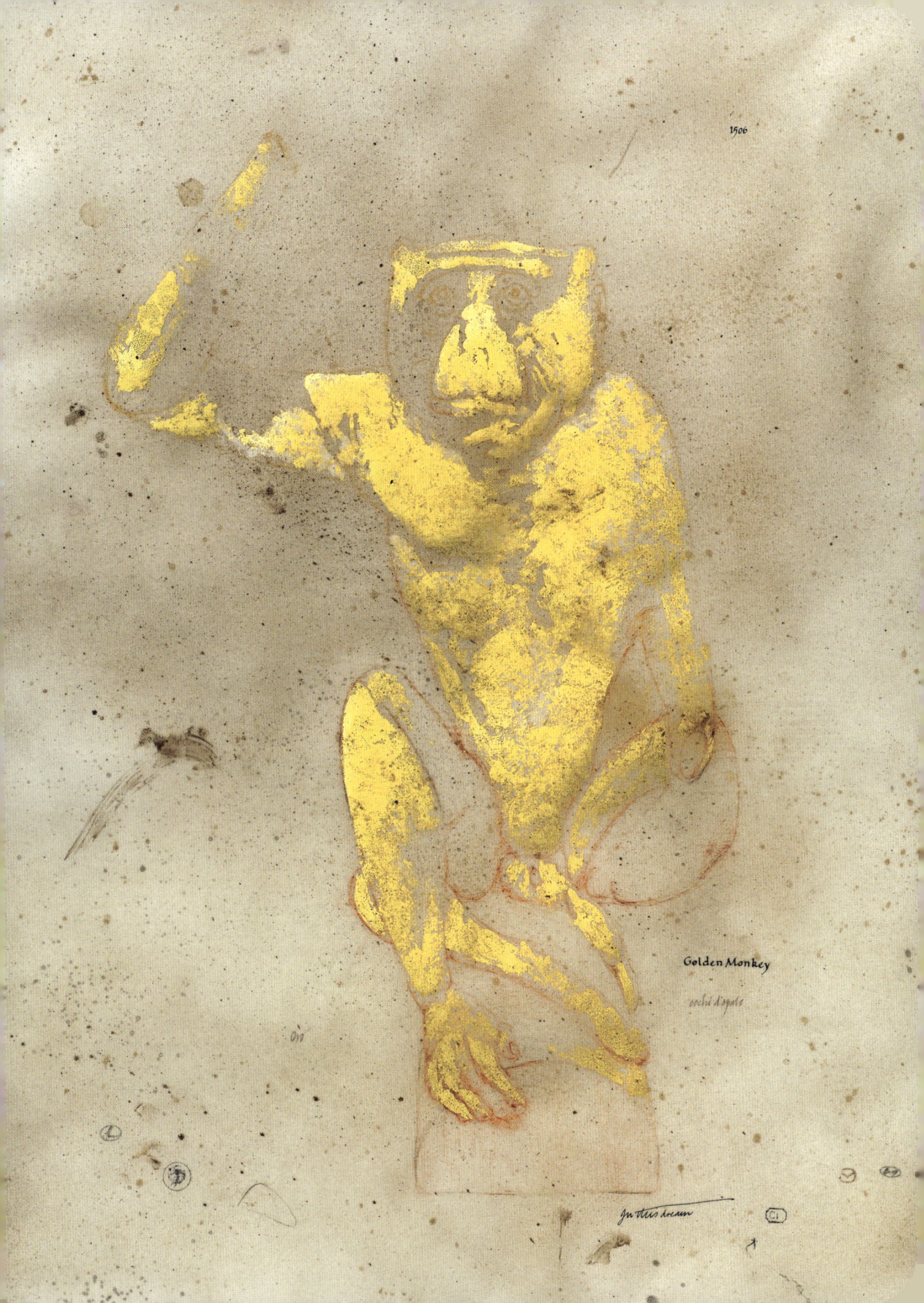

1506

Golden Monkey

oclù d'opals

In die Zukunft zeichnen

Elsy Lahner

1988 präsentierte Damien Hirst erstmals Werke, die später als *Spot Paintings* zu einem seiner Markenzeichen werden sollten. In der von ihm organisierten bahnbrechenden Ausstellung *Freeze* in den London Docklands entstanden die beiden frühen Gemälde *Edge* und *Row* direkt auf der Wand im Inneren des Gebäudes. Eine Zeichnung aus dem Jahr 1987 zeigt Hirsts frühe Auseinandersetzung mit der systematischen Anordnung der Punkte dieser Gemälde: Auf einem kleinen Blatt (S. 34) skizzierte er *Edge* und *Row*, indem er zwei Raster aus jeweils 10 × 15 handgezeichneten Kreisen anlegte. Spätere Zeichnungen dokumentieren die weitere Planung und gedankliche Entwicklung der *Spot Paintings* sowie ihrer Untergruppe der *Pharmaceutical Paintings*, wenn der Künstler Maße und Anweisungen auf dem Blatt notiert, auf diesem verschiedene Formen und Größen der zu verwendenden Leinwände definiert oder Kompositionen auf Millimeterpapier erprobt. Doch auch Hirsts skulpturale und installative Arbeiten werden für gewöhnlich von grafischen Darstellungen begleitet und kommentiert, die im Sinne klassischer Bildhauerzeichnungen als Skizzen und Entwurfszeichnungen oder eigenständige Werke von ihm geschaffen werden. Dabei kam vor allem in den Anfangsjahren seines Schaffens häufig Papier zum Einsatz, das ihm gerade untergekommen war. Auf einer Einladungskarte (S. 22) hat er 1988 erste Überlegungen zu *A Hundred Years* (1990) und *A Thousand Years* (1990) umrissen – große Glaskästen, mit denen er anhand frisch geschlüpfter Fliegen und einer elektrischen Fliegenfalle den Lebenszyklus unmittelbar erfahrbar macht. *The Physical Impossibility of Death in the Mind of Someone Living* (1991), den ikonischen in Formaldehyd konservierten Tigerhai, skizzierte er 1989 als frühe Studien auf einer Buchseite (S. 59) oder einem aufgefalteten braunen Rechnungskuvert (S. 58). Auf einem aus

Drawing into the Future

Elsy Lahner

In 1988, Damien Hirst first exhibited works that later became known as *Spot Paintings*, one of his trademark styles. Two of those early paintings, *Edge* and *Row,* were executed directly on an interior wall as part of the groundbreaking exhibition *Freeze*, which he organised in London's Docklands. A drawing from the previous year shows Hirst's early preoccupation with the systematic arrangement of the spots in these paintings: on a small sheet of paper (p. 34), he sketched *Edge* and *Row* by creating two 10 × 15 grids of hand-drawn circles. Later drawings document the further planning and conceptual development of the *Spot Paintings* and their sub-group, the *Pharmaceutical Paintings*; in these drawings, the artist notes dimensions and instructions on the sheet, defines different shapes and sizes of the canvas to be used, or tests compositions on graph paper. Hirst's sculptures and installations are also usually accompanied and commented on by graphic representations, which he creates as sketches and drafts in the sense of a classical sculptor's drawings, or as independent works. Especially early in his career, he often used whatever paper happened to be at hand. On an invitation card (p. 22) from 1988, for example, he sketched out his initial ideas for *A Hundred Years* (1990) and *A Thousand Years* (1990)— the large glass vitrine works in which he used freshly hatched flies and an electric flytrap to make the cycle of life vividly apparent. Early sketches of *The Physical Impossibility of Death in the Mind of Someone Living* (1991), the iconic tiger shark preserved in formaldehyde, were sketched in 1989 on a book page (p. 59) and an unfolded brown invoice envelope (p. 58). On a sheet of lined paper

einem Heft oder Block herausgerissenen linierten Blatt (S. 101) findet sich eine kleine Skizze seines mit Diamanten besetzten Totenkopfs, *For the Love of God* (2007). Während einige seiner Entwürfe spontan und schnell entstehen – oft ergänzt durch schnell aufgeschriebene Notizen, Listen von möglichen Materialien und Berechnungen, die strukturelle Überlegungen zu seinen Kunstwerken wiedergeben –, sind andere detaillierter ausgearbeitet. Diese Zeichnungen fertigt Hirst meist auf Zeichenpapier und in größeren Formaten an, viele davon parallel oder auch nach der Realisierung der jeweiligen skulpturalen Arbeiten.

Hirst versteht das Zeichnen als zentralen Bestandteil seiner künstlerischen Praxis.[1] Es ermöglicht ihm, Erinnerungen zu bewahren, Ideen im Moment ihres Entstehens festzuhalten und Konzepte zu erarbeiten. Zudem erlaubt es ihm, räumliche Dimensionen und Proportionen auf dem Papier zu erproben, bevor ein Werk tatsächlich realisiert wird – und fungiert damit als wesentliche Brücke zwischen Gedanken und materieller Umsetzung. Er nutzt diese Technik, um Ähnlichkeiten und Details zu erfassen oder den Entwicklungsprozess eines Werks im Vergleich zu Vorstudien nachzuvollziehen. Ebenso dient sie der Erstellung von Visualisierungen, damit sein Team Skulpturen und Installationen nach seinen Vorstellungen umsetzen kann. Zugleich beschreibt Hirst, dass ihm das Zeichnen die Möglichkeit gebe, Gefühle auszudrücken und seine Wahrnehmung von Menschen, Dingen und der Welt zu vermitteln, ohne Worte zu benutzen. Er betrachtet es als fortlaufenden Prozess, der sich über verschiedene Phasen hinweg entwickelt hat und bereits in seiner Kindheit begann, als seine Mutter ihm Stift und Papier gab, um ihn zu beschäftigen. Er erzählt, dass sie ständig neue Blätter an seine Zeichnungen anfügte, sodass diese immer größer und größer wurden: „Und so habe ich schließlich angefangen, über die Grenzen des Papiers hinauszudenken."

Das Faszinierende an Hirsts Zeichnungen ist, dass sie Einblick in seine Denkweise und die Bandbreite seiner Ideen geben. Sie offenbaren, wann sich

(p. 101), torn from a notebook or pad, is a small sketch of his diamond-studded skull, *For the Love of God* (2007). While some of his designs are spontaneous and quick—often accompanied by hastily scribbled notes, lists of possible materials, and suggested calculations—others are more detailed. Hirst usually creates these more detailed designs on drawing paper and in larger formats, often in parallel with or even after the realisation of the respective sculptural works.

Hirst sees drawing as a central part of his artistic practice.[1] It allows him to preserve memories, capture ideas as they arise, and develop concepts. With drawings, he can test spatial dimensions and proportions on paper before a work is realised— using them as an essential bridge between thoughts and their material realisation. This technique enables him to capture similarities and details, or to understand the development process of a work in comparison to preliminary studies. It is also used to create visualisations so that his team can produce sculptures and installations according to his ideas. At the same time, Hirst describes how drawing allows him to express feelings and convey his perceptions of people, things, and the world without using words. He sees it as an ongoing process that has developed through various stages, starting in his childhood when his mother gave him a pen and paper to keep him occupied. He says that she would add new pages to his drawings so that they would get bigger and bigger: 'So I ended up sort of thinking beyond the limits of the paper.'

What is fascinating about Hirst's drawings is that they give an insight into his way of thinking and the range of his ideas. They show when these ideas begin to take shape, how they gradually change, how they diverge from what is realised in three dimensions and actually move beyond that form, beyond space or time. For this reason, but also because some ideas would be impossible to produce,

diese Ideen zu formieren beginnen, wie sie sich schrittweise verändern, wie sie von dem, was plastisch umgesetzt wird, abweichen und sich tatsächlich über diese Gestalt, über Raum oder Zeit hinausbewegen. Nicht nur aus diesem Grund, nicht nur aufgrund der Tatsache, dass manche Ideen überhaupt nicht umsetzbar wären, bleiben viele Entwürfe unrealisiert und reine Gedankenspiele. Auf andere greift Hirst erst Jahre später in einem anderen Kontext oder als Ausgangspunkt eines neuen Projekts zurück, wenn er beim Durchblättern alter Notizbücher auf eine vergangene Idee stößt und denkt: „Verdammt, das hätte ich machen sollen."

Schon in jungen Jahren hat er seine Einfälle und spontanen Eingebungen auch in Notizbüchern festgehalten. Während seiner Zeit am Goldsmiths College zeichneten er und seine Kommilitonen sich gegenseitig in ihre Hefte, um einander zu zeigen und zu erklären, woran sie gerade arbeiteten. Auch heute trägt Hirst immer ein Notizbuch bei sich, das inzwischen vor allem schriftliche Notizen enthält, während Skizzen für dreidimensionale Werke seltener geworden sind. Derzeit arbeitet er jedoch an einem bemerkenswerten Projekt, das auf seinen Notizbuchzeichnungen beruht und dem er den Titel „Posthumous Paintings" gegeben hat. In exakt 200 Büchern entwirft Hirst fortlaufend Werke – Gemälde, doch ebenso Skulpturen und Installationen –, die sukzessive erst nach seinem Tod als solche realisiert werden sollen, wobei ein Buch jeweils für ein Jahr steht und jedes Buch rund 50 Anleitungen für Werke enthält. So ist neben kleinen *Spin Drawings*[2] die Vorgabe zu lesen: „Mach auf Grundlage dieser Farben einen Eineinhalb-Meter-Spin." Hirsts Planung zufolge werden die Instruktionen mit der Zeit zunehmend vager und lauten etwa: „Finde ein Objekt, gieße es in Bronze" und schließlich schlicht: „Mach, was du willst, nenne es, wie du willst, in jedem Material, das du willst, in jeder Größe, die du willst, in jeder Dimension." Darüber hinaus enthalten die Bücher eine besondere Sektion, die Hirst „Historic Works" nennt. In dieser beschreibt er Werke, die aus

many designs remain unrealised and purely intellectual exercises. Others Hirst only returns to years later in a different context or as a starting point for a new project when, leafing through old notebooks, he comes across a past idea and thinks: 'Damn, I should have made that.'

Even as a young man, he used to record his ideas and spontaneous inspirations in notebooks. During his time at Goldsmiths College, he and his fellow students would draw in each other's notebooks to show and explain what they were currently working on. Nowadays, Hirst carries a notebook with him at all times, which mainly contains written notes, while sketches for three-dimensional works have become less common. Currently, he is working on a remarkable project based on his notebook drawings, which he has titled *Posthumous Paintings*. In exactly 200 books, Hirst is continuously developing works—paintings, as well as sculptures and installations—to be realised one after the other only after his death, with each book representing one year and containing around fifty work instructions. Alongside small *Spin Drawings*,[2] for example, the instructions read: 'Based on these colours, make a five-foot spin.' According to Hirst's plan, the instructions become increasingly vague over time and read something like 'Find an object, cast it in bronze', and finally, simply, 'Do what you want, call it what you want, in any material you want, any size you want, any dimension.' The collection also includes a special section that Hirst calls 'Historic Works'. In this section, he describes works from different phases of his earlier creative output—from 1992, for example: 'And I'm going to draw it', he says, 'and I'm going to go, this is a work from '92, which can't be made until I die, and it can be made in this date.' He developed this idea of delayed realisation further: 'When you get to book 20, maybe you can make a historic work from book one.' In this way, Hirst creates a working principle that not only extends

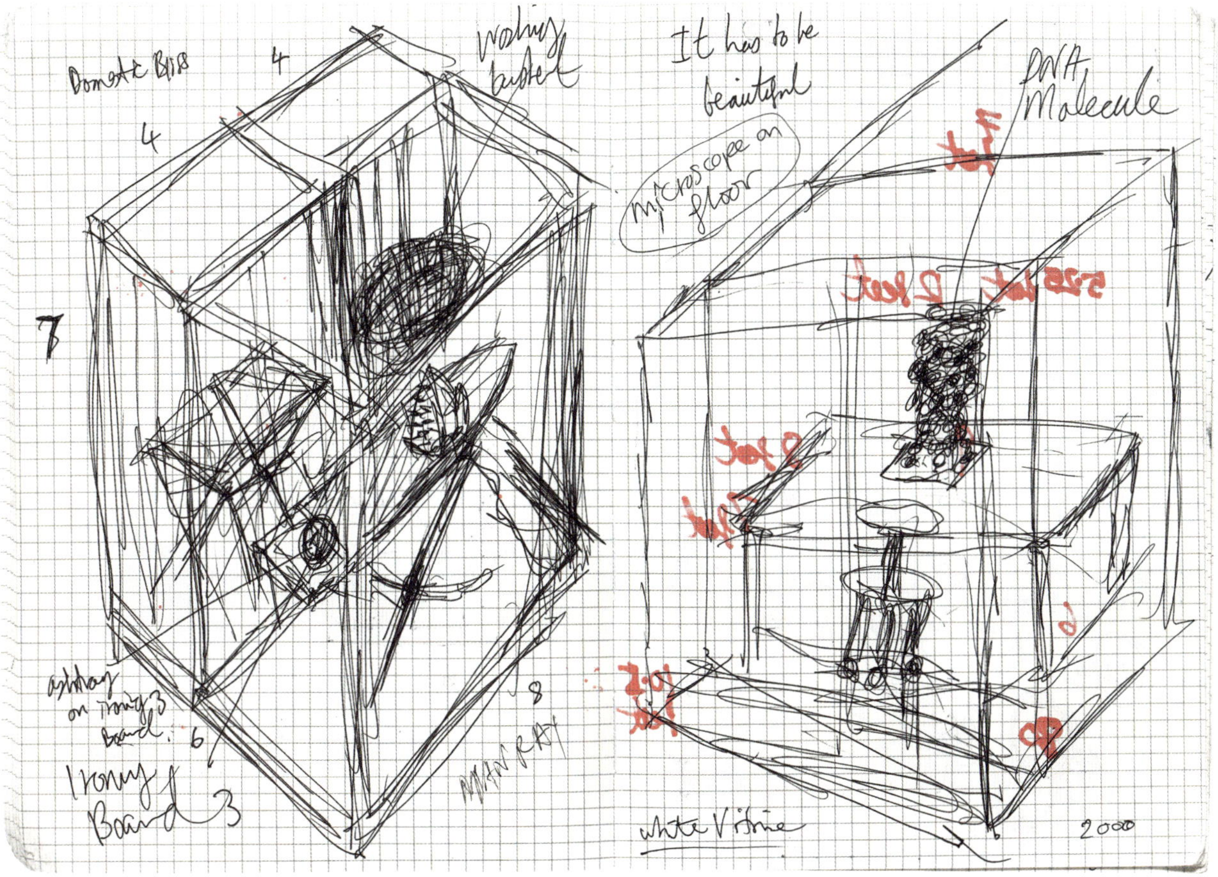
It has to be beautiful
DNA Molecule
microscope on floor
Ironing Board 3
white Vitrine
2000

Vorbereitende Skizzen für Kunstwerke im Notizbuch | *Preparatory sketches for artworks in notebook*

verschiedenen Phasen seines bisherigen Schaffens stammen – etwa aus dem Jahr 1992. „Ich werde sie zeichnen", sagt er, „und ich werde dazu schreiben: Das ist ein Werk von '92, das erst ab diesem Datum gemacht werden kann". Diese Idee der zeitverzögerten Umsetzung entwickelt er noch weiter: „Wenn du bei Buch 20 angelangt bist, kannst du vielleicht ein historisches Werk aus Buch 1 machen." Damit schafft Hirst ein Werkprinzip, das mit Anweisungen für künftige Generationen nicht nur über seinen Tod hinausreicht und einer posthumen Weiterführung seines künstlerischen Œuvres entspricht, sondern auch eine Art Selbstreferentialität in sich trägt – eine Struktur, die sich immer wieder auf frühere Ideen bezieht und doch in der Zukunft verankert bleibt.

beyond his death with instructions for future generations and a posthumous continuation of his artistic oeuvre but also contains a kind of self-referentiality—a structure that repeatedly refers to earlier ideas while remaining anchored in the future. Hirst's drawings thus reflect the past and, as thought experiments, sketch out new possibilities. However, Hirst's graphic oeuvre is much more diverse than these works suggest. In the early 1990s, the artist experimented with mechanised drawing and painting techniques. It was during this period that he created the first *Spin Paintings*, for which he and his artist colleague Angus Fairhurst used a modified car mechanism to rotate canvases. From this first playful and somewhat dangerous experiment, Hirst developed a series of other devices. In 1994, while

Hirsts Zeichnungen reflektieren somit Vergangenes und entwerfen als Gedankenexperimente neue Möglichkeiten. Neben diesen Werken ist Hirsts zeichnerisches Œuvre allerdings noch weitaus facettenreicher. In den frühen 1990er-Jahren experimentierte der Künstler mit mechanisierten Zeichen- und Maltechniken. In dieser Zeit entstanden die ersten *Spin Paintings*, für die er zusammen mit seinem Künstlerkollegen Angus Fairhurst eine umgebaute Automechanik verwendete, um Leinwände rotieren zu lassen. Aus diesem ersten gemeinsamen spielerischen und nicht ungefährlichen Versuch entwickelte Hirst eine Reihe weiterer Apparaturen. 1994 stellte er während seines Aufenthalts in Berlin im Rahmen eines DAAD-Stipendiums erstmals eine Zeichnungsmaschine unter dem Titel *Making Beautiful Drawings* (S. 123) aus. Er beschreibt diese als recht simpel: „Es war ein Handbohrer darunter, mit einem Stück Holz, auf das man einfach drückte, wodurch sich der Bohrer drehte. Während der Show haben wir den Motor ein paar Mal durchbrennen lassen und mussten den Bohrer ersetzen. Es war sehr handgemacht. Es war eine gute Maschine."

Mit *Making Beautiful Drawings* rückt Hirst den Prozess des Zeichnens selbst in den Mittelpunkt. Zum einen lagert er das Zeichnen, das doch gemeinhin als persönlichste und individuellste künstlerische Ausdrucksform gilt, da sie die direkte und unmittelbare Verbindung von Kopf und Hand sichtbar macht, an eine Maschine aus, zum anderen ermöglicht er den Besucherinnen und Besuchern seiner Ausstellungen, diese Maschine zu bedienen, wodurch eigene *Spin Drawings* nach ihren Vorgaben entstehen, und eröffnet dadurch einen partizipativen Zugang. Mit diesem Ansatz stellt Hirst traditionelle Vorstellungen von künstlerischer Handschrift und Authentizität zur Disposition.

Ähnliches gilt für jene Zeichnungen, die der Künstler von seinen Assistentinnen und Assistenten im Studio ausführen lässt, um Werke zu dokumentieren – eine Aufgabe, die er früher schlicht durch Fotografien löste, etwa um ein Gemälde später leichter in eine

in Berlin on a DAAD grant, he exhibited a drawing machine for the first time under the title *Making Beautiful Drawings* (p. 123). He describes it as quite simple: 'It was a hand drill underneath with a piece of wood that you just pressed on and it made the drill spin. We burned out the motor a few times in the show and had to replace the drill. It was very handmade. It was a good one.'

With *Making Beautiful Drawings*, Hirst shifts the focus to the process of drawing itself. He outsources drawing—which is generally considered to be the most personal and individual form of artistic expression because it reveals the direct and immediate connection between head and hand—to a machine. At the same time, he allows visitors to his exhibitions to operate this machine, thereby creating their own *Spin Drawings* according to their specifications, thus opening up a participatory approach. In this way, Hirst challenges traditional notions of unique artistic style and authenticity. The same goes for the drawings produced by Hirst's studio assistants to document works—a task that the artist used to solve simply by taking photographs, for example to make it easier to translate a painting into a print at a later date. For Hirst this is less about a conceptual engagement with ideas and authorship than it is about a practical means to an end. What matters to Hirst is that the work lives up to his expectations. Whether it is made by him or his team makes no difference. He likens this approach to architecture: 'Architects don't build their own houses. You definitely know that is a Gehry house. But he didn't build it himself. It's a Gehry house because he made sure that every part of it is 100% how he wanted it.'

The meticulous crayon and pencil drawings not only give him a new perspective on his own work but are also essential intermediate steps in the creation of works based on specific objects. For the series *Art & Artists* (pp. 145–51), for example, hyper-real

Druckgrafik zu übersetzen. Für ihn selbst steht hierbei daher aber weniger eine konzeptuelle Auseinandersetzung mit Idee und Autorschaft im Vordergrund als vielmehr das praktische Mittel zum Zweck. Entscheidend ist für Hirst, dass die Arbeiten seinen Vorstellungen entsprechen. Ob sie von ihm selbst oder von seinem Team ausgeführt werden, macht für ihn keinen Unterschied. Er vergleicht diesen Ansatz mit der Architektur: „Architekten bauen ihre Häuser nicht selbst. Du weißt genau, dass das ein Haus von Gehry ist. Aber er hat es nicht selbst gebaut. Es ist ein Gehry-Haus, weil er dafür gesorgt hat, dass jeder Teil zu 100 % so ist, wie er es haben wollte."

Die akribischen Bunt- und Bleistiftzeichnungen eröffnen ihm jedoch nicht nur eine neue Perspektive auf sein eigenes Werk, sondern sind ebenso wesentliche Zwischenschritte in der Entstehung von Arbeiten, die auf bestimmten Objekten basieren. Für die Werkserie *Art & Artists* (S. 145–151) beispielsweise werden hyperreale Zeichnungen von Spielzeugen mit Hinweisen zu großformatigen skulpturalen Versionen versehen.

Auf Grundlage dieser Zeichnungen entstanden seine Skulpturen, vergrößerte Adaptionen der ursprünglichen Figuren. Bei den *Pipe Cleaner Animals* (S. 163–169) hingegen verlief der Prozess anders: Hirst lud zuerst Eltern mit ihren Kindern ins Studio ein, um Tiere aus Pfeifenputzern zu erstellen. Dann wählte er seine Lieblingsstücke aus und setzte sie in größerem Maßstab um, bevor Zeichnungen auf Basis von Fotos der großen Versionen angefertigt wurden.

Auch in Hirsts umfangreichem Projekt *Treasures from the Wreck of the Unbelievable* (S. 171–193) spielen Zeichnungen eine wesentliche Rolle. In diesem konstruierte der Künstler die fiktive Geschichte um ein vor ca. 2 000 Jahren gesunkenes Schiff eines Kunstsammlers, Cif Amotan II., und erschuf vorgetäuschte antike Skulpturen, die 2017 als vermeintlich geborgene Kunstschätze in einer umfangreichen Ausstellung präsentiert wurden. Zudem produzierte Hirst einen Film[3], der das Projekt erweitert. Zur gleichen Zeit auf Netflix veröffentlicht,

drawings of toys are then annotated with directions for large-scale sculptural versions. For the *Pipe Cleaner Animals* (pp. 163–69), the process was different: first, Hirst invited parents and their children to his studio to make animals out of pipe cleaners. Hirst then selected his favourites and enlarged them before making drawings based on photographs of the larger versions.

Drawings also play an important role in Hirst's comprehensive *Treasures from the Wreck of the Unbelievable* (pp. 171–93). In this project, the artist constructed the fictional story of a ship belonging to an art collector, Cif Amotan II, which sank some 2,000 years ago, and created fake ancient sculptures that were presented as supposedly recovered art treasures in a major exhibition in 2017. Hirst also produced a film[3] that extended the project. Released simultaneously on Netflix, it staged the fictional discovery of the shipwreck, thereby reinforcing the illusion of a real archaeological sensation. The aesthetics of a serious documentary blur the lines between truth and staging, drawing the audience into the narrative. However, the illusion gradually crumbles: one of the coral-covered figures recovered from the depths of the sea looks like Mickey Mouse, and a supposed sculpture of the collector bears an uncanny resemblance to Hirst himself—obvious signs that the story cannot be true. The artist plays with authenticity, the manipulation of perception, and the belief in the genuineness of objects.

His drawings for this project follow the same idea. They are not mere preliminary studies, but part of the staging itself. Hirst's idea is that they should not appear as salvaged artefacts from the time of Cif Amotan II or even earlier, but as drawings based on handed-down stories about the lost sculptures. 'So the drawings are supposed to be younger than the treasures. That's how I got over that hurdle. I had to kind of fix it because I knew the drawings couldn't survive on the sunken ship.' In this way,

inszenierte er die fiktive Entdeckung des Schiffswracks und verstärkte dadurch die Illusion einer realen archäologischen Sensation. Durch die Ästhetik einer seriösen Dokumentation verschwimmen die Grenzen zwischen Wahrheit und Inszenierung, wodurch das Publikum in die Erzählung hineingezogen wird. Nach und nach jedoch bröckelt die Illusion: eine der aus den Tiefen des Meeres geborgenen und mit Korallen bewachsenen Figuren sieht aus wie Micky Maus und eine angebliche Skulptur des Sammlers weist eine verblüffende Ähnlichkeit mit Hirst selbst auf – offenkundige Hinweise darauf, dass die Geschichte so nicht stimmen kann. Der Künstler spielt mit Authentizität, der Manipulation von Wahrnehmung und dem Glauben an die Echtheit von Objekten. Seine Zeichnungen zu diesem Projekt knüpfen genau hier an. Sie sind nicht bloße Vorstudien, sondern Teil der Inszenierung selbst. Nach Hirsts Vorstellung sollen sie nicht als geborgene Artefakte aus der Epoche Cif Amotans II. oder gar früher erscheinen, sondern als Zeichnungen, die sich auf überlieferte Erzählungen der verlorenen Skulpturen stützen. „Die Zeichnungen sollen also jünger sein als die Schätze. So habe ich diese Hürde überwunden. Ich musste es irgendwie in Ordnung bringen, weil ich wusste, dass die Zeichnungen auf dem gesunkenen Schiff nicht überleben konnten." Damit etabliert Hirst die Idee, dass die Zeichnungen aus den Erinnerungen von Menschen stammen, die die Geschichte des gesunkenen Schatzes über Jahrhunderte hinweg tradiert haben. Es sind keine klassischen Skizzen oder Entwürfe, sondern bewusst gestaltete Elemente eines künstlerischen Narrativs, das zwischen Realität und Fiktion oszilliert.

Ein besonderer Aspekt dieser Zeichnungen ist ihr bewusst gewählter Stil. Da sie nach Fotografien der Skulpturen entstehen, erhalten die Zeichnungen aufgrund der Kameraeinstellung und der Perspektive der Aufnahmen eine zeitgenössische Anmutung. Hirst war sich bewusst, dass auch der Hyperrealismus, den er in diesen Werken erkennt, in der Antike nicht existierte. Dennoch bezog er ihn gezielt ein,

Hirst establishes the idea that the drawings come from the memories of people who have passed on the story of the sunken treasure over the centuries. They are not classic sketches or drafts, but consciously designed elements of an artistic narrative that oscillates between reality and fiction. A particular aspect of these drawings is their deliberately chosen style. Because they are made from photographs of the sculptures, the drawings take on a contemporary look through the camera angle and perspective of the photographs. Hirst was aware that the hyper-realism he saw in these works did not exist in antiquity. Nevertheless, he deliberately incorporated it, but at the same time made the drawings look old. To create a sense of historical authenticity, the drawings were executed on goatskin parchment and aged paper, while those on new paper were intended as preparatory studies. A projector was used to trace the outlines and details of photographs of the sculptures. Hirst and his assistants studied historical drawing techniques. They used silverpoint and inks specially made for the project. In studio meetings, the team experimented with different techniques to make the sheets look as if they had aged over centuries. Conservators were consulted to age the paper artificially, giving the impression that the images were from a bygone era. Hirst also included subtle clues that the drawings could not really be old, for example by inserting car brand logos. With details like these, he played with the notion of authenticity and pointed to the central question of the whole project: How is history constructed and how easily are we led by narratives?

By reflecting on the past and the present while simultaneously thinking them into the future— whether as a draft for a later work, as posthumous instructions, or as part of a manipulated history— Hirst makes clear that he views his art as a dynamic, ongoing game of possibilities and illusions.

ließ die Zeichnungen aber zugleich alt erscheinen. Um historische Authentizität vorzutäuschen, wurde auf Pergament aus Ziegenhaut sowie gealtertem Papier gezeichnet, wobei jene auf Papier im Sinn von vorbereitenden Studien gedacht waren. Mithilfe eines Projektors wurden die Fotoaufnahmen der Skulpturen auf die Oberflächen projiziert, um die Umrisse und Details festzuhalten. Hirst studierte mit seinen Assistentinnen und Assistenten historische Zeichentechniken. Sie verwendeten unter anderem Silberstift und Tinten, die sie eigens für dieses Projekt herstellten. In Studio-Meetings experimentierte das Team mit verschiedenen Verfahren, um die Blätter so erscheinen zu lassen, als seien sie über Jahrhunderte gealtert. Restauratorinnen und Restauratoren wurden hinzugezogen, um das Papier künstlich altern zu lassen und so den Eindruck zu erwecken, es handle sich um Grafiken aus einer längst vergangenen Zeit. Hirst integrierte zudem subtile Hinweise darauf, dass die Zeichnungen nicht wirklich alt sein können, etwa durch das Einfügen der Logos von Automarken. Mit Details wie diesen spielte er mit dem Konzept von Echtheit und verwies auf die zentrale Fragestellung des gesamten Projekts: Wie wird Geschichte konstruiert und wie leicht lassen wir uns von Erzählungen leiten?

Indem Hirst mit seinen Zeichnungen über Vergangenes und Bestehendes reflektiert und sie gleichzeitig in die Zukunft denkt – sei es als Entwurf für ein späteres Werk, als posthume Anleitungen oder als Teil einer manipulierten Geschichte –, unterstreicht er die Auffassung von seiner Kunst als ein dynamisches, fortlaufendes Spiel mit Möglichkeiten und Illusionen.

---

[1] Die folgenden Informationen sowie die Zitate des Künstlers stammen aus einem Gespräch mit der Autorin am 27.01.2025.
[2] Als *Spin Drawings* bezeichnet Hirst seine durch die Zentrifugalkraft entstandenen Zeichnungen, bei denen Farbe auf ein rotierendes Blatt Papier aufgetragen wird.
[3] Der Film ist mittlerweile auf YouTube verfügbar, um einen uneingeschränkten Zugang zu ermöglichen.

[1] The following information and quotes from the artist are taken from a conversation with the author on 27 January 2025.
[2] Hirst refers to his drawings created by centrifugal force as *Spin Drawings*, made on rotating sheets of paper.
[3] The film is now available on YouTube to ensure unrestricted access.

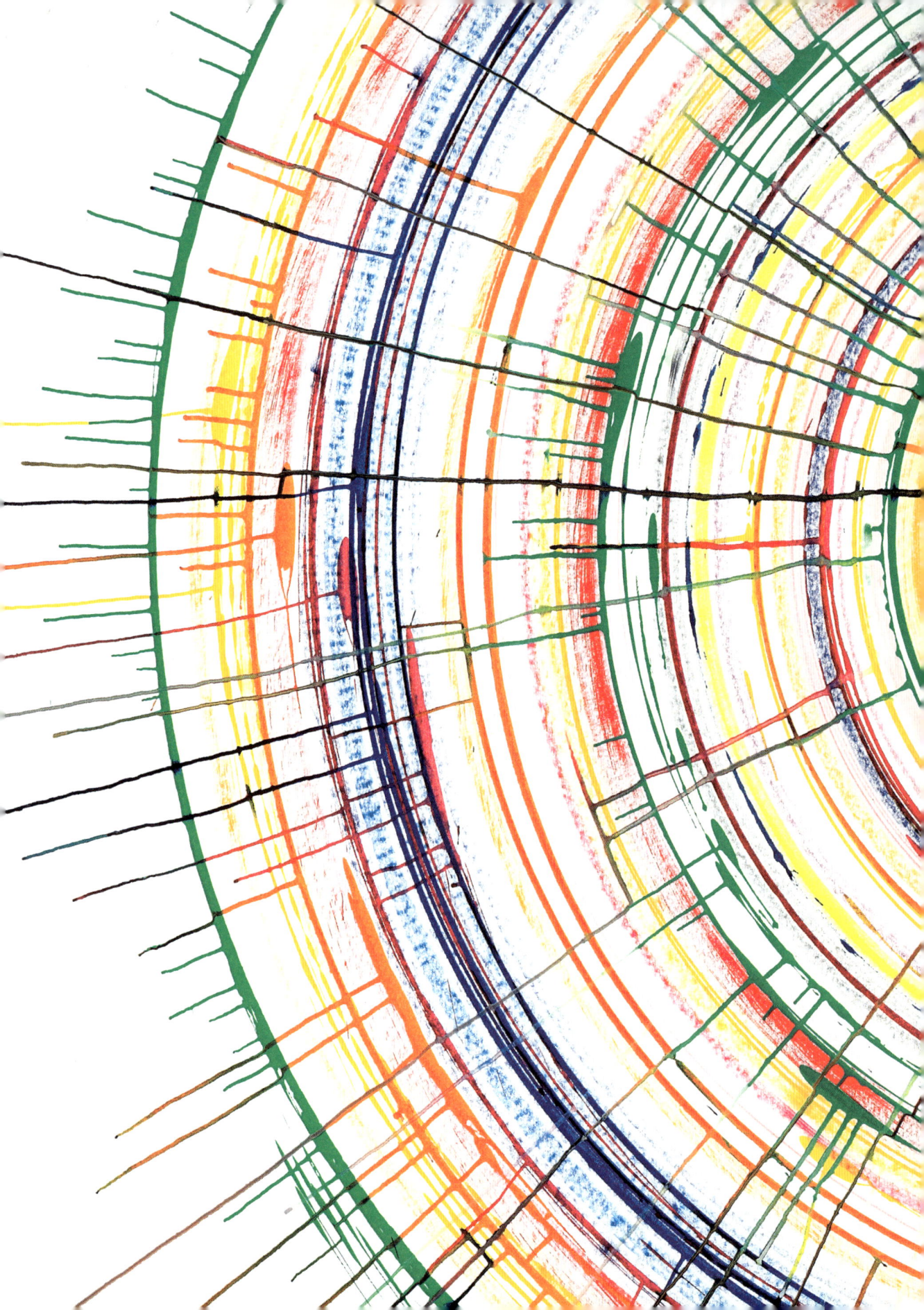

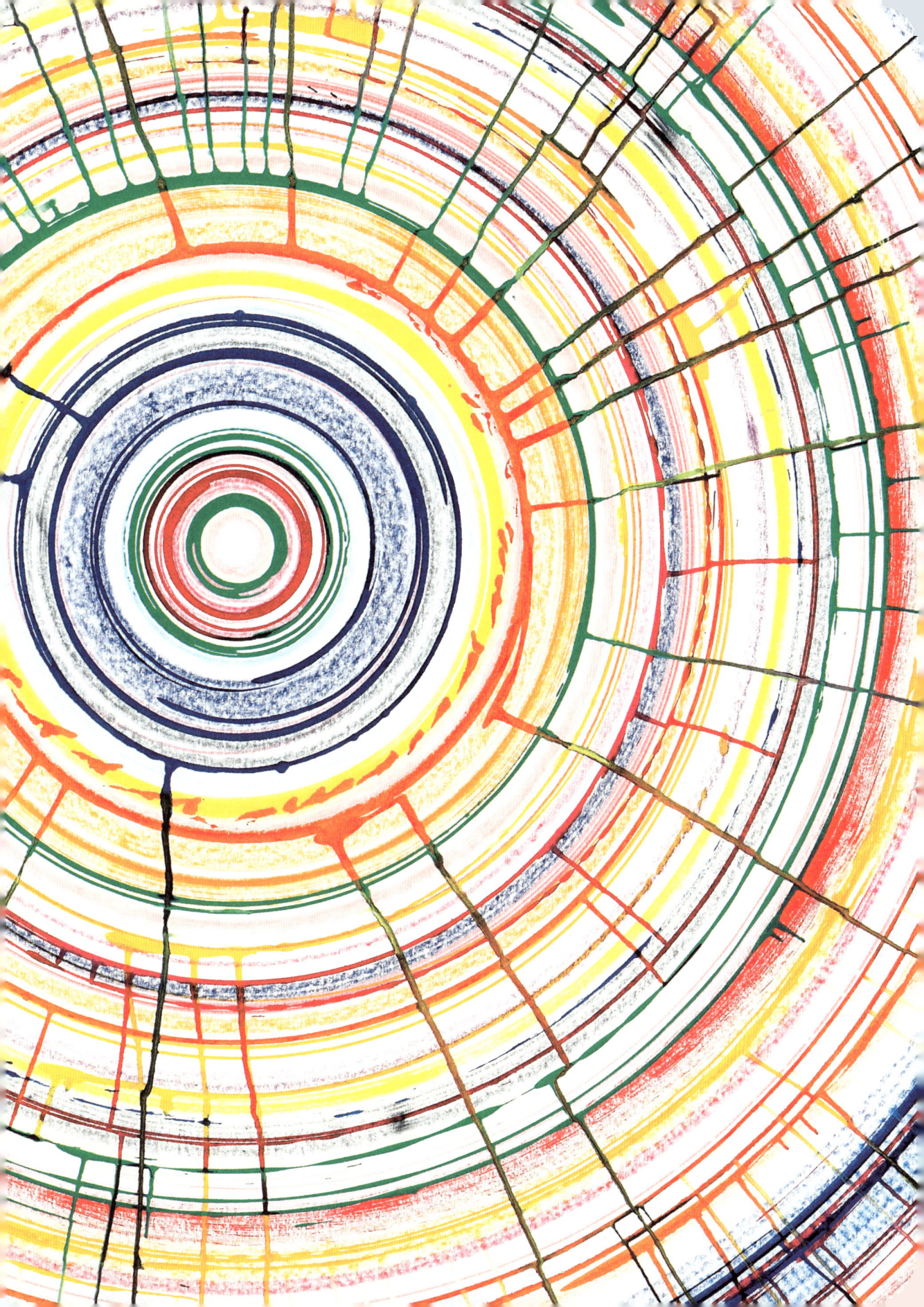

„Das Tolle am Zeichnen ist, dass es
billig ist. So kann man sehr teure Ideen
und Dinge sehr günstig visualisieren,
während man sich noch in der Bleistift-
und-Papier-Phase befindet. Wenn man
eine sehr teure Skulptur machen
möchte, ist es sehr gut, mit dem
Zeichnen zu beginnen."

'The great thing about drawing is
it's cheap, so you can visualise very
expensive ideas and things very
cheaply while you're on the pencil-
and-paper stage. If you want to do
a very expensive sculpture, it's very
good to start with drawing.'

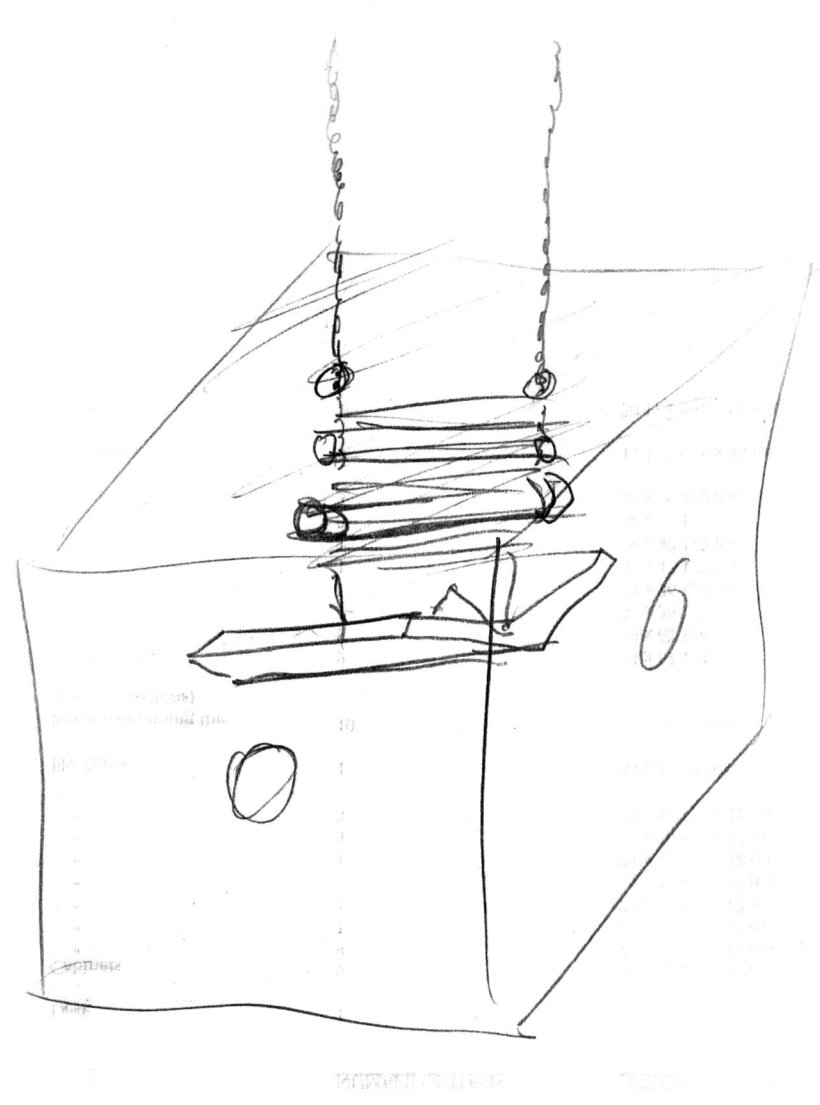

Cube Fly Killer, 1992 | Bleistift auf Papier | Pencil on paper | 28 × 22 cm

a whole life cycle
your born you look around, you die.

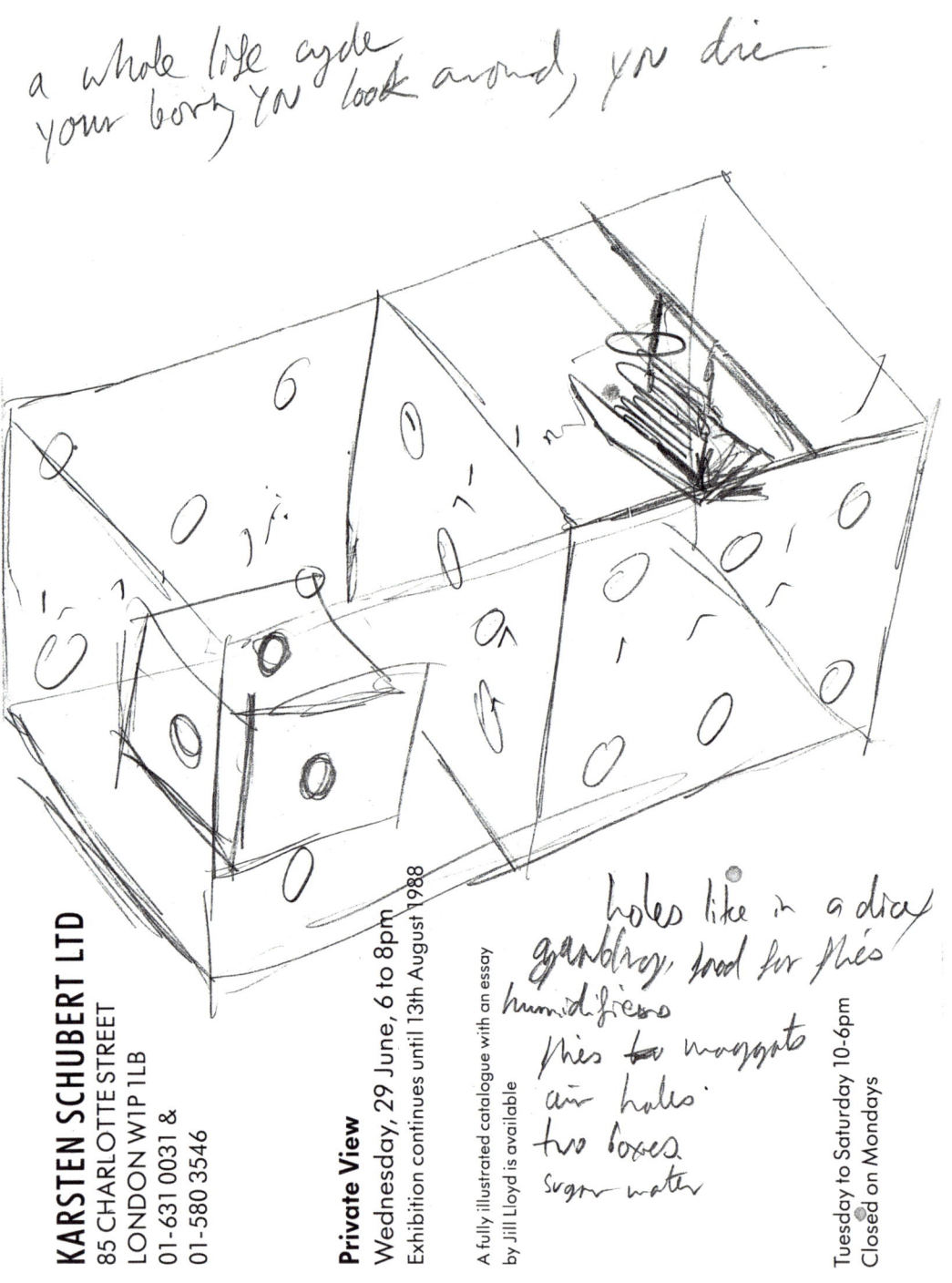

KARSTEN SCHUBERT LTD
85 CHARLOTTE STREET
LONDON W1P 1LB
01-631 0031 &
01-580 3546

Private View
Wednesday, 29 June, 6 to 8pm
Exhibition continues until 13th August 1988

A fully illustrated catalogue with an essay
by Jill Lloyd is available

Tuesday to Saturday 10-6pm
Closed on Mondays

holes like in a diary
gangbang, food for flies
humidifiers
flies to maggots
air holes
two boxes
sugar water

A Whole Life Cycle: You're Born, You Look Around, You Die, 1988
Bleistift auf Karton | Pencil on card | 18 × 13 cm

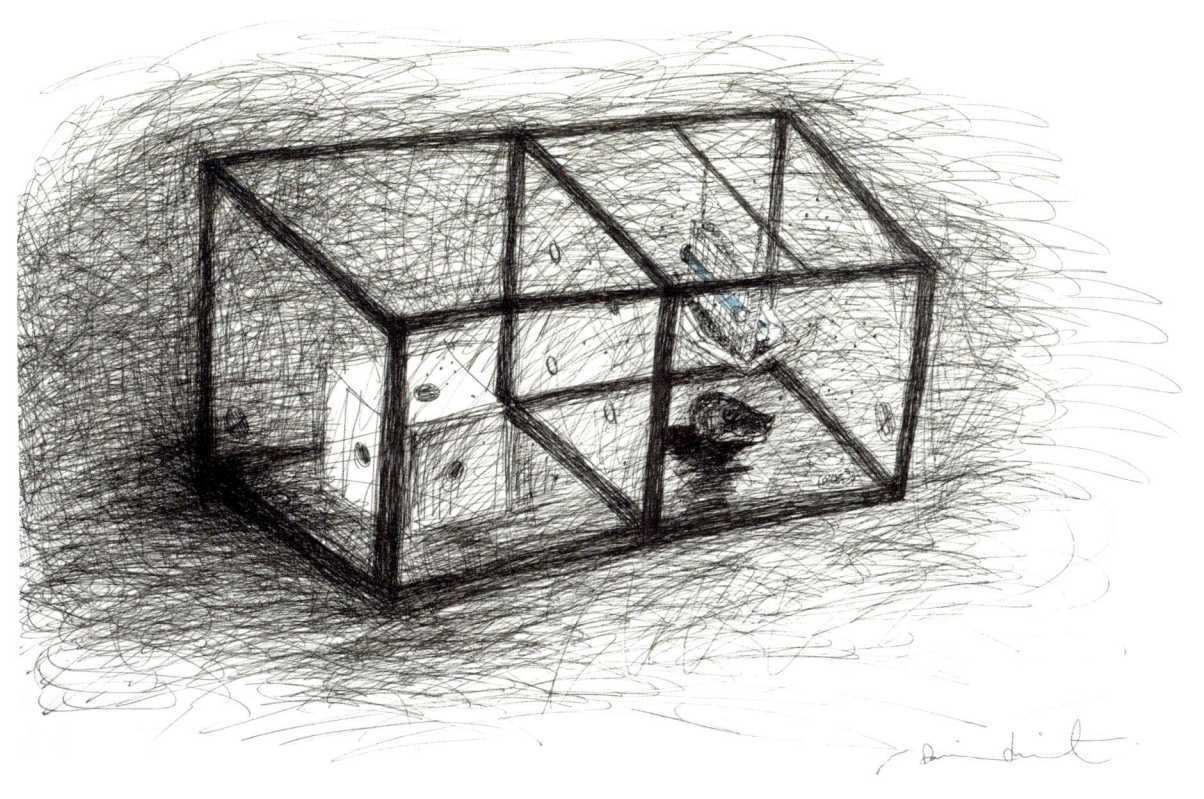

A Thousand Years, 2004 | Tinte und Textmarker auf Papier | Ink and highlighter on paper | 59 × 84 cm

23

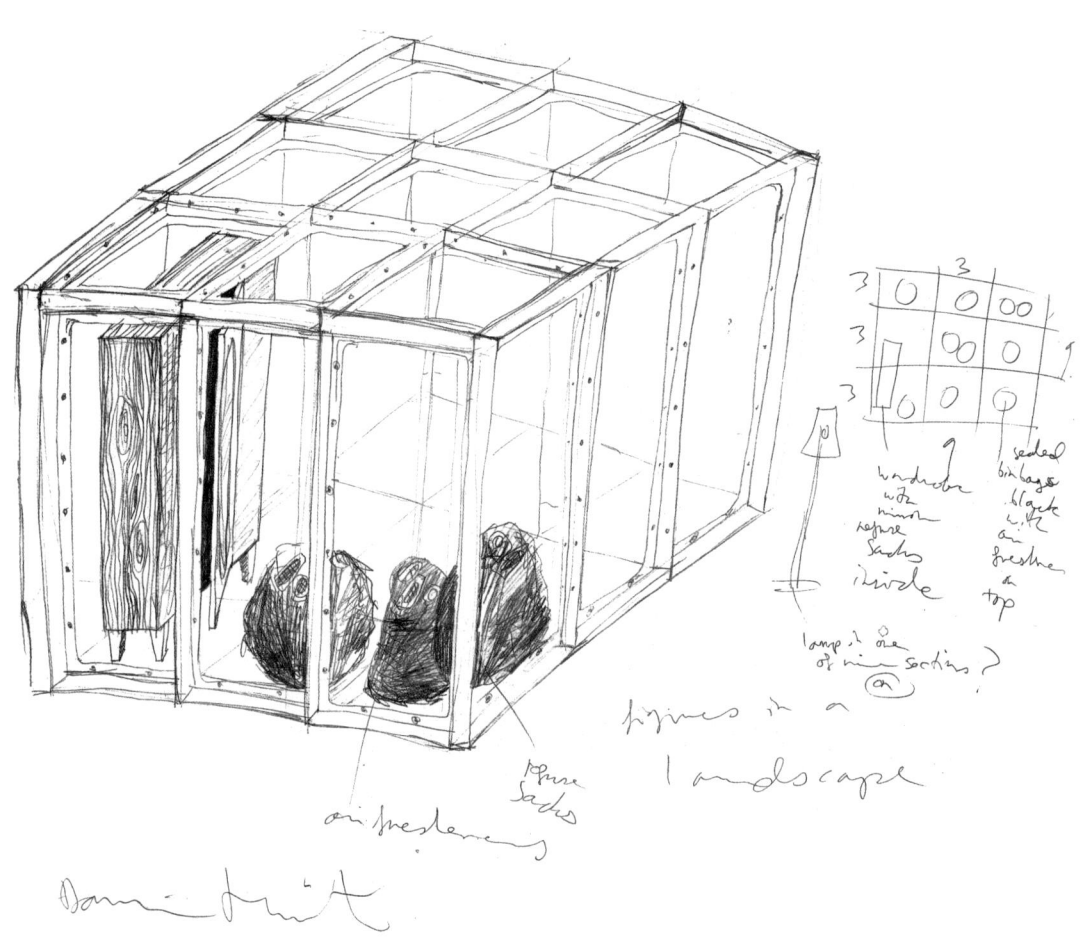

Figures in a Landscape, 1988 | Bleistift auf Papier | Pencil on paper | 70 × 95 cm

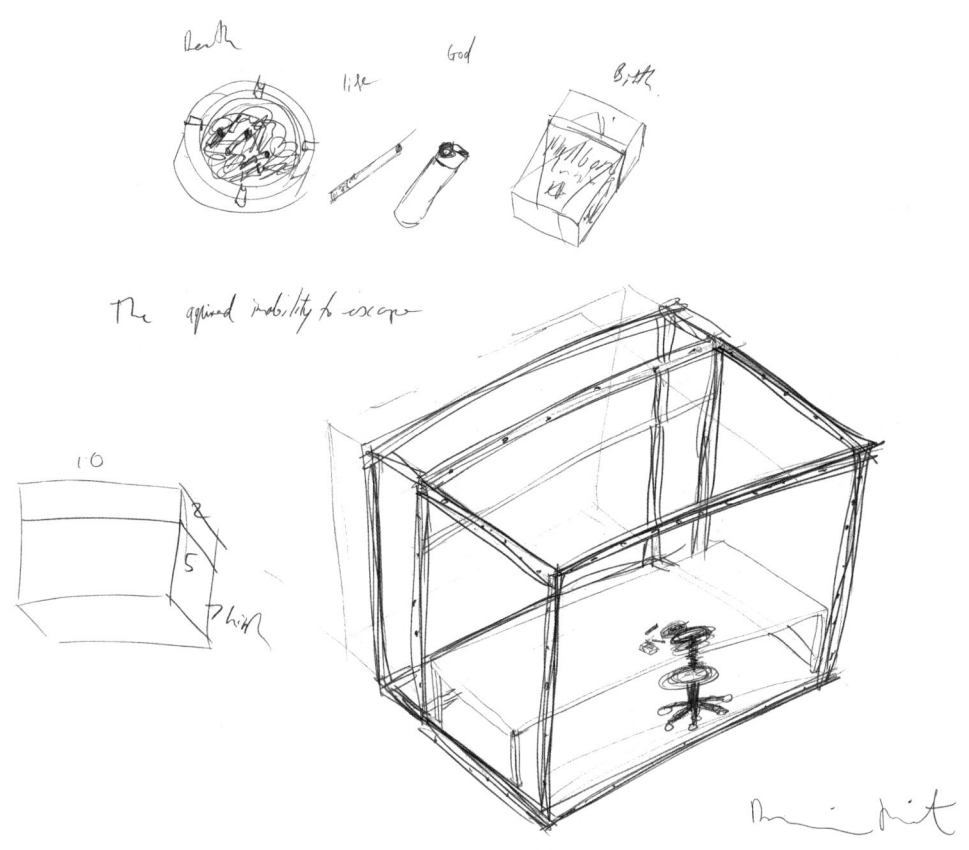

Death   Life   God   Birth

The acquired inability to escape

10

8

5

The Acquired Inability to Escape (Death, Life, God, Birth), 2002 | Bleistift auf Papier | Pencil on paper | 75 × 110 cm

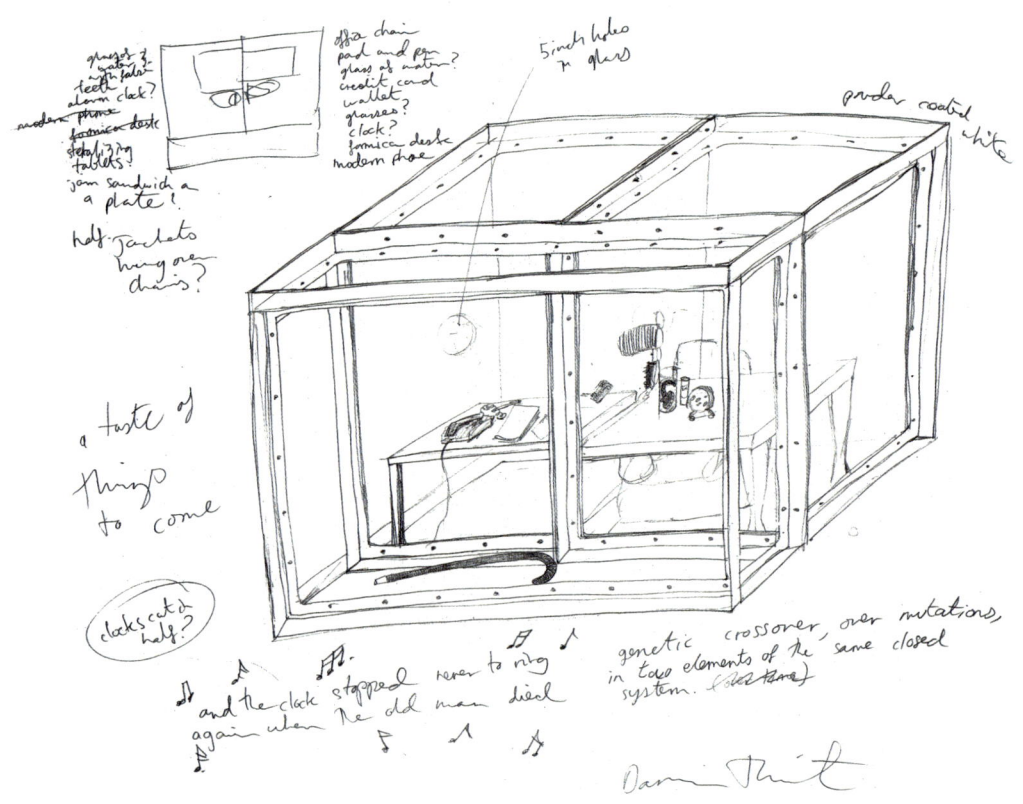

quagat of water
teeth false
alarm clock?
modern phone
formica desk
stabalizing
tablets!
jam sandwich a
a plate !.

half. jackets
hung over
chairs?

office chair
pad and pen
glass of water?
credit card
wallet
glasses?
clock?
formica desk
modern phone

5 inch holes
in glass

powder coated
white

a taste of

things

to come

clocks cut in
half?

♫. and the clock stopped never to ring again when the old man died

genetic crossover, over mutations,
in two elements of the same closed
system. (electrons)

Damien Hirst

From the Cradle to the Grave (And the Clock Stopped Never to Ring Again When the Old Man Died), 1998 | Bleistift auf Papier | Pencil on paper | 70 × 95 cm

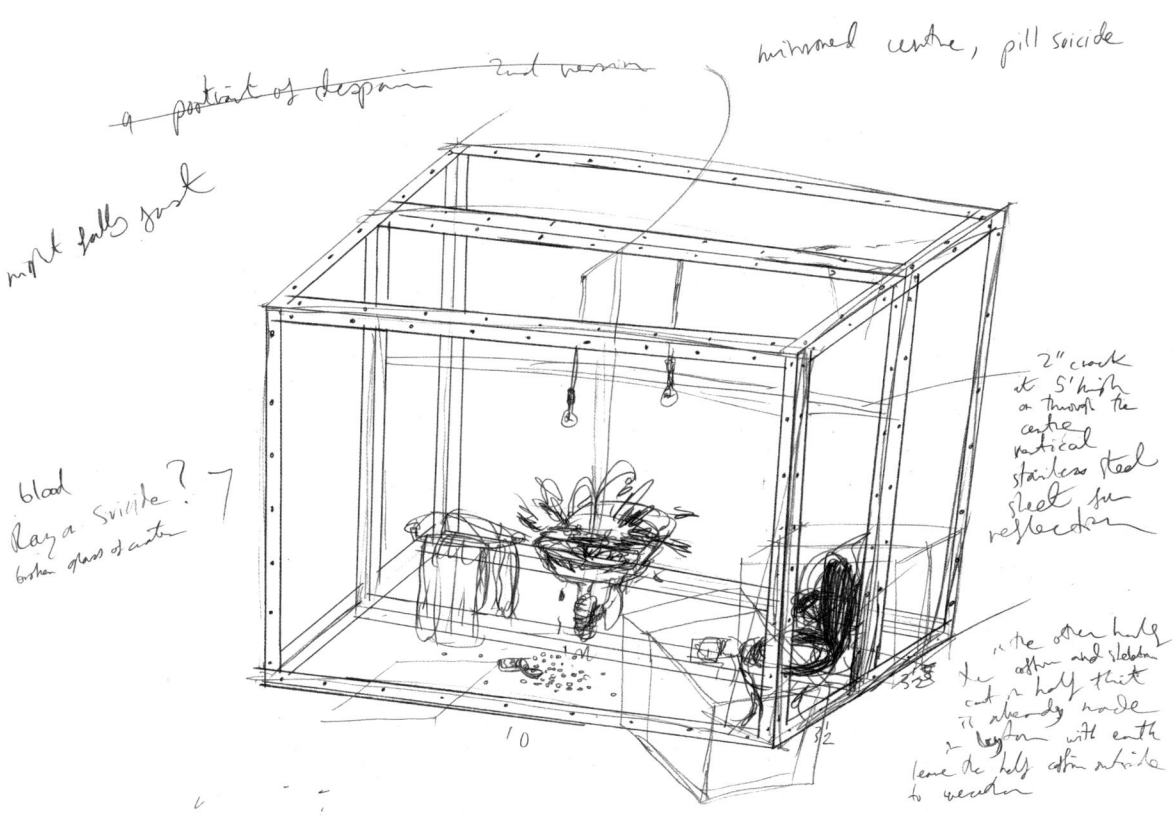

a portrait of despair 2nd version   mirrored centre, pill suicide

night falls fast

blood
Raza suicide? 7
broken glass of centre

2" crack
at 5' high
or through the
central
vertical
stainless steel
sheet for
reflection

A Portrait of Despair/Night Falls Fast, 2000 | Bleistift auf Papier | Pencil on paper | 75 × 110 cm

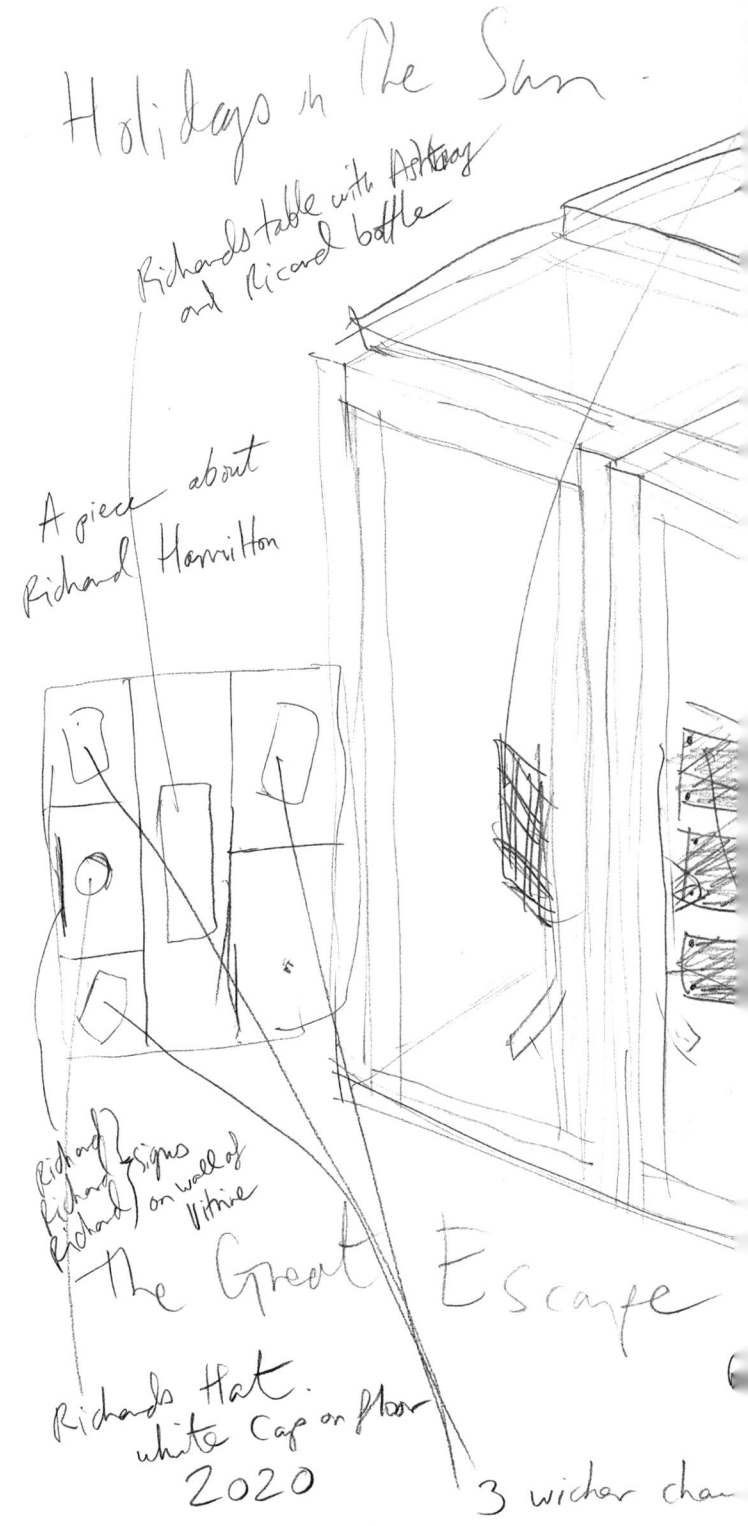

Holidays in The Sun.

Richards table with Ashtray
and Ricard bottle

A piece about
Richard Hamilton

Richard
Richard } signs
Richard } on wall of
Vitrine

The Great Escape

Richards Hat.
white Cap on floor
2020

3 wicker chai

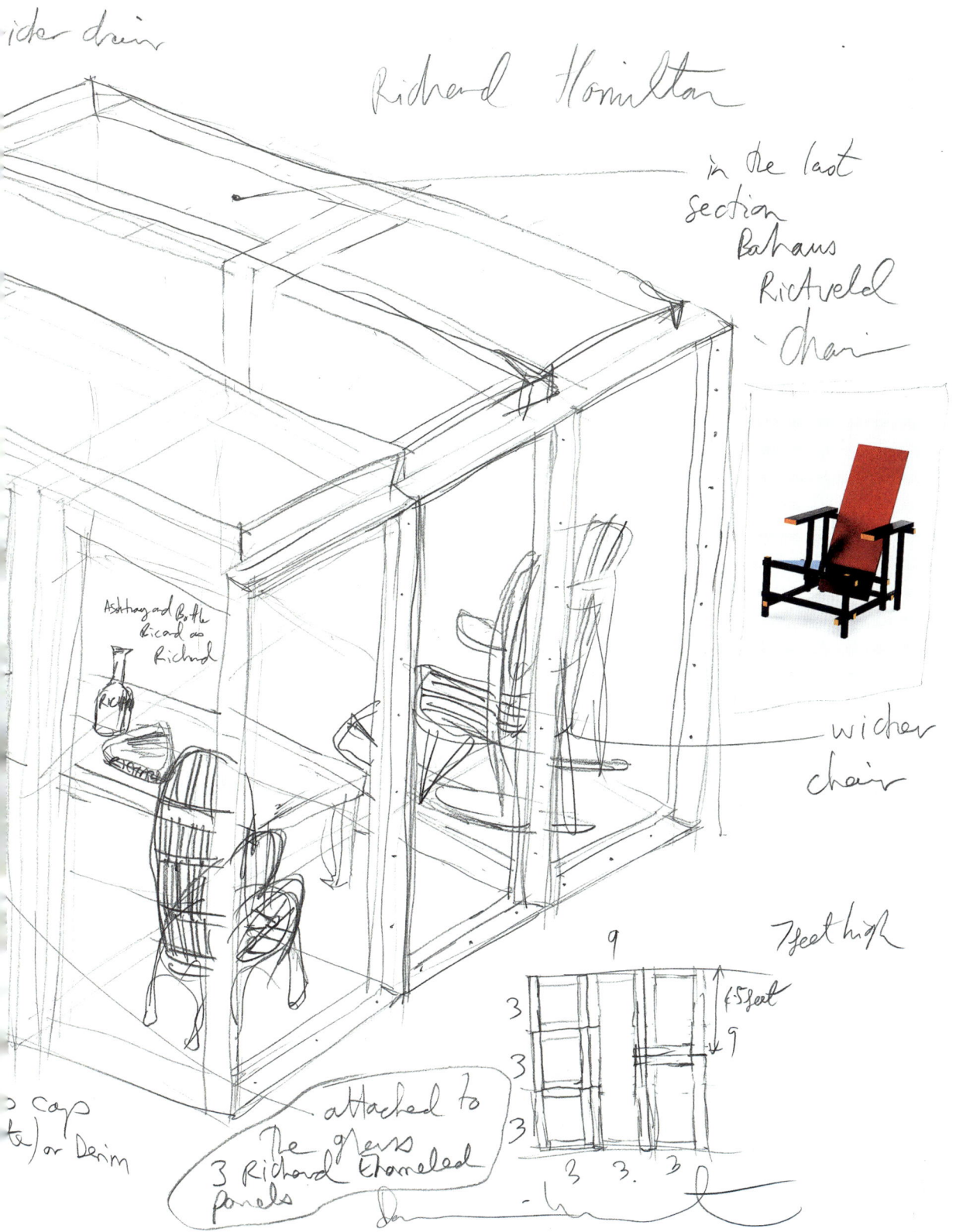

icker chair

Richard Hamilton

in the last
section
Bauhaus
Rietveld
chair

Ashtray and Bottle
Ricard as
Richard

RICARD

wicker
chair

7 feet high

9

3   +5 feet

3   ←9

3

5 cap
te) or Denim

attached to
the glass
3 Richard enameled
panels
Denim

3   3.   3

„Ich mag die sich verändernden Spot
Paintings: Das Produkt verändert
sich, der Maßstab verändert sich,
die Farbe verändert sich, doch die
Form bleibt gleich."

'I like the changing life of the spot
paintings: the product changes, the
scale changes, the colour changes,
but the form does not.'

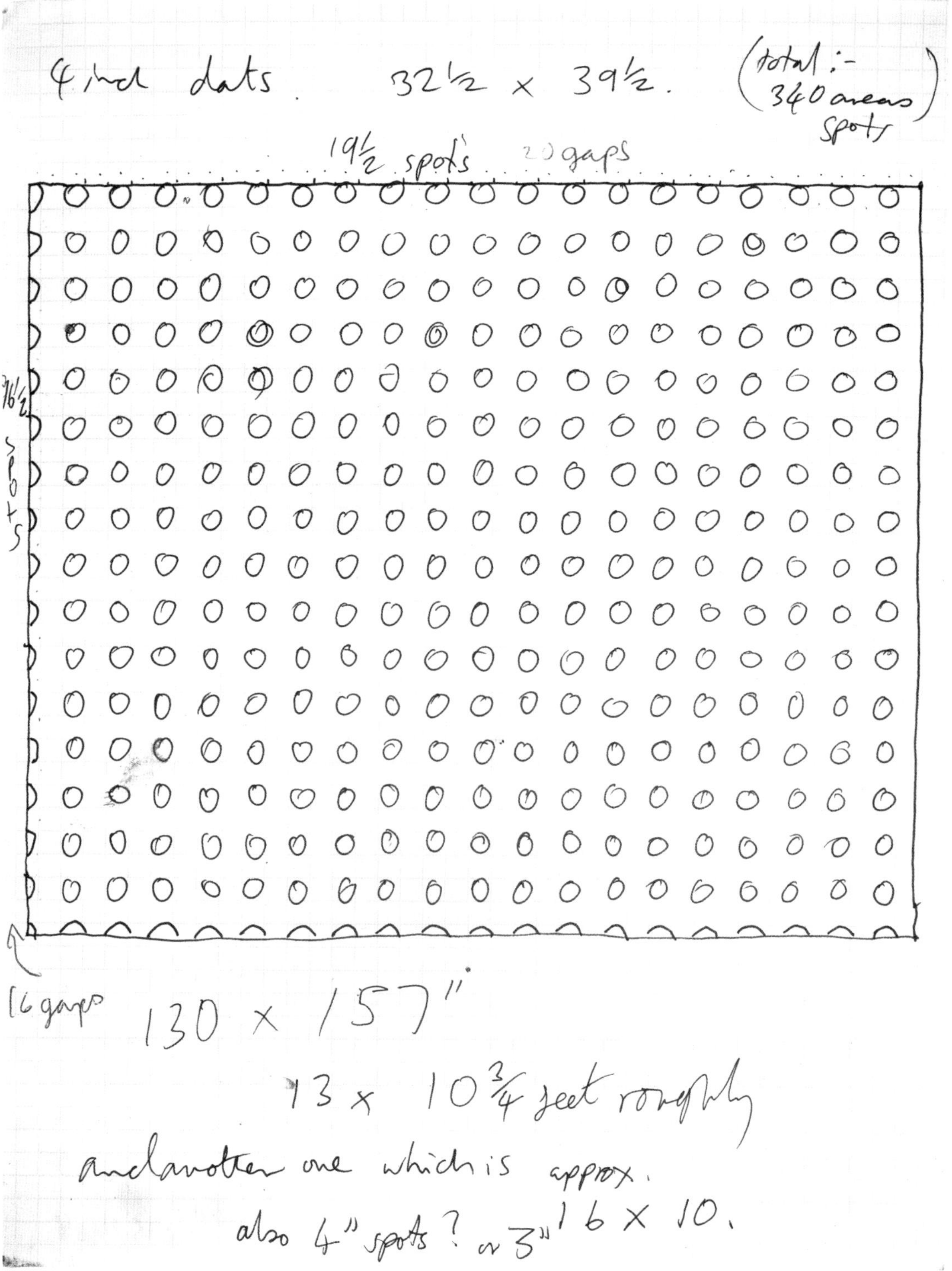

4 inch dots.   32½ × 39½.   (total :- 340 areas) spots

19½ spots   20 gaps

16½ spots

16 gaps   130 × 157″

13 × 10¾ feet roughly

and another one which is approx.

also 4″ spots? or 3″ 16 × 10.

32½ × 39½, 1992 | Tinte auf Papier | Ink on paper | 28 × 21 cm

2.

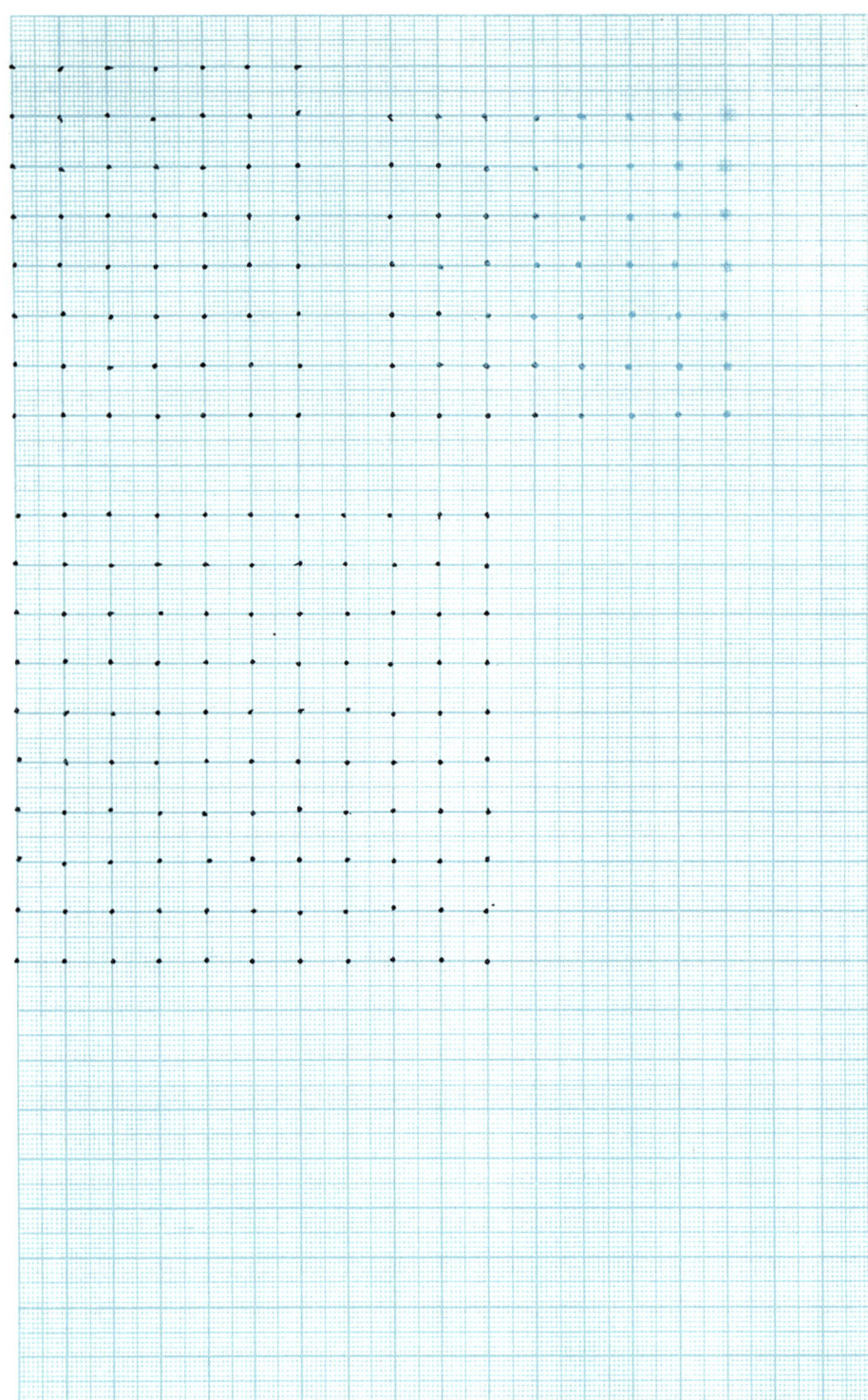

Preparatory Studies for Spot Paintings, 1993 | Tinte auf Papier | Ink on paper |
Aus einer 9-teiligen Serie, je | From a series of 9 parts, each: 32 × 21 cm

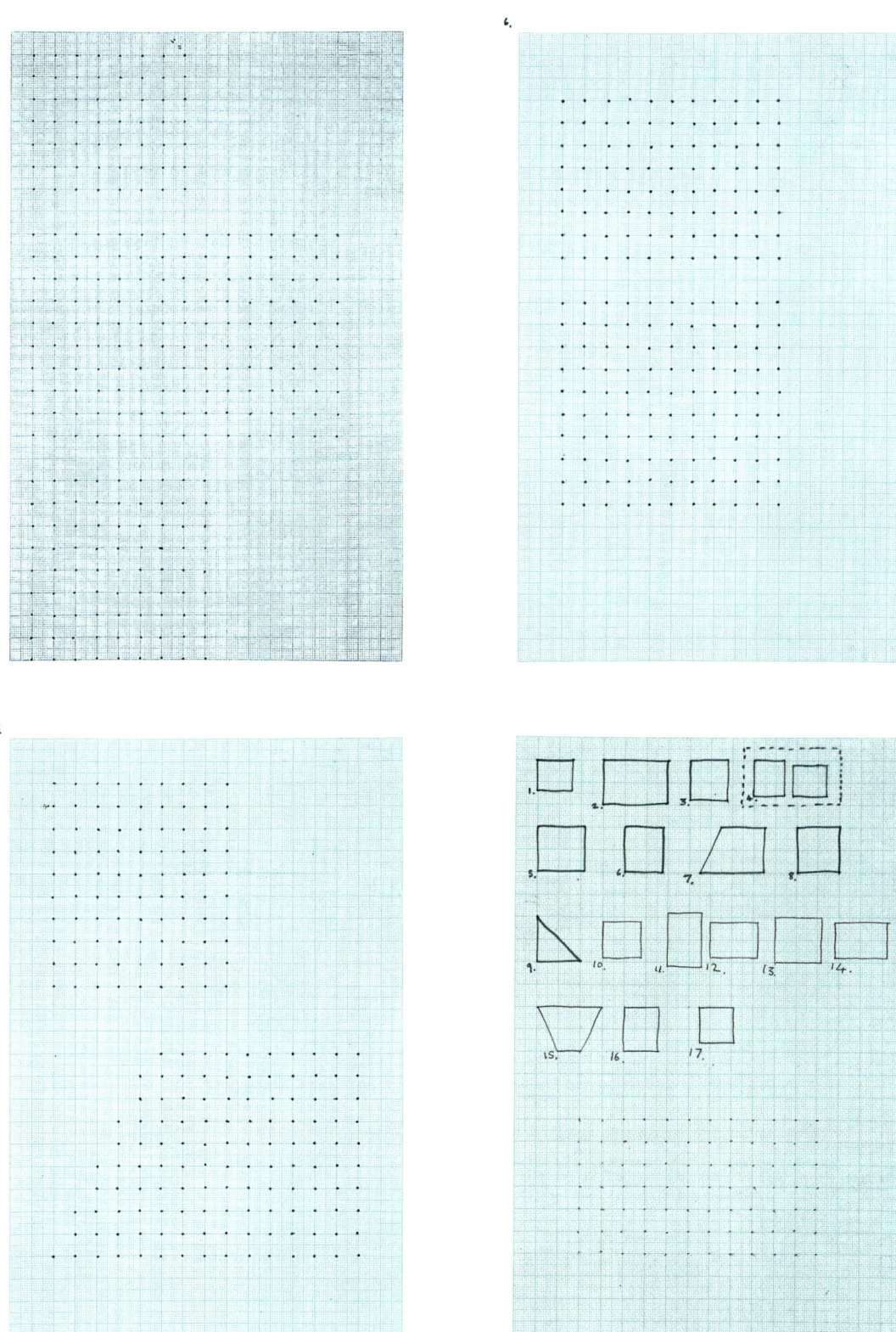

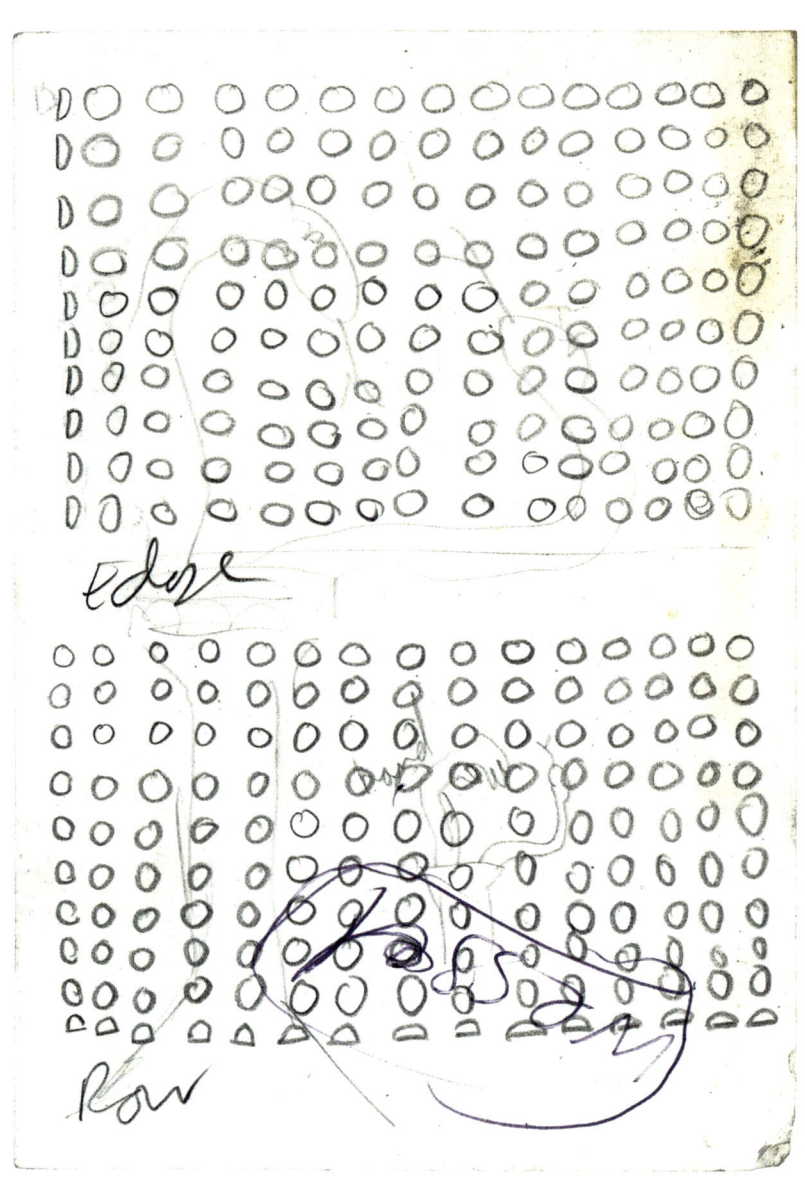

Edge/Row, 1987 | Bleistift und Tinte auf Papier | Pencil and ink on paper | 15 × 10 cm

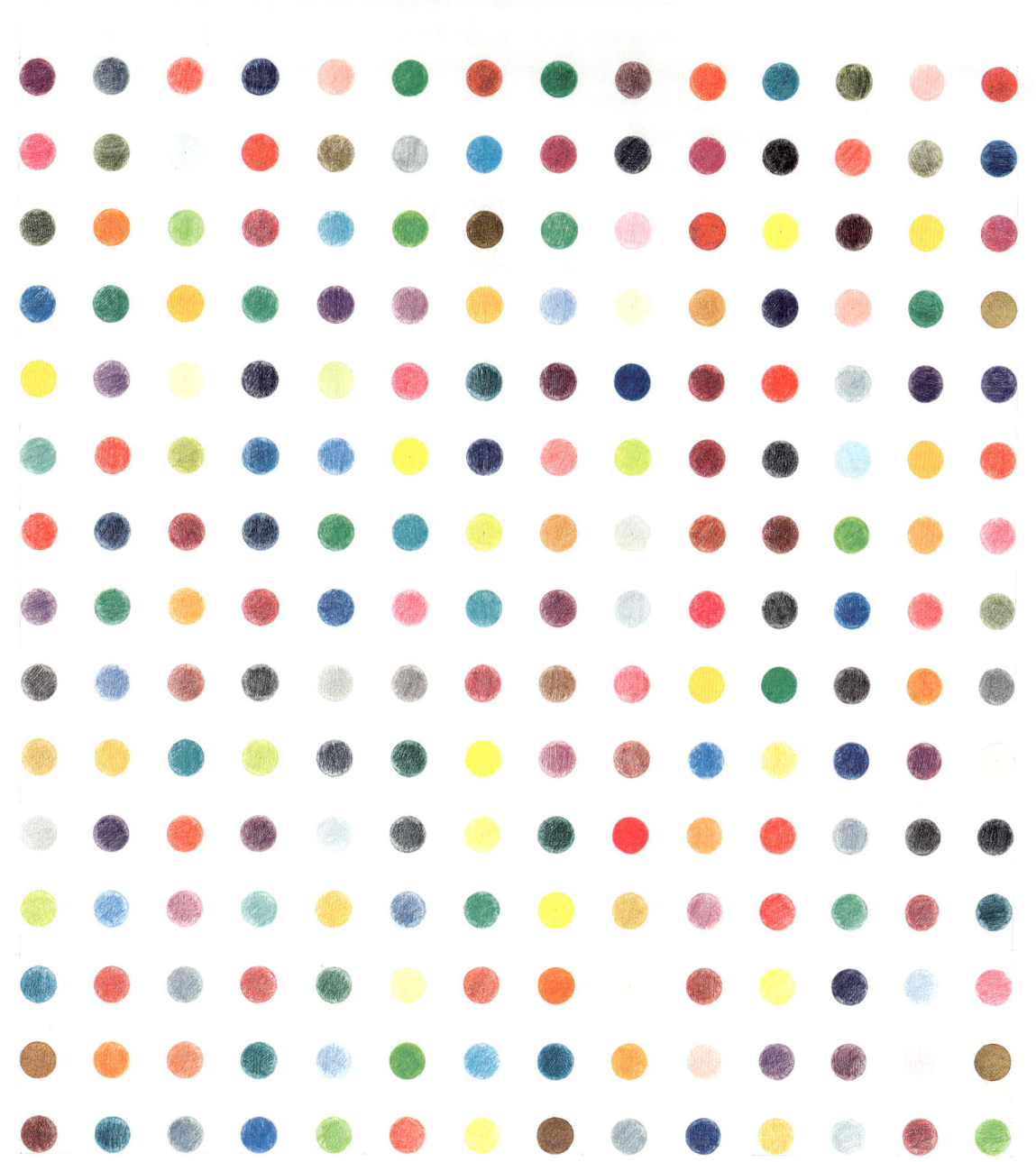

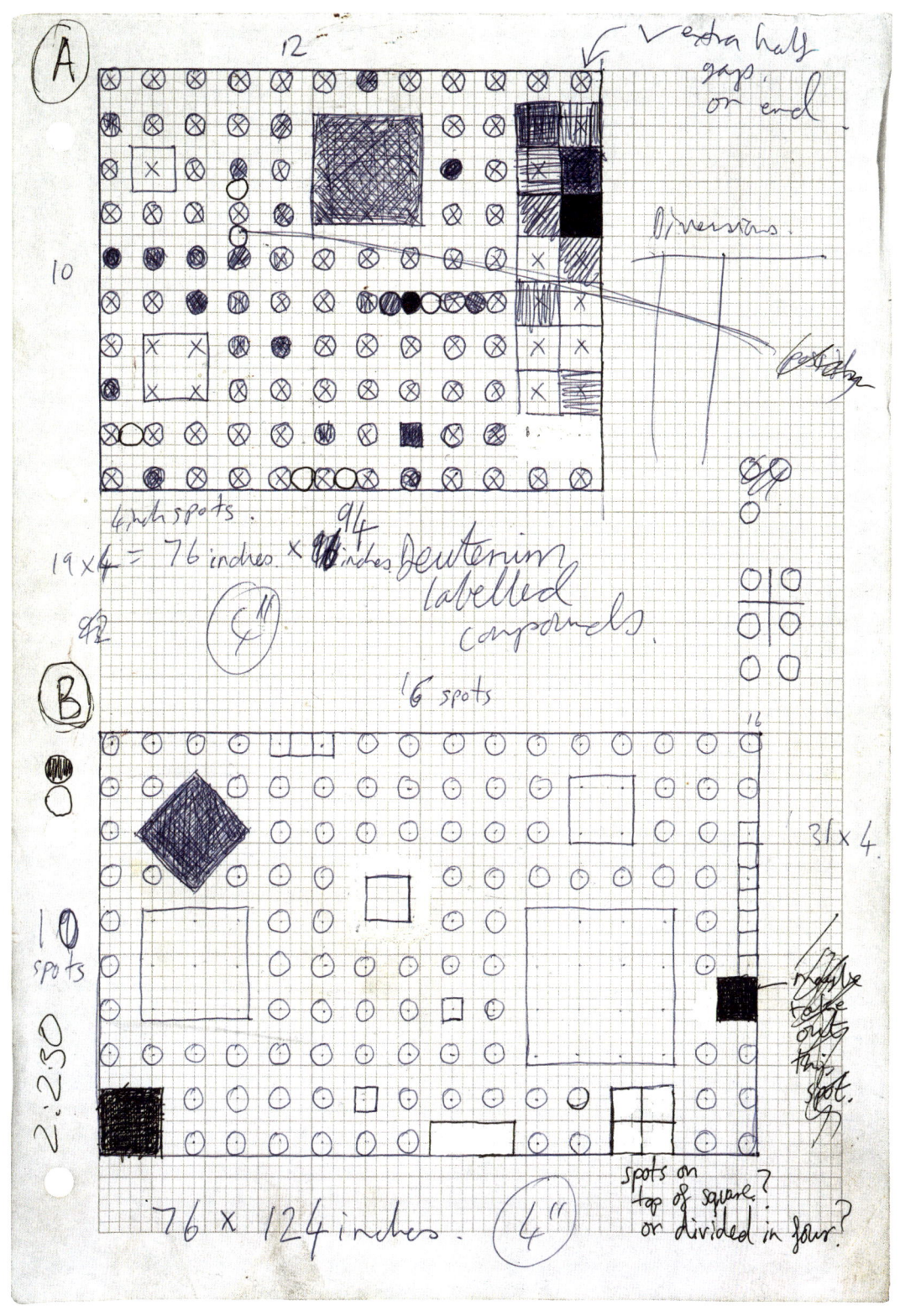

Deuterium Labelled Compounds, 1992 | Tinte und Korrekturflüssigkeit auf Papier |
Ink and correction fluid on paper | 30 × 21 cm

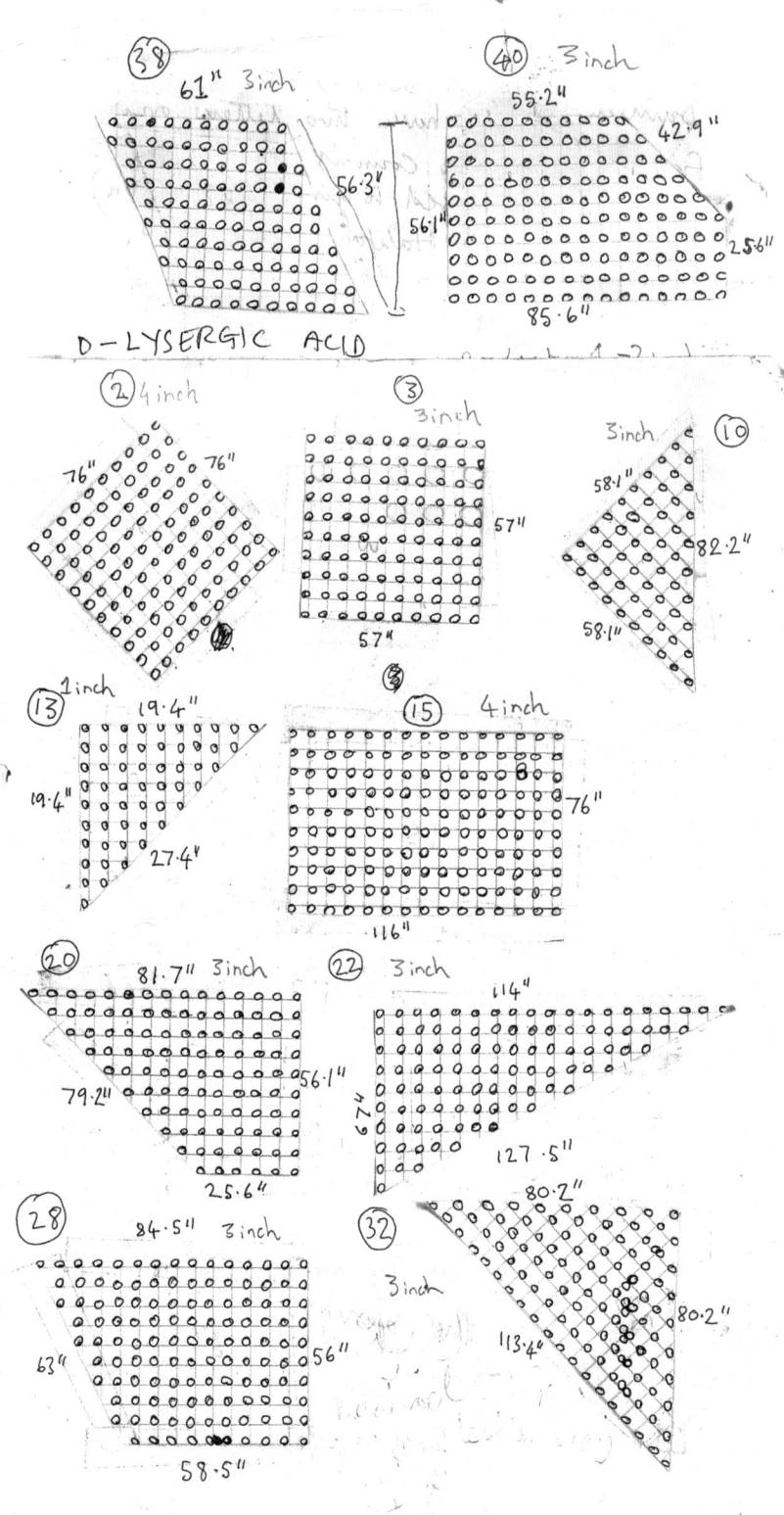

D—LYSERGIC ACID

Controlled Collage, 1993 | Tinte, Bleistift und Klebeband auf Papier | Ink, pencil, and adhesive tape on paper | 39 × 21 cm

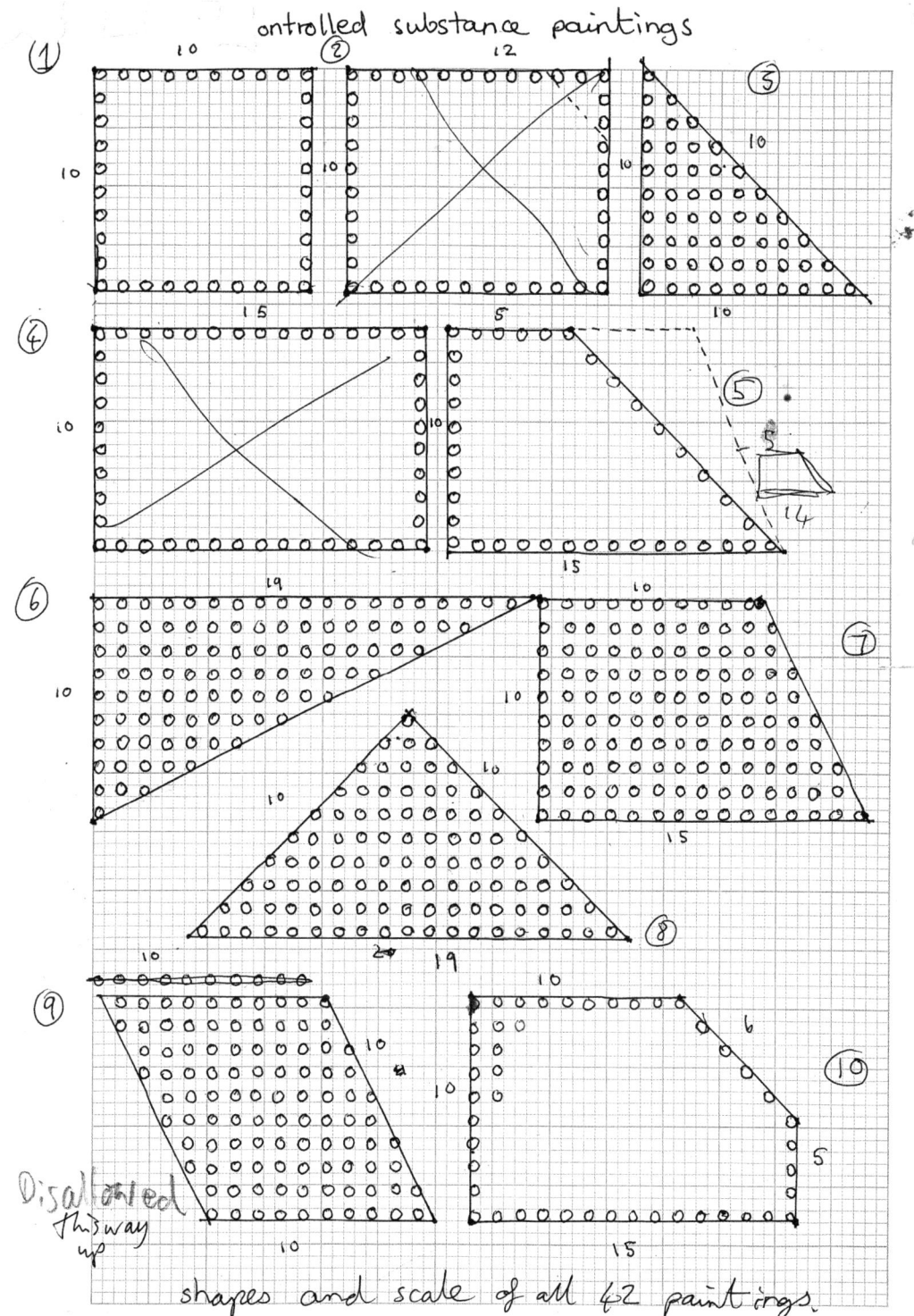

ontrolled substance paintings

shapes and scale of all 42 paintings.

ALL MEASUREMENTS ARE IN INCHES.

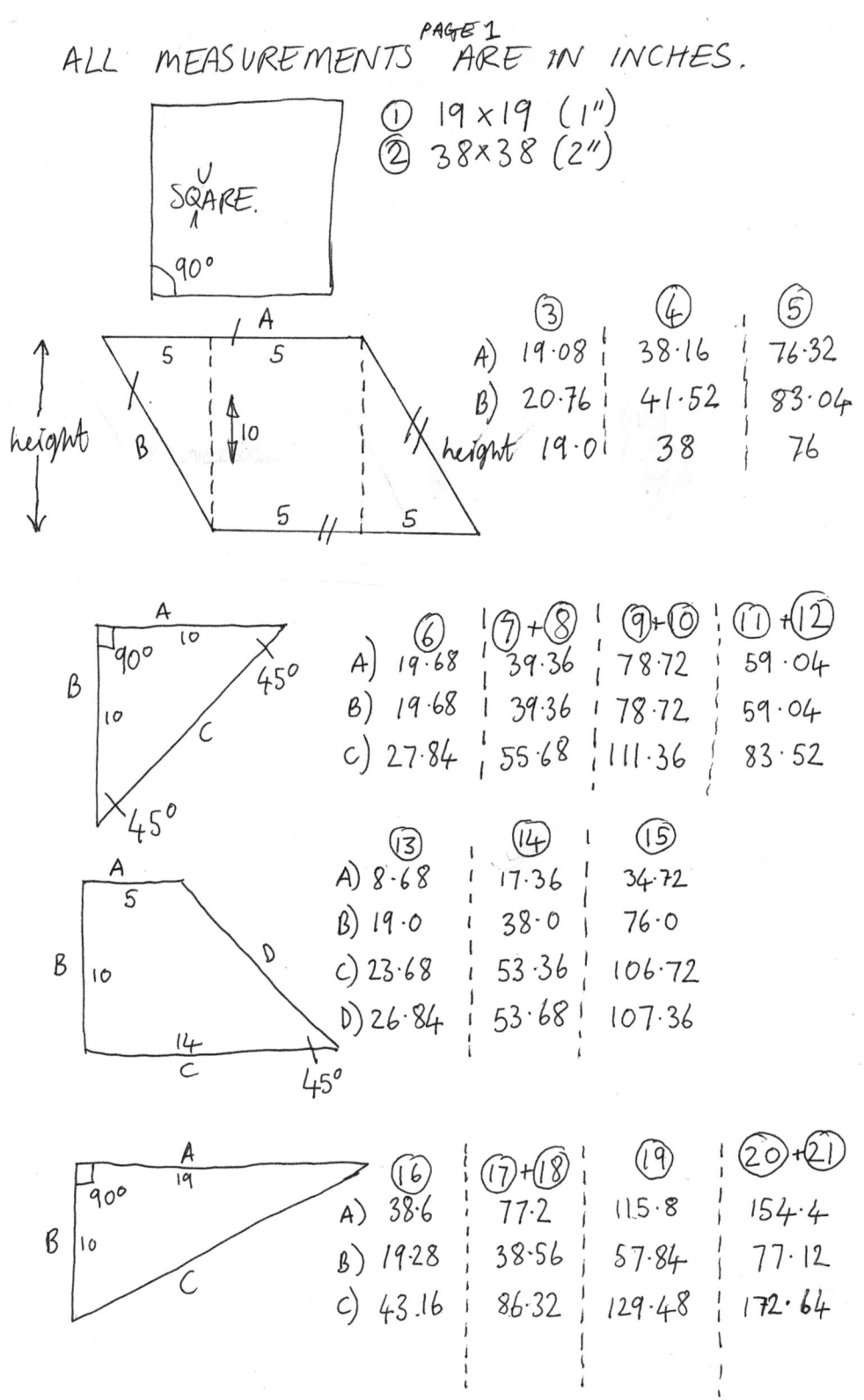

① 19 × 19 (1")
② 38 × 38 (2")

SQARE.

90°

	③	④	⑤
A)	19.08	38.16	76.32
B)	20.76	41.52	83.04
height	19.0	38	76

A 5   5
B height

	⑥	⑦+⑧	⑨+⑩	⑪+⑫
A)	19.68	39.36	78.72	59.04
B)	19.68	39.36	78.72	59.04
C)	27.84	55.68	111.36	83.52

A 10   90°   45°
B 10   C   45°

	⑬	⑭	⑮
A)	8.68	17.36	34.72
B)	19.0	38.0	76.0
C)	23.68	53.36	106.72
D)	26.84	53.68	107.36

A 5   B 10   D   14 C   45°

	⑯	⑰+⑱	⑲	⑳+㉑
A)	38.6	77.2	115.8	154.4
B)	19.28	38.56	57.84	77.12
C)	43.16	86.32	129.48	172.64

A 19   90°   B 10   C

Study for Controlled Substance Paintings, 1993 | Tinte auf Papier | Ink on paper | 30 × 42 cm

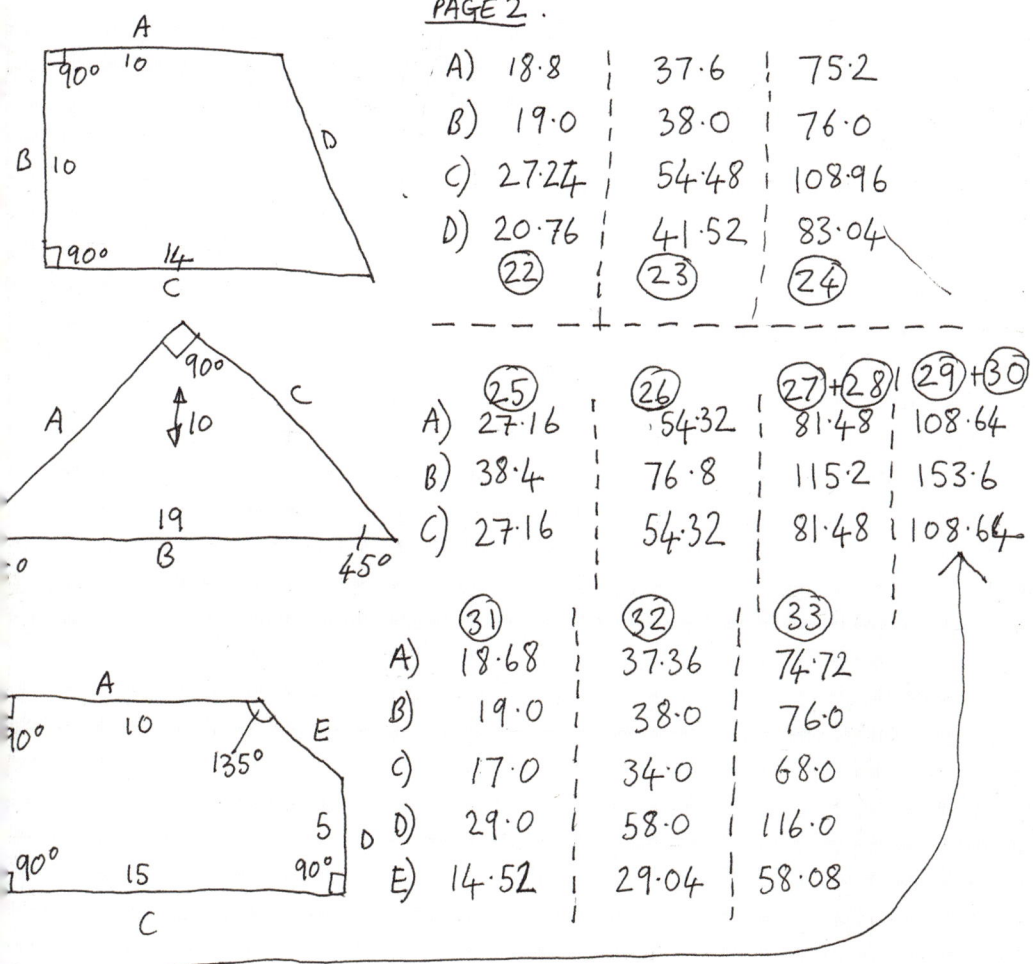

PAGE 2.

	22	23	24
A)	18.8	37.6	75.2
B)	19.0	38.0	76.0
C)	27.24	54.48	108.96
D)	20.76	41.52	83.04

	25	26	27+28	29+30
A)	27.16	54.32	81.48	108.64
B)	38.4	76.8	115.2	153.6
C)	27.16	54.32	81.48	108.64

	31	32	33
A)	18.68	37.36	74.72
B)	19.0	38.0	76.0
C)	17.0	34.0	68.0
D)	29.0	58.0	116.0
E)	14.52	29.04	58.08

The numbers in the circles eg ① represent individual paintings where there are two numbers -like here, there are two stretchers. (they go different ways on the wall   33 stretchers in total Hugh can you ask Stuart if he can work out the angles of the parralellogram again if Mick needs it, he may not need it .

FOLGENDE SEITEN | FOLLOWING PAGES: *34 Boxes (with Hole), 1987* | Haushaltspolitur auf Pappkartons | Household gloss on cardboard boxes | 105 × 257 × 71 cm

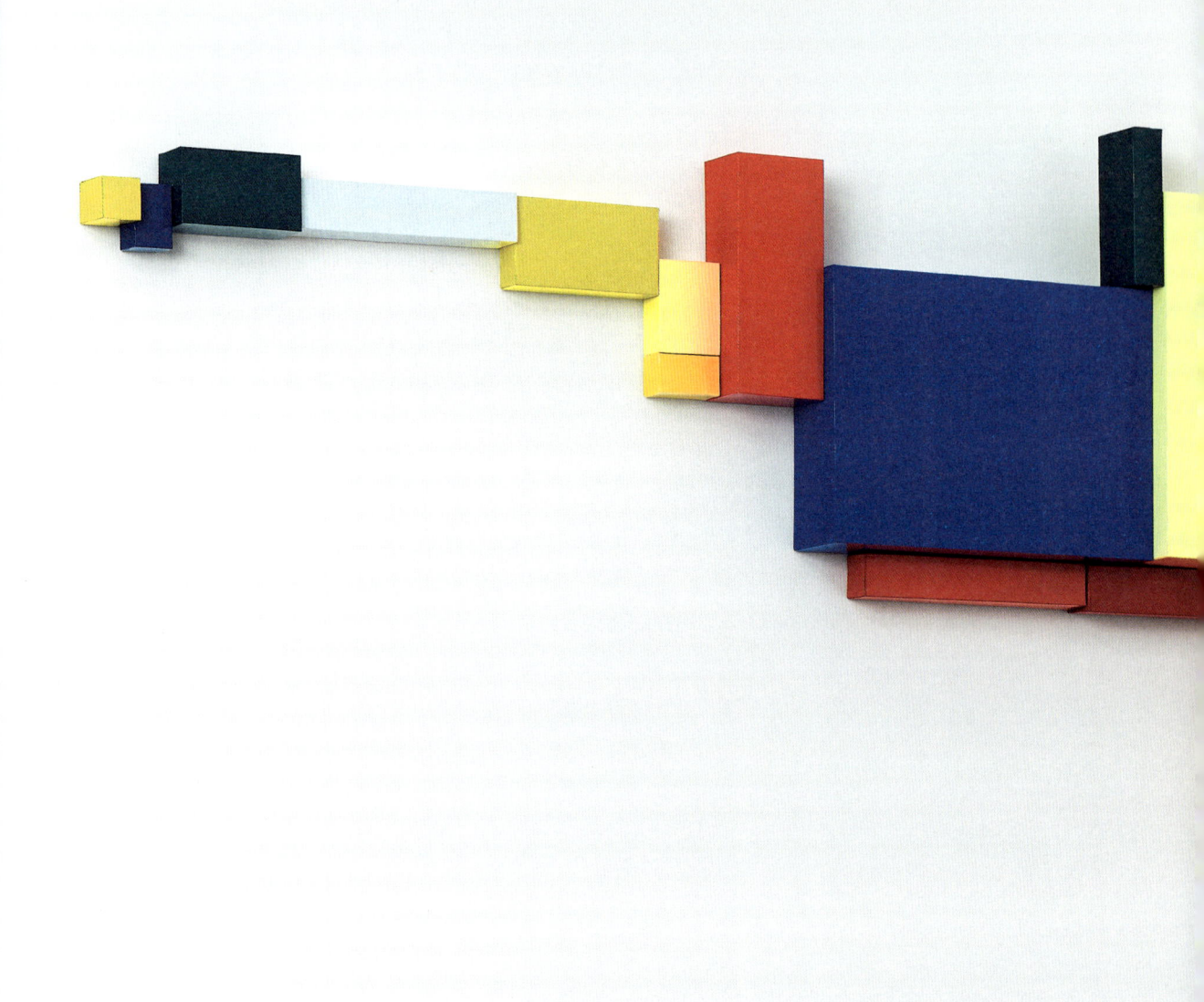

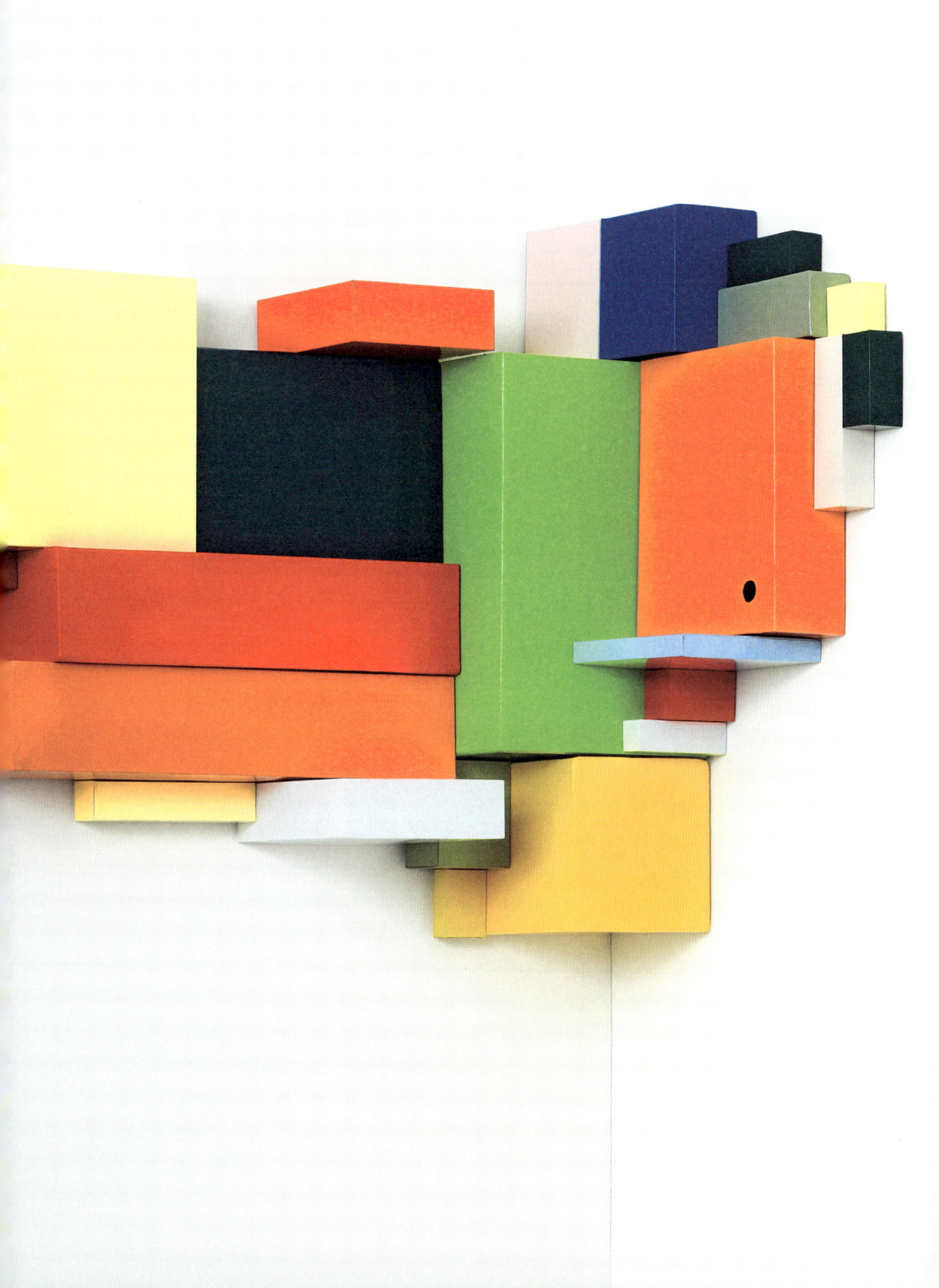

„Ich habe Medizinschränke immer als
Körper gesehen, aber auch als eine Art
Stadtlandschaft oder Zivilisation, mit einer
Art Hierarchie darin. Es ist auch wie ein
zeitgenössisches Museum des Mittelalters.
In 100 Jahren wird das wie eine alte
Apotheke aussehen. Ein Museum für
etwas, das es heute noch gibt."

'I've always seen medicine cabinets
as bodies, but also like a cityscape or
civilization, with some sort of
hierarchy within it. It's also like a
contemporary museum of the Middle
Ages. In 100 years' time this will look
like an old apothecary. A museum of
something that's around today.'

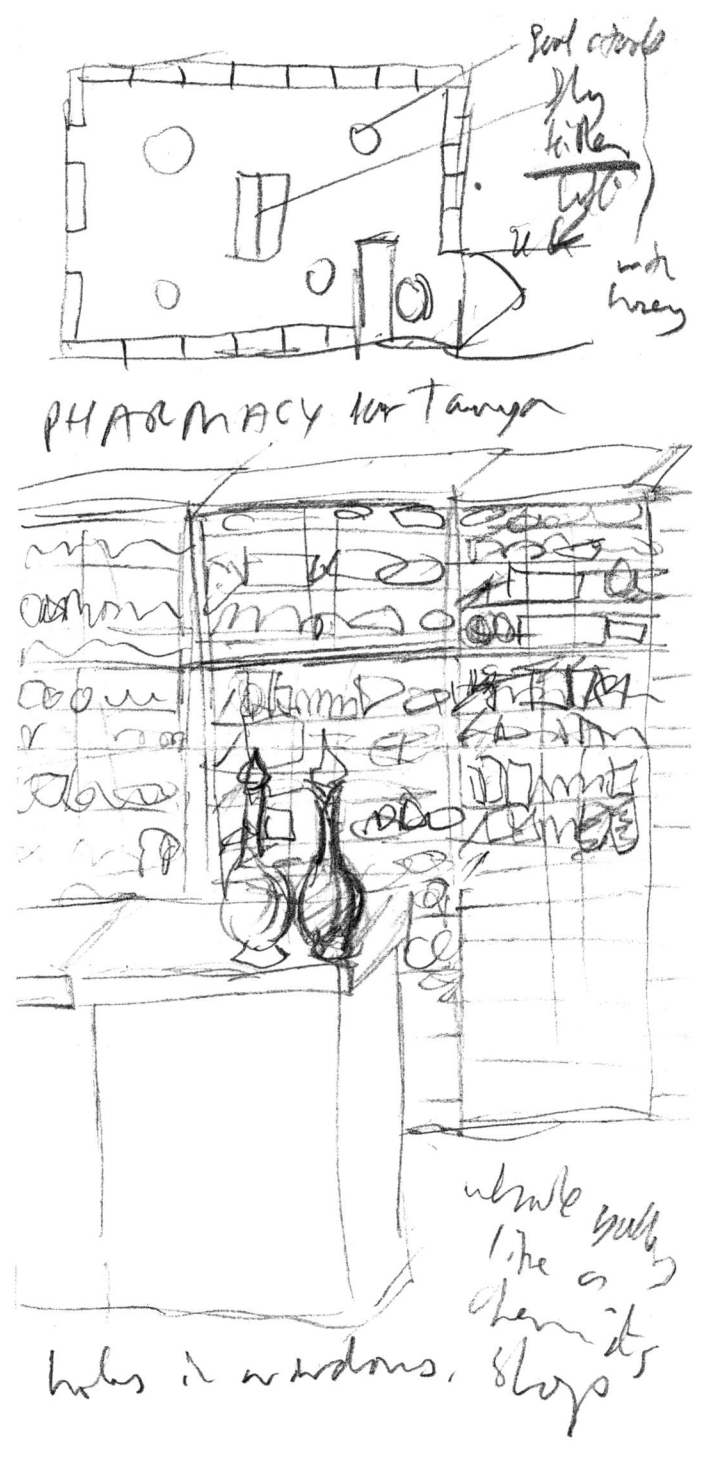

PHARMACY for Tanya

Pharmacy for Tanya, 1990–1991 | Bleistift auf Papier | Pencil on paper | 21 × 10 cm

45

Bodies, 1989 | Glas, beschichtete Spanplatte, Buche, Kunststoff, Aluminium und Arzneimittelpackung | Glass, faced particleboard, beech, plastic, aluminium, and pharmaceutical packaging | 137 × 102 × 23 cm

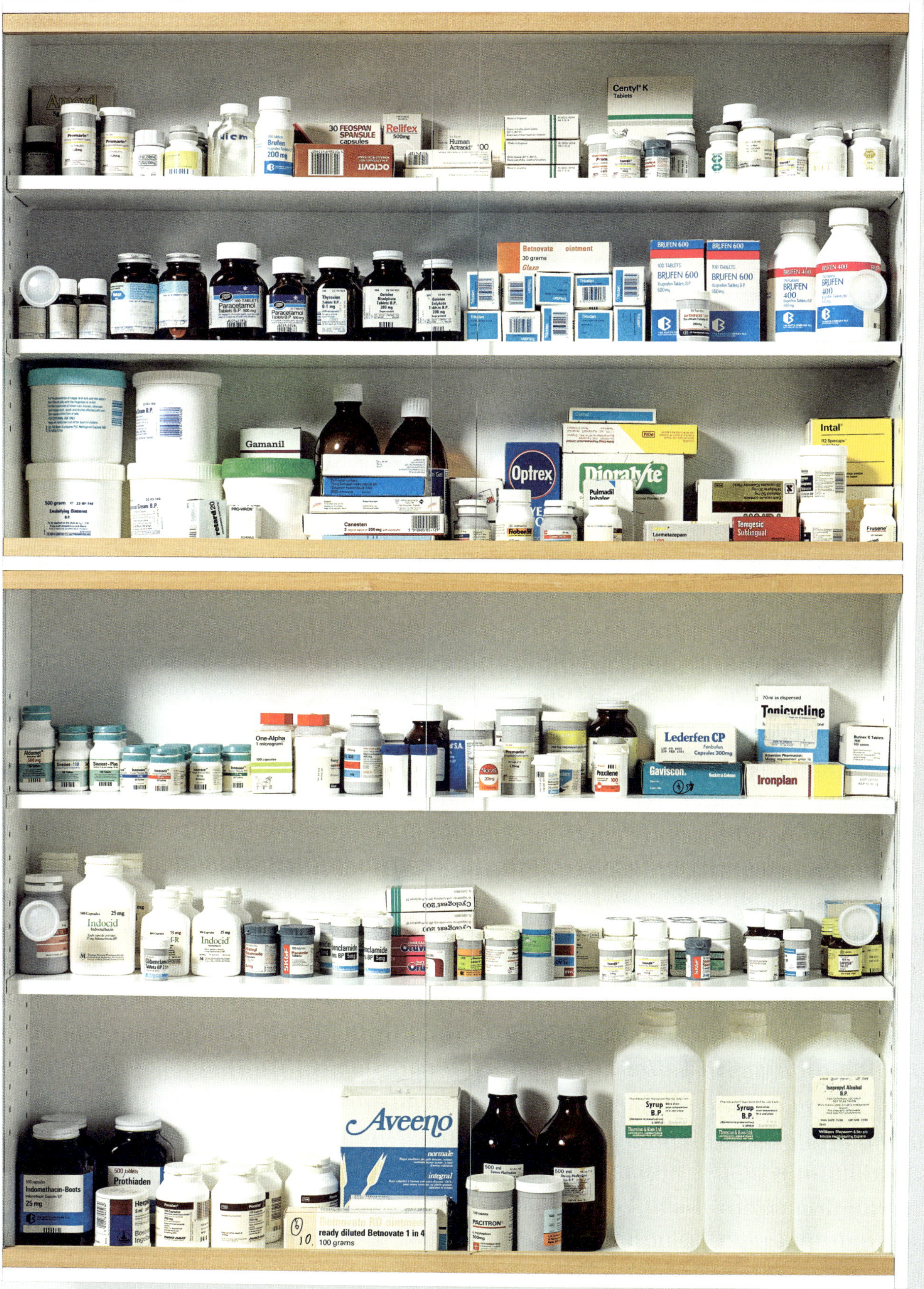

Centyl K
Tablets
30 FEOSPAN SPANSULE capsules
Relifex
500mg
Brufen
200 mg
Human Actrapid
Betnovate ointment
30 grams
Glaxo
BRUFEN 600
BRUFEN 400
Paracetamol
Gamanil
Optrex
Dioralyte
Pulmadil Inhaler
Intal
Canesten
Lormetazepam
Temgesic Sublingual
Frusene
One-Alpha
Lederfen CP
Fenbufen
Capsules 300mg
Tonicycline
Gaviscon
Ironplan
Proxilene
Indocid
Cyclogest 200
Aveeno
normale
integral
Syrup B.P.
Isopropyl Alcohol B.P.
Indomethacin-Boots
25 mg
500 tablets
Prothiaden
ready diluted Betnovate 1 in 4
100 grams
PACITRON
500 ml

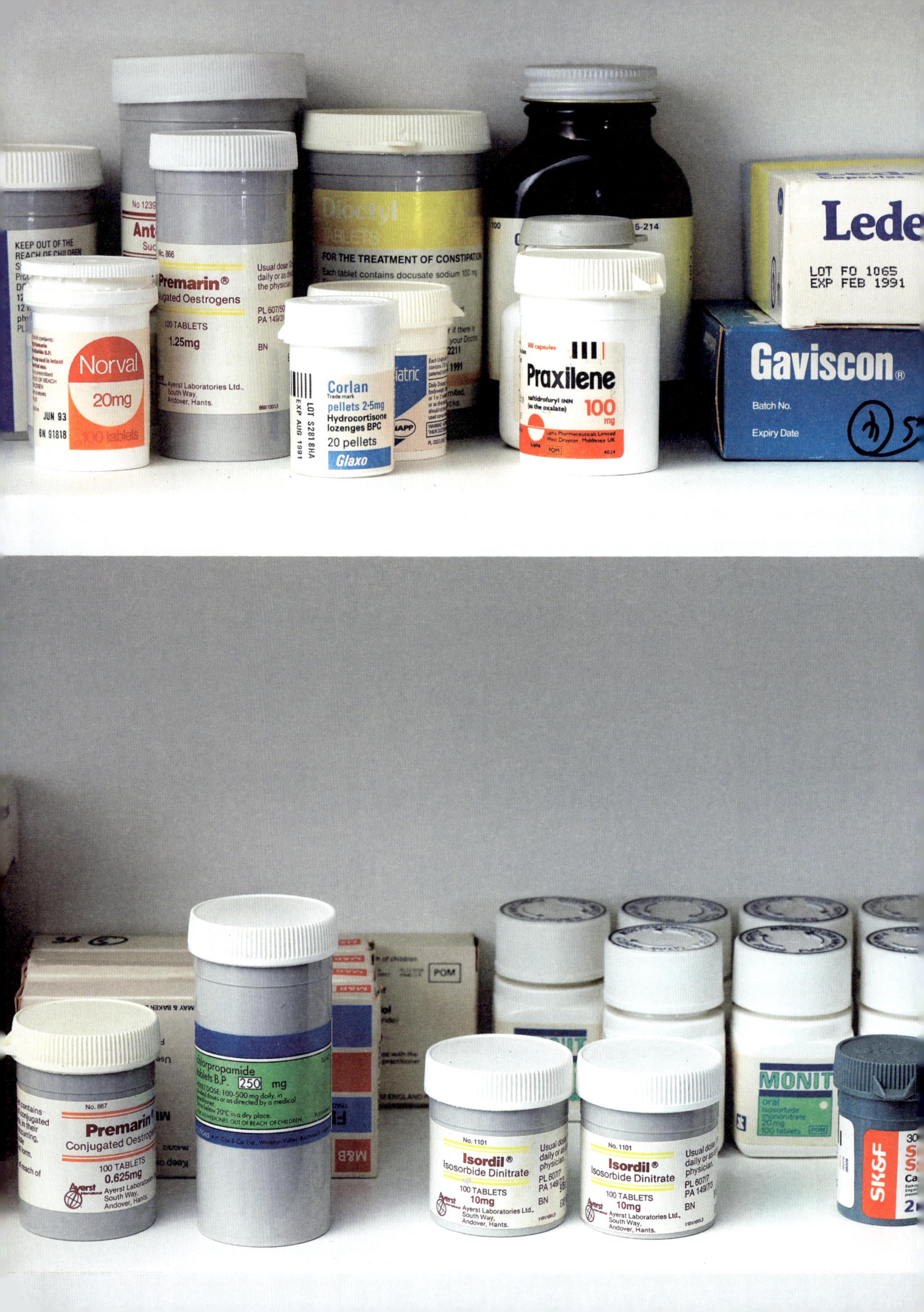
KEEP OUT OF THE REACH OF CHILDREN
Premarin®
100 TABLETS
1.25mg
Ayerst Laboratories Ltd., South Way, Andover, Hants.
Norval
20mg
100 tablets
JUN 93
Dioctyl
FOR THE TREATMENT OF CONSTIPATION
Each tablet contains docusate sodium 100 mg
Corlan
pellets 2·5mg
Hydrocortisone lozenges BPC
20 pellets
Glaxo
LOT S2818HA
EXP AUG 1991
Praxilene
100 mg
Lede
LOT FO 1065
EXP FEB 1991
Gaviscon
Batch No.
Expiry Date
POM
Premarin®
Conjugated Oestrogens
100 TABLETS
0.625mg
chlorpropamide
250 mg
M&B
No. 1101
Isordil®
Isosorbide Dinitrate
100 TABLETS
10mg
Ayerst Laboratories Ltd., South Way, Andover, Hants.
MONIT
SK&F

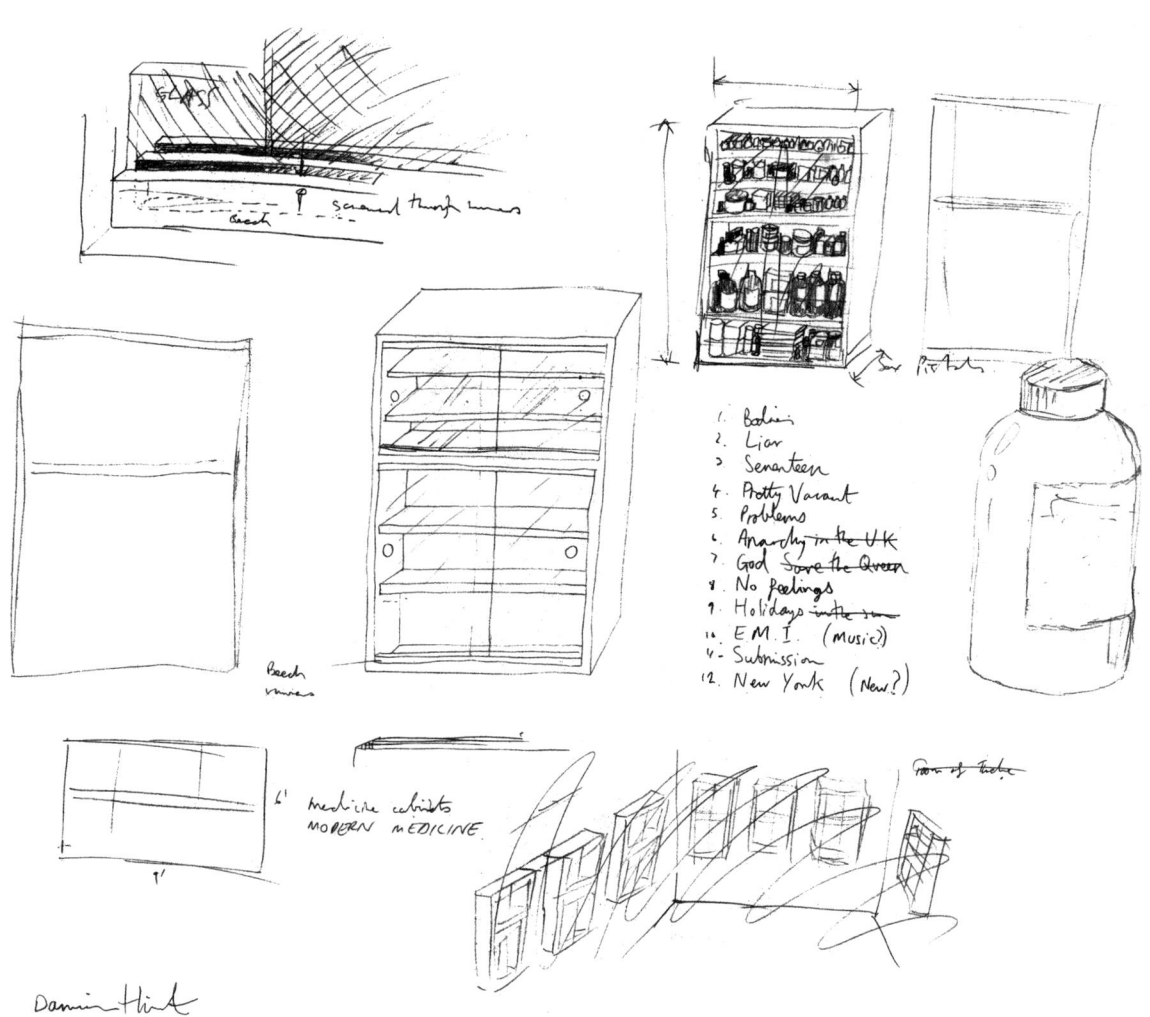

1. Bodies
2. Liar
3. Seventeen
4. Pretty Vacant
5. Problems
6. Anarchy in the UK
7. God Save the Queen
8. No feelings
9. Holidays in the sun
10. E.M.I. (music?)
11. Submission
12. New York (New?)

medicine cabinets
MODERN MEDICINE

Damien Hirst

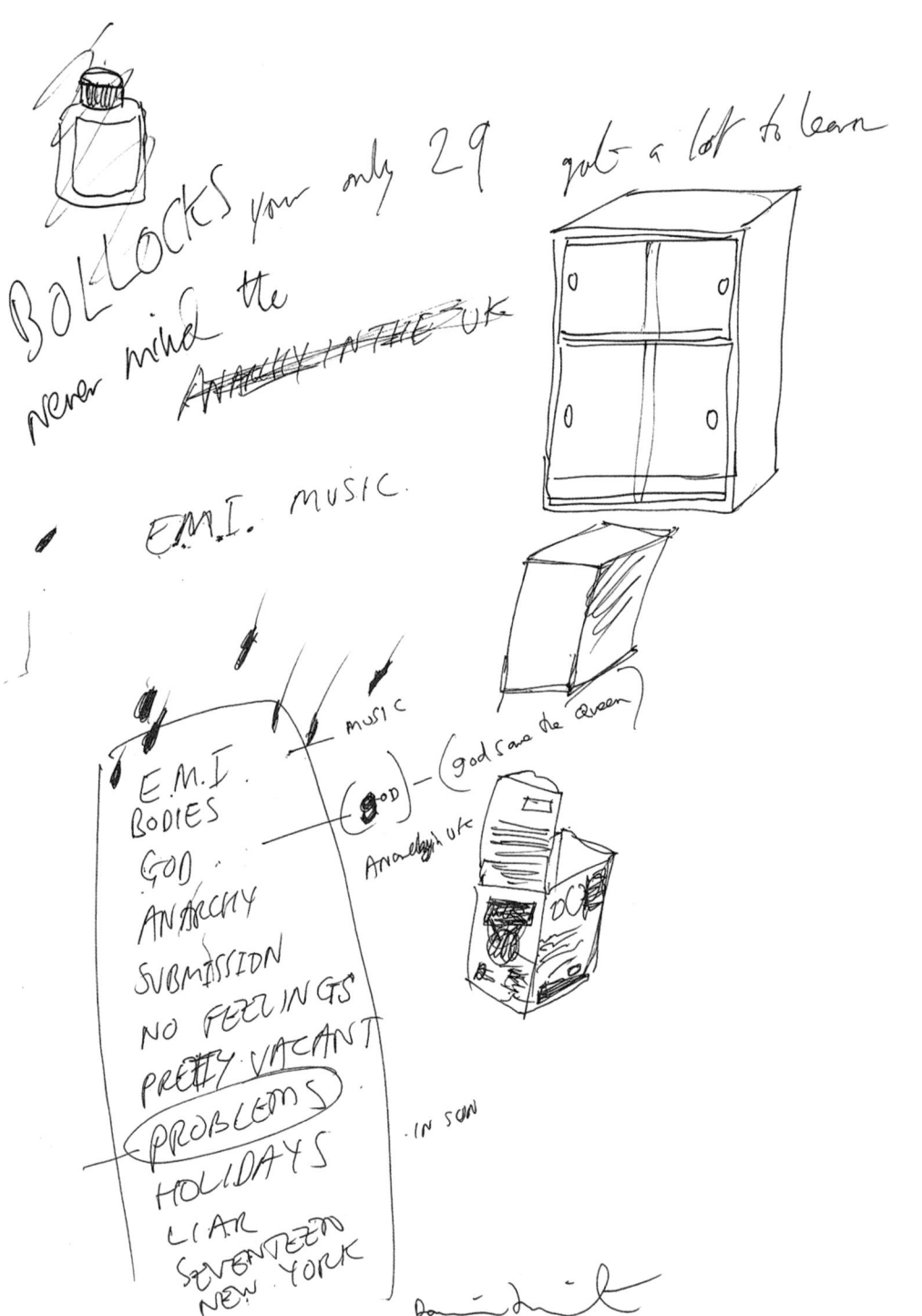

BOLLOCKS you only 29 got a lot to learn

never mind the ~~ANARCHY IN THE UK~~

E.M.I. MUSIC.

music

(GOD) — (god save the Queen)

Anarchy in UK

E.M.I.
BODIES
GOD
ANARCHY
SUBMISSION
NO FEELINGS
PRETTY VACANT
PROBLEMS
HOLIDAYS
LIAR
SEVENTEEN
NEW YORK

. IN SUN

Untitled (Drawing with Cabinet and Medical Packaging), 1989 | Tinte auf Papier | Ink on paper | 42 × 30 cm

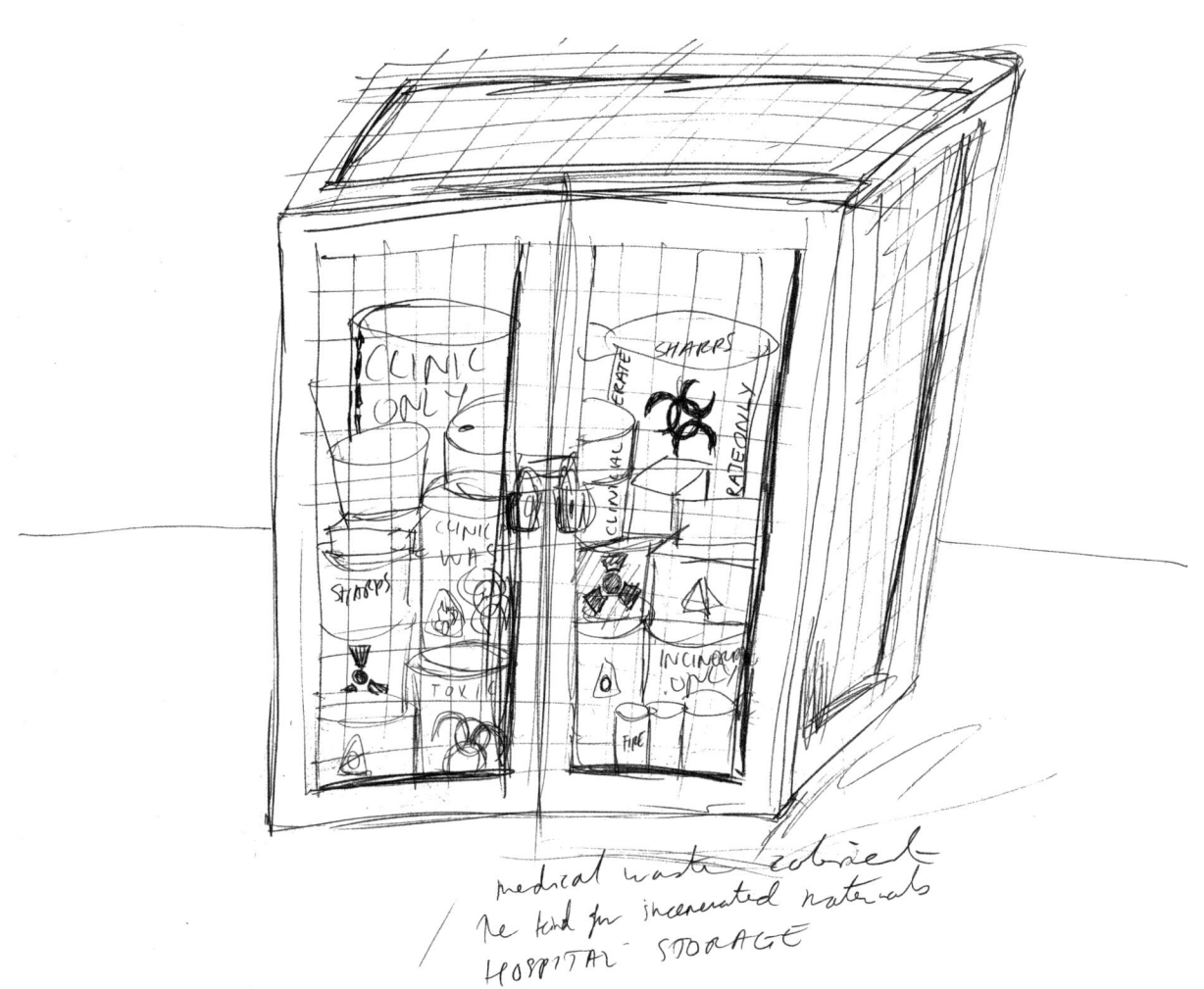

Medical Waste Cabinet, 2003 | Bleistift auf Papier | Pencil on paper | 75 × 78 cm

'Somewhere Over T

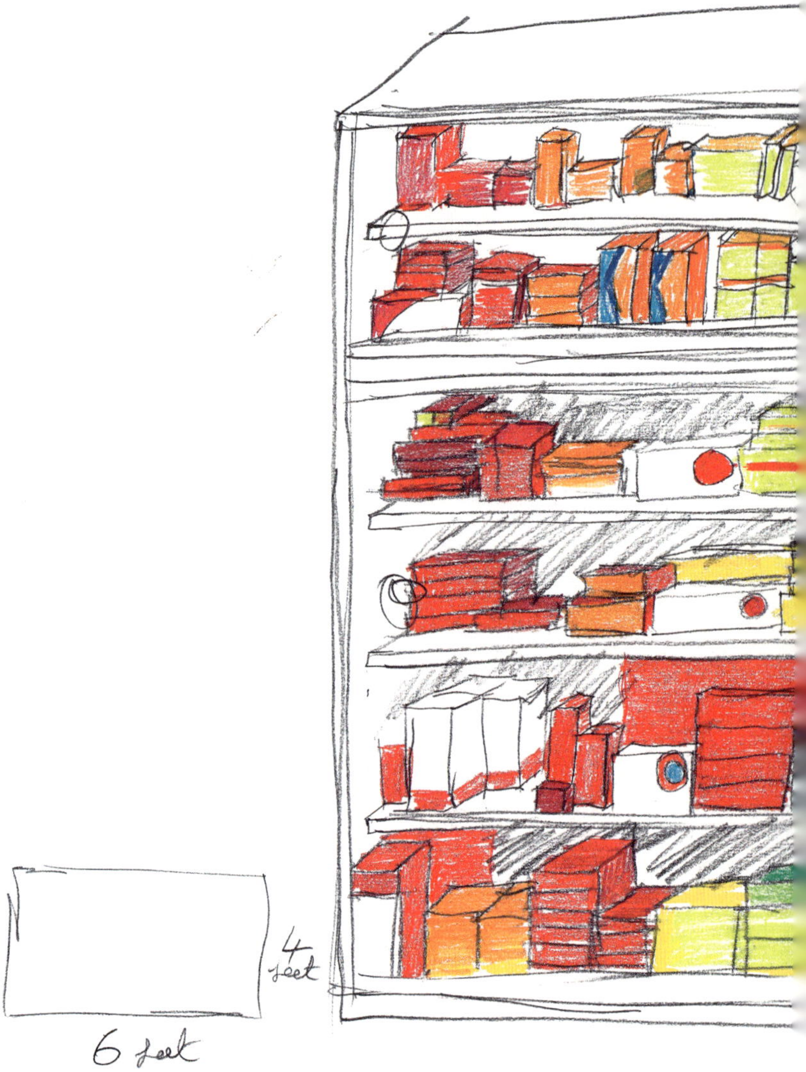

6 feet

4 feet

Rainbow M
The spe

2015

52

Rainbow'

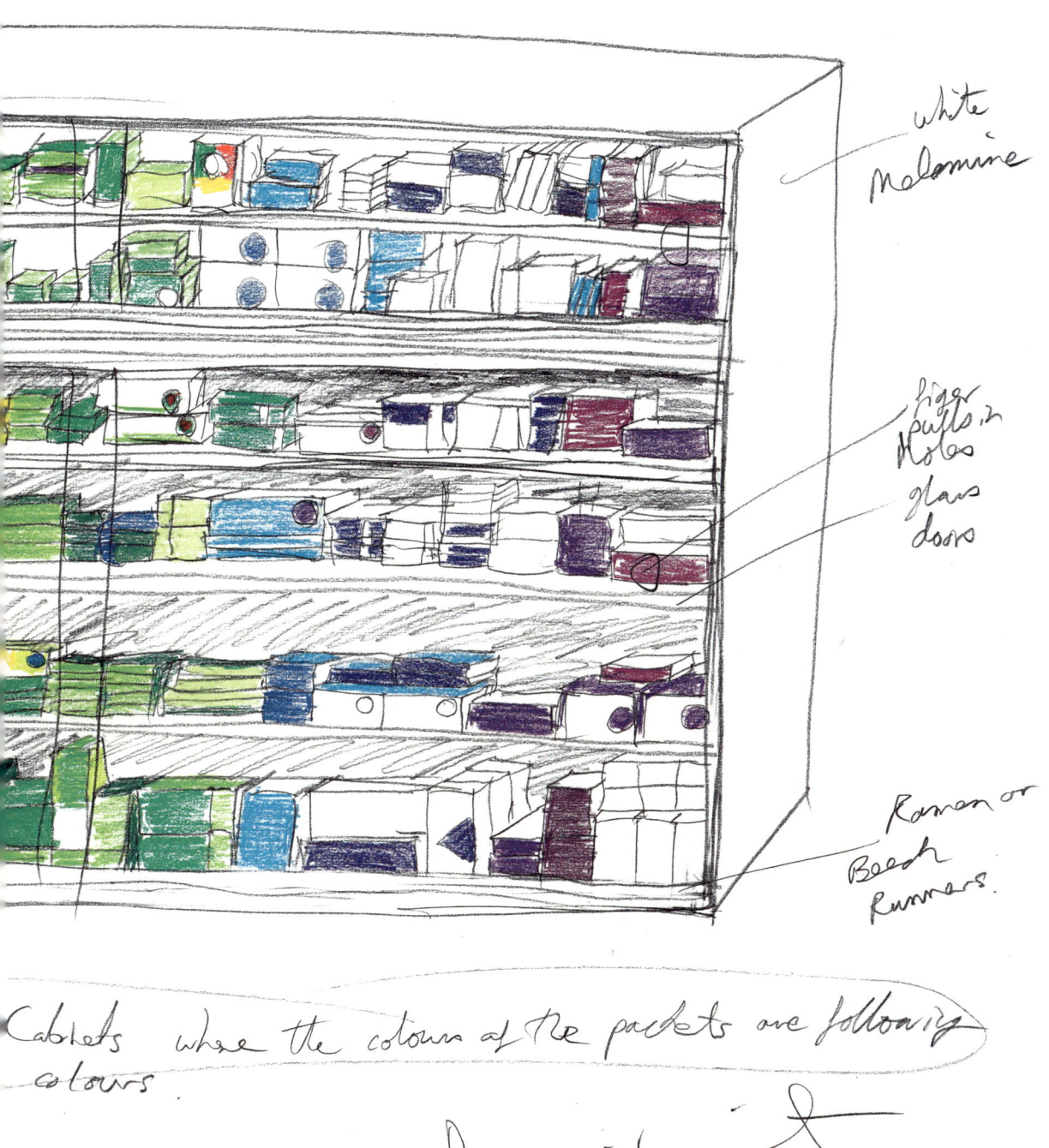

white
Melamine

finger
pulls in
Holes
glass
doors

Ramin or
Beech
Runners.

Cabinets where the colours of the packets are following
colours.

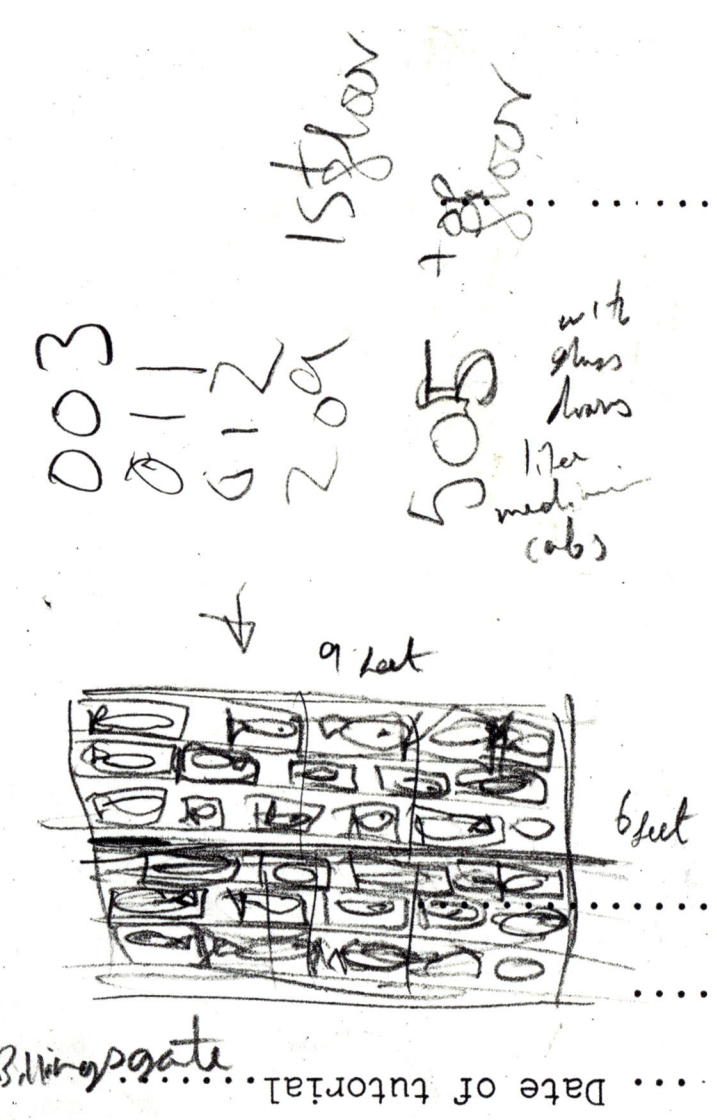

1st glov

+ 2f glour

DO3
1 1 2
Ø G ? 0

505

with
glass
doors

liter
medium
(obs)

9 feet

6 feet

Billingsgate ..... Date of tutorial ....

Study for Isolated Elements Swimming in the Same Direction for the Purpose of Understanding, 1989 | Bleistift auf Papier | Pencil on paper | 11 × 7 cm

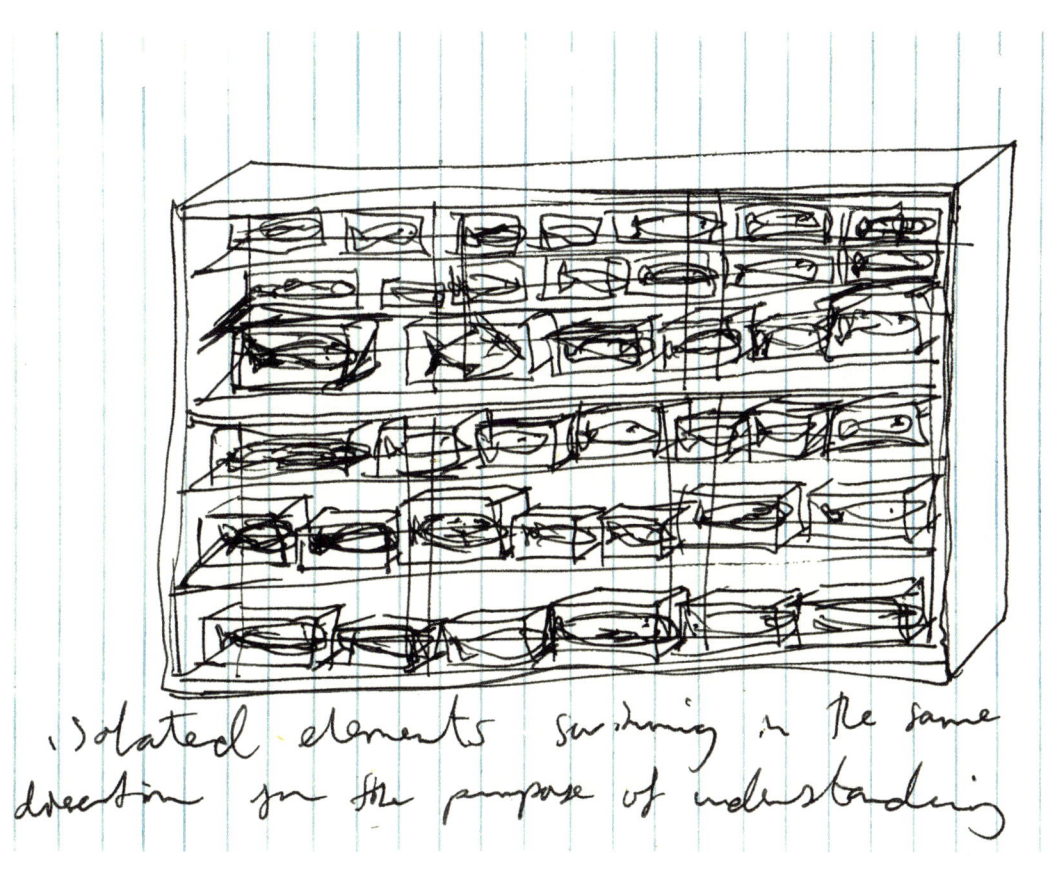

Isolated Elements Swimming in the Same Direction for the Purpose of Understanding (Right), 1991 | Tinte auf Papier | Ink on paper | 10 × 15 cm

„Ich habe mich schon immer für das
Leben interessiert, deshalb
verwende ich tote Tiere, um sie real
werden zu lassen und Kunst zu
schaffen, die lebt."

'I've always been interested in
life, that's why I use the dead
animals, to make them real, to
make art that lives.'

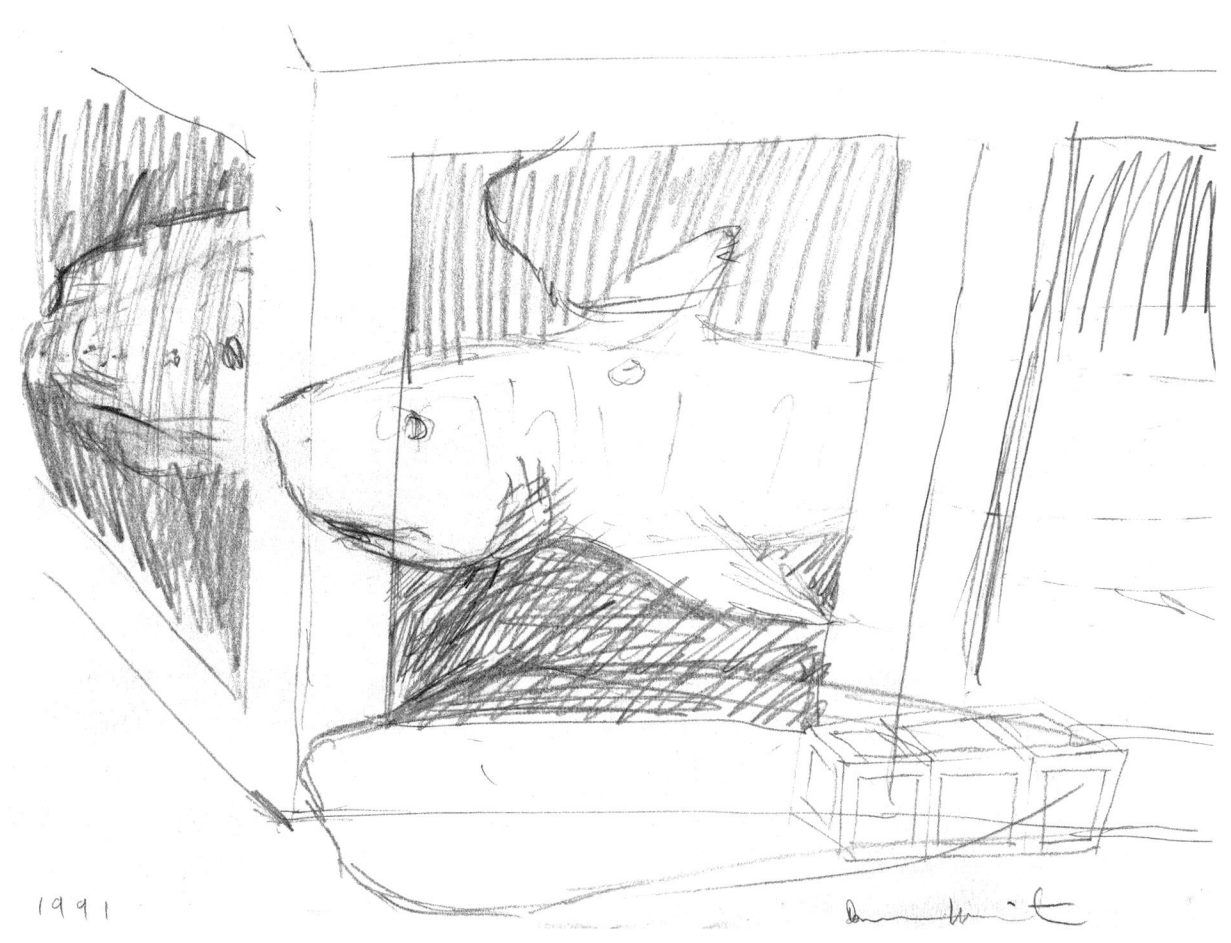

1991

The Physical Impossibility, 1991 | Bleistift auf Papier | Pencil on paper | 30 × 41 cm

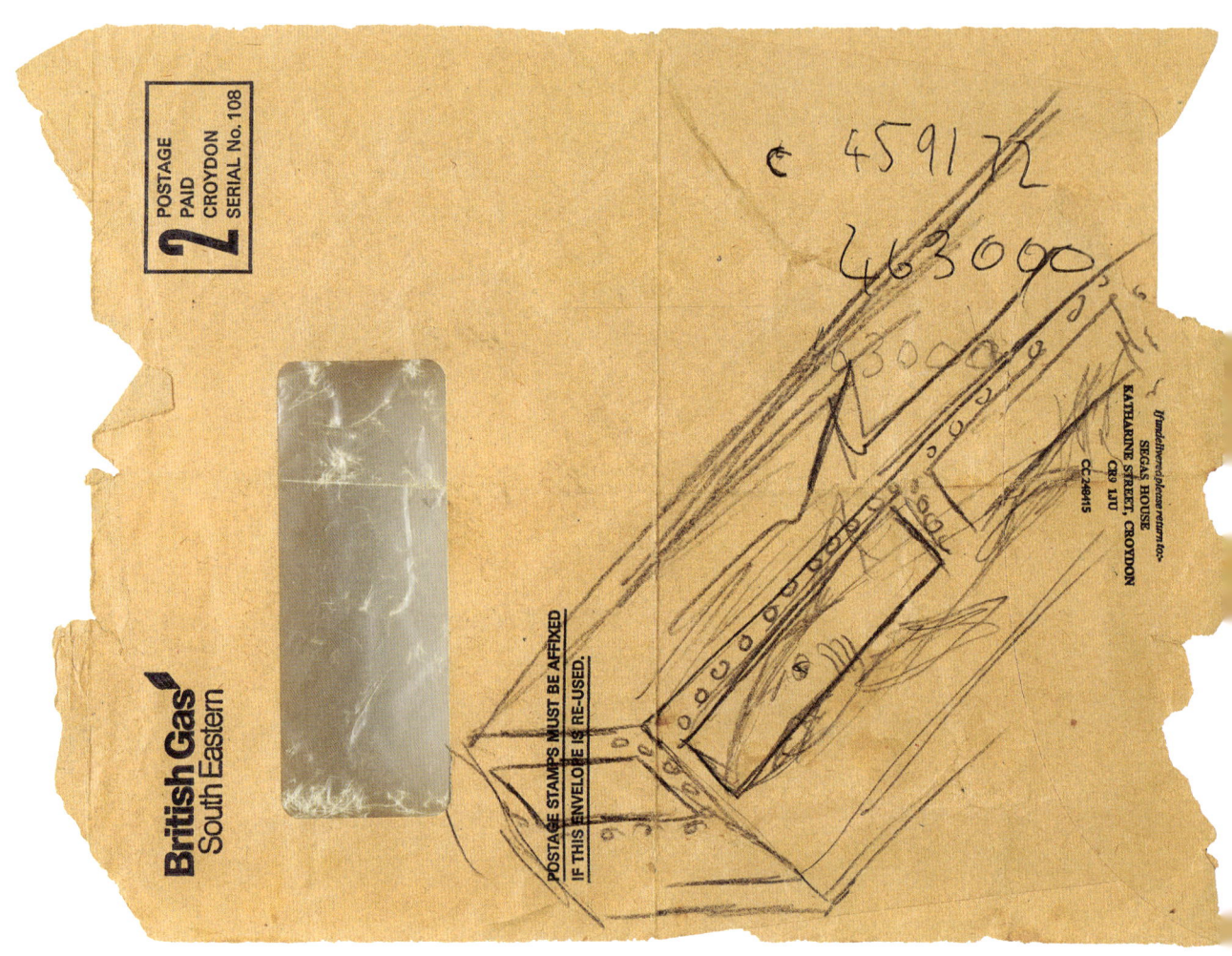

Early Study for the Physical Impossibility of Death in the Mind of Someone Living, 1989
Bleistift auf Papier | Pencil on paper | 18 × 23 cm

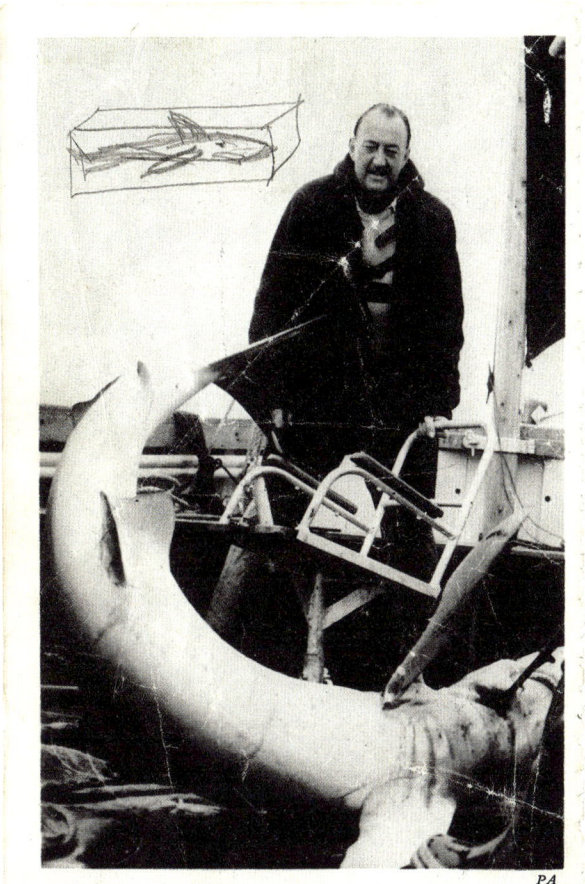

Above and opposite The Cornish coast was infested with sharks during the warm summer of 1957. Local fishermen bemoaned the damage to their nets, but caught the sharks and used them as bait for lobster pots.

The Physical Impossibility of Death in the Mind of Someone Living, 1989
Bleistift auf Buchseite | Pencil on book page | 18 × 11 cm

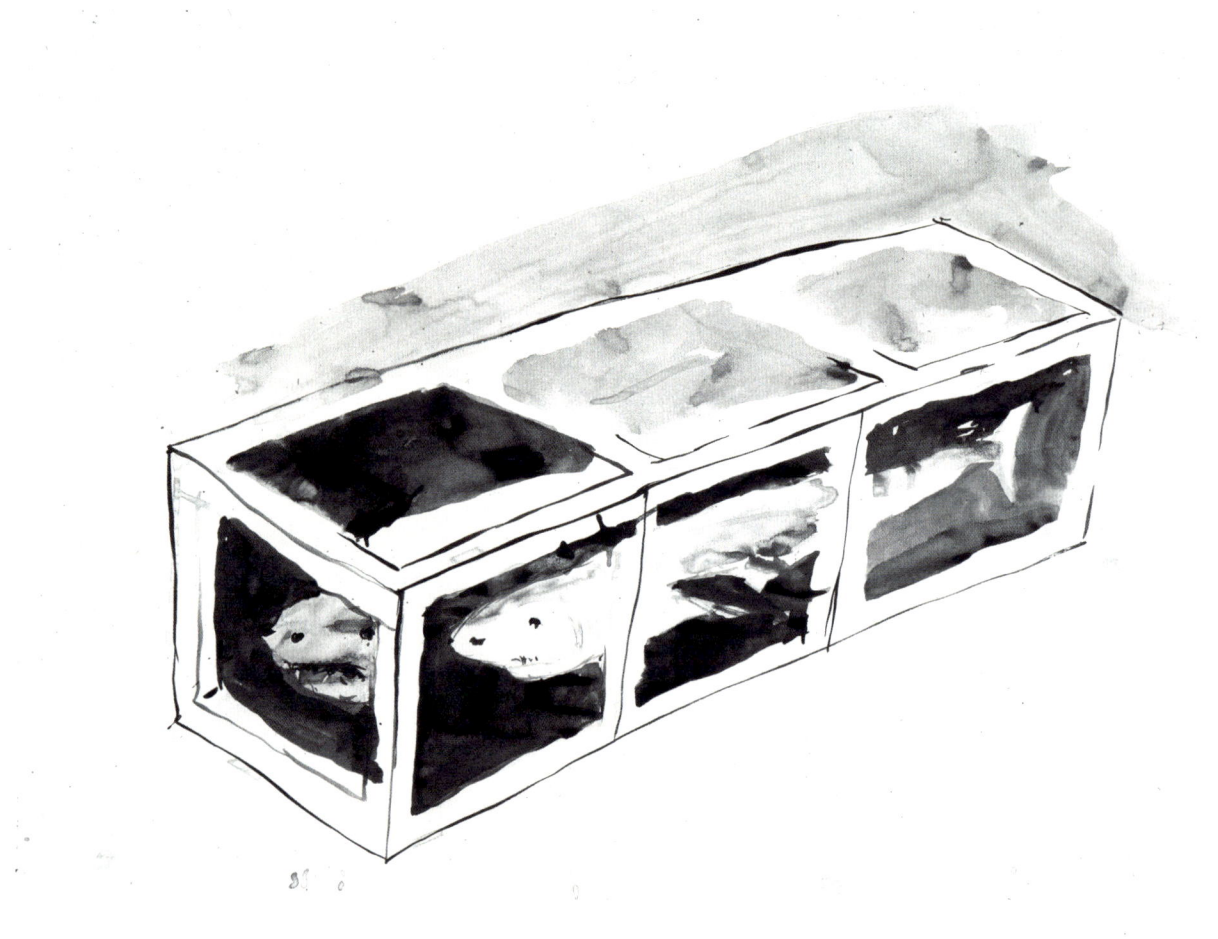

The Physical Impossibility of Death in the Mind of Someone Living, 1991
Tinte auf Papier | Ink on paper | 59 × 84 cm

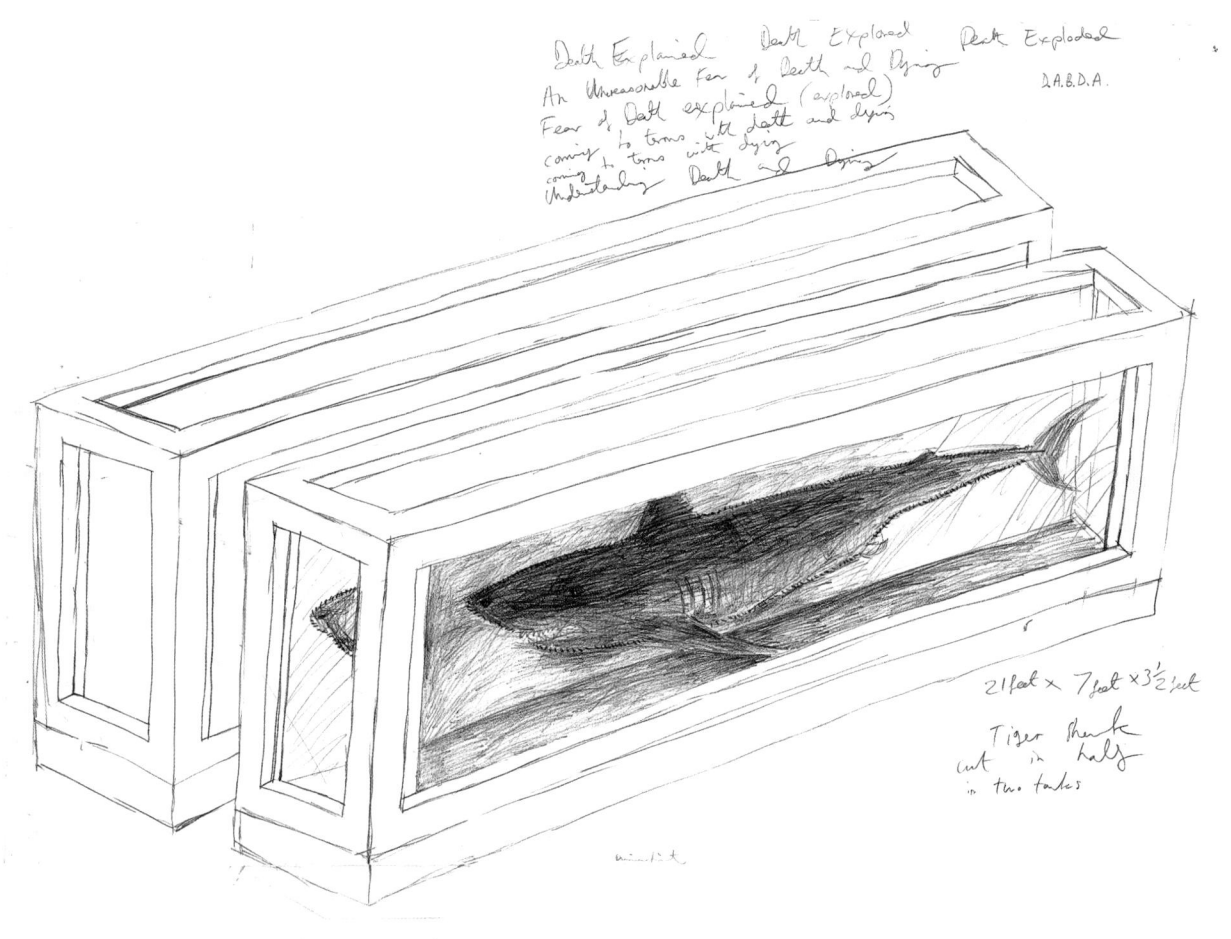

Death Explained   Death Explained   Death Exploded
An Unreasonable Fear of Death and Dying
Fear of Death explained (exploded)
coming to terms with death and dying
coming to terms with dying
Understanding Death and Dying

D.A.B.D.A.

21 feet × 7 feet × 3½ feet

Tiger Shark
cut in half
in two tanks

Untitled (Tiger Shark in Tank), 2003 | Bleistift auf Papier | Pencil on paper | 83 × 110 cm

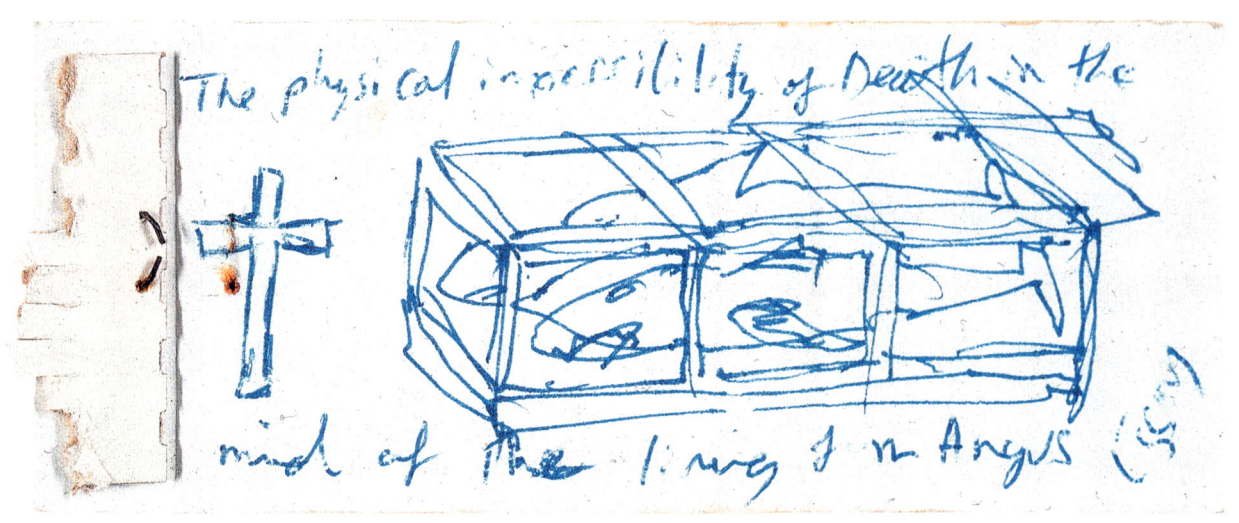

The Physical Impossibility of Death in the Mind of the Living for Angus, 1996 |
Tinte auf Streichholzbriefchen-Deckel | Ink on matchbook cover | 4 × 11 cm

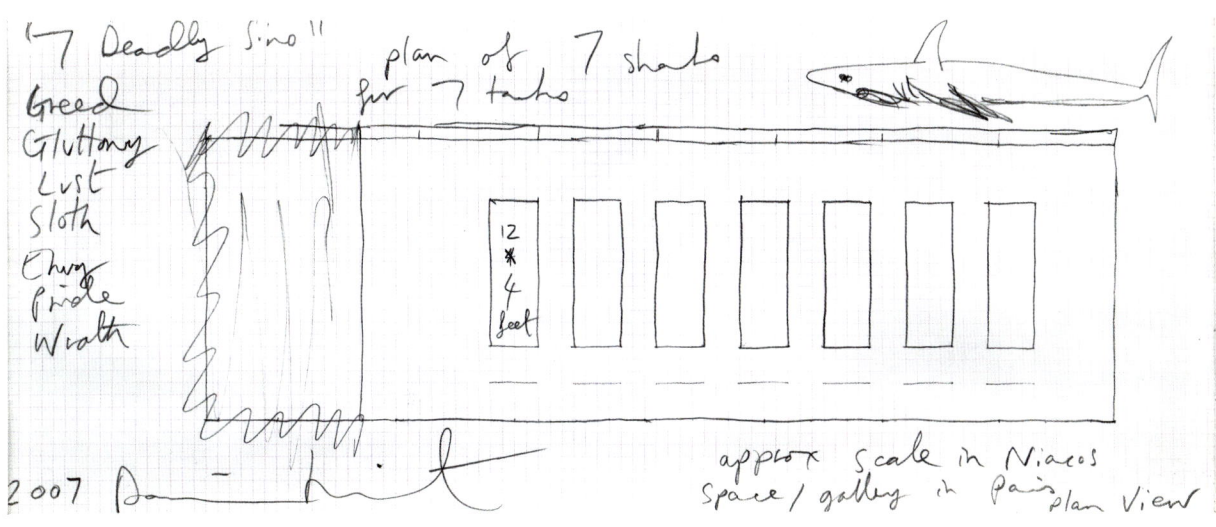

Seven Deadly Sins – Greed, Gluttony, Lust, Sloth, Envy, Pride, Wrath, 2007 | Tinte auf Papier |
Ink on paper, 20 × 51 cm

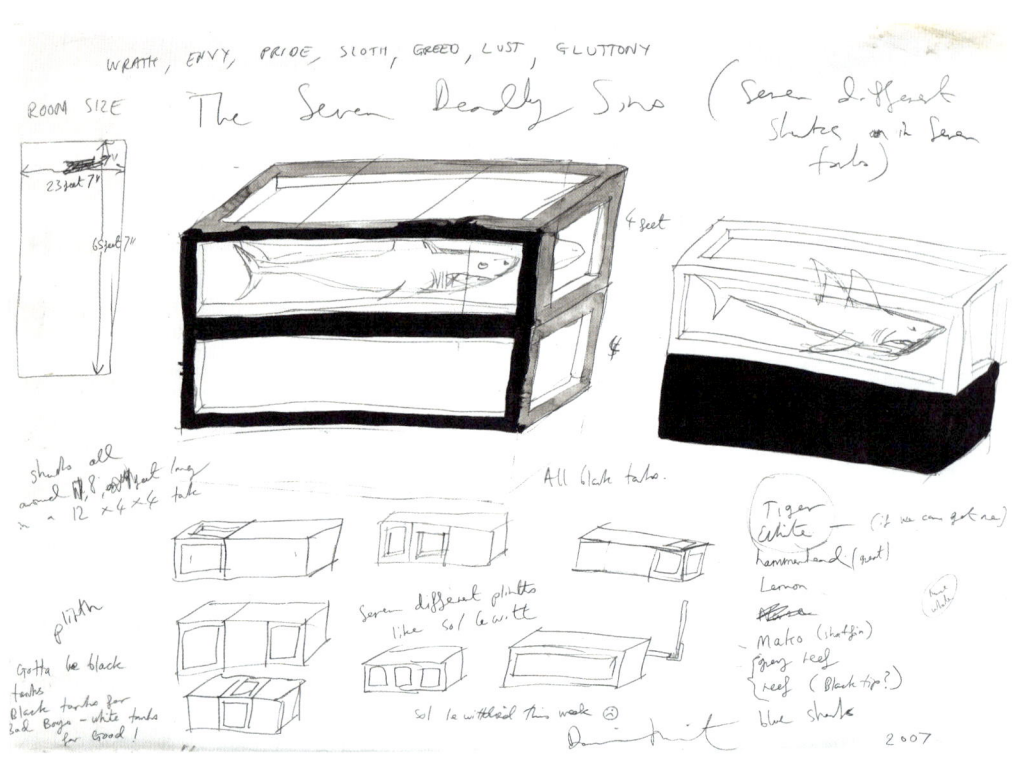

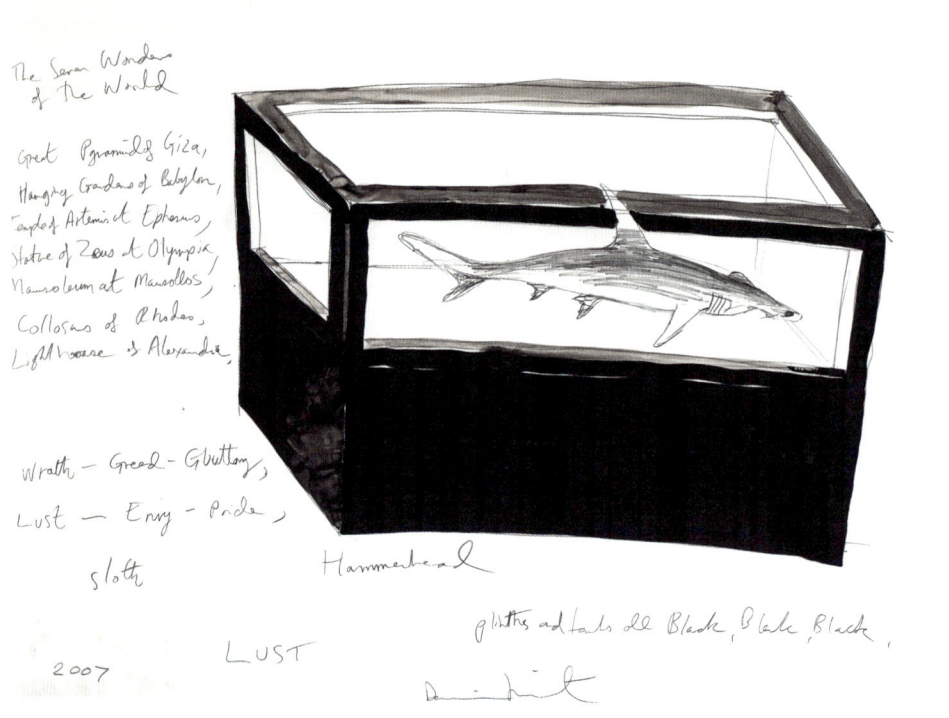

The Seven Deadly Sins (Seven Different Sharks in Seven Tanks), 2007 | Bleistift und Tinte
auf Papier | Pencil and ink on paper | 83 × 117 cm
The Seven Deadly Sins, 2007 | Bleistift und Tinte auf Papier | Pencil and ink on paper |
In sieben Teilen, je: | In seven parts, each: 83 × 117 cm

Gluttony — Reef shark

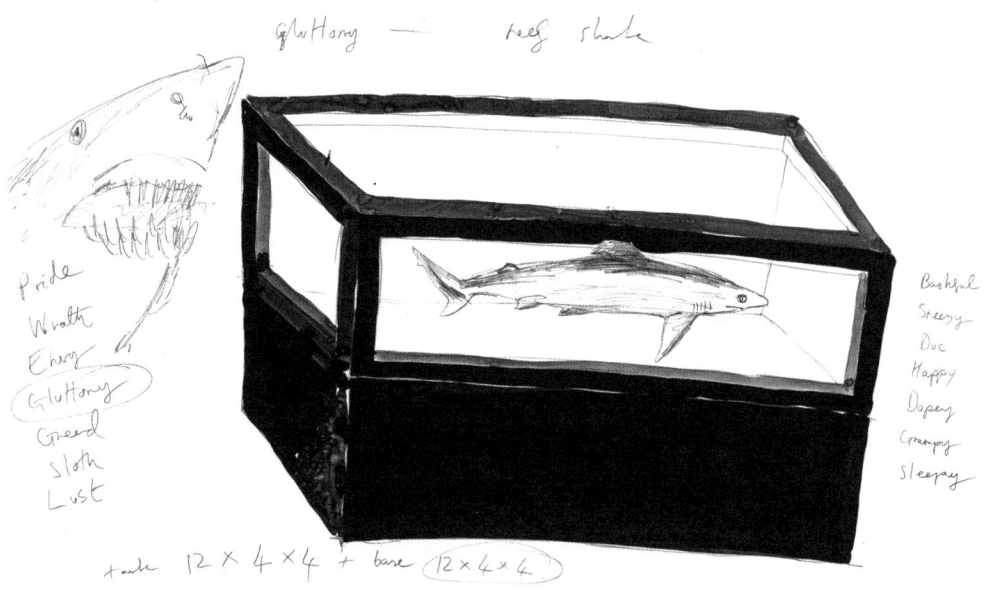

Pride
Wrath
Envy
Gluttony
Greed
Sloth
Lust

Bashful
Sneezy
Doc
Happy
Dopey
Grumpy
Sleepy

tank 12 × 4 × 4 + base (12 × 4 × 4)

all tanks Black!

Damien Hirst   2007

'Greed'

Great White

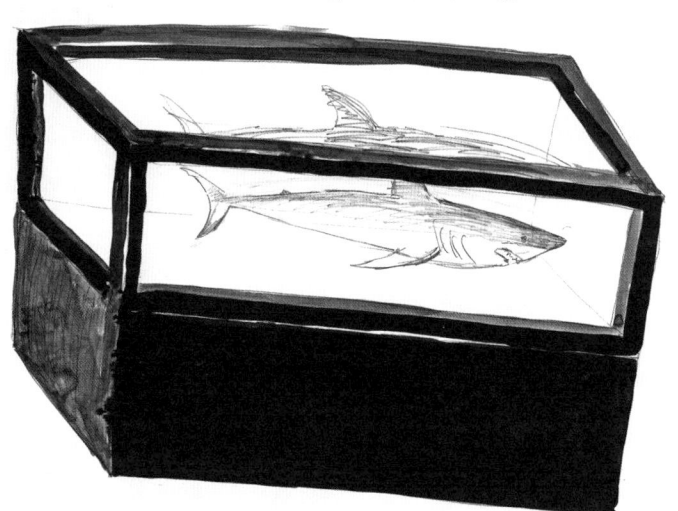

Seven Brides for
Seven Brothers

also called pointer shark

Damien Hirst   2007

"The Seven Deadly Sins"

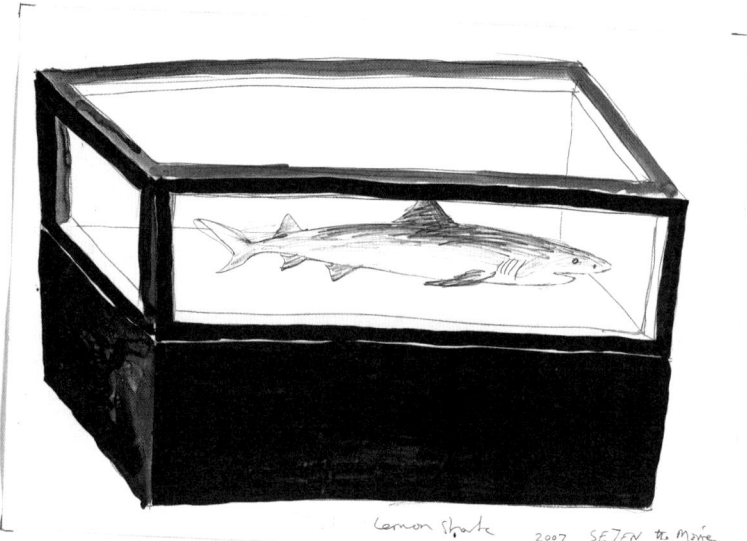

The
magnificent
Seven
—
Yul Brynner

Lemon Shark   2007 SE7EN the Movie

SLOTH   Damien Hirst   2007

"Wrath"

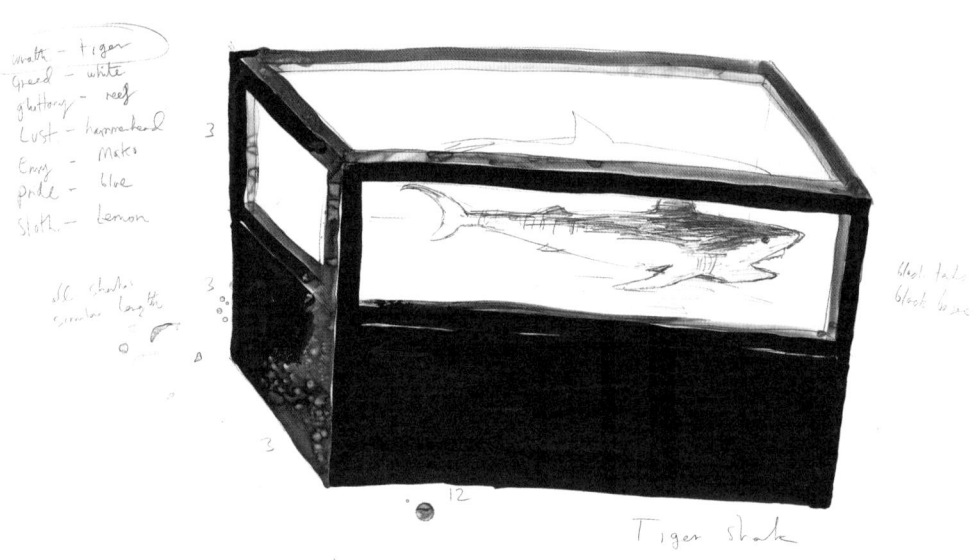

wrath – tiger
Greed – white
gluttony – reef
Lust – hammerhead
Envy – Mako
Pride – blue
Sloth – Lemon

all sharks
similar lengths

                                                    Glass tank
                                                    black base

                                3
                            3

                    3
                        12

                                    Tiger Shark

tank – 8 or 9 feet long

Damien Hirst   Damien Hirst   2007

'The Seven Deadly Sins'

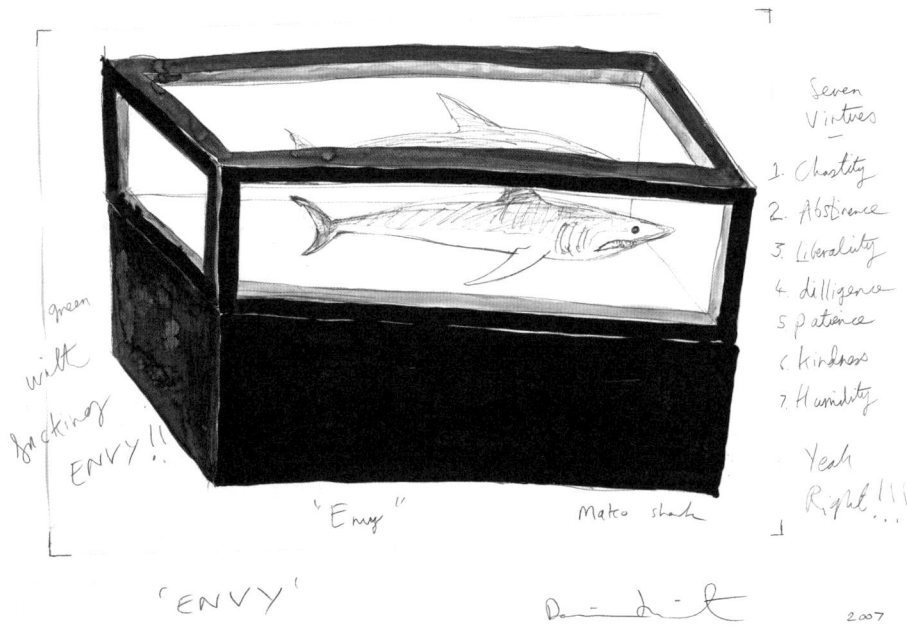

Seven
Virtues

1. Chastity
2. Abstinence
3. Liberality
4. dilligence
5. patience
6. kindness
7. Humility

Yeah
Right!!!

green
with
lacking
ENVY!!

"Envy"   Matco shark

'ENVY'

2007

"The Seven Deadly Sins"

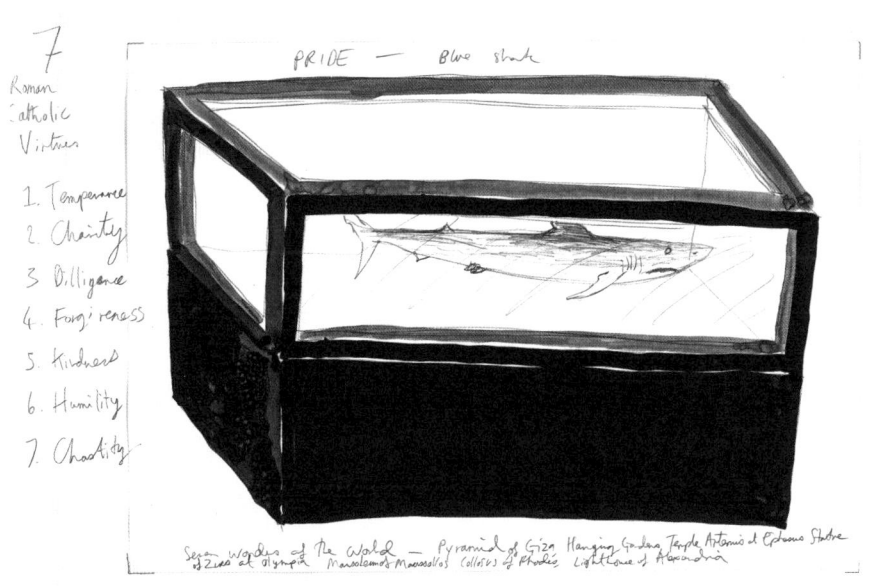

7
Roman
Catholic
Virtues

1. Temperance
2. Chastity
3. Dilligence
4. Forgiveness
5. Kindness
6. Humility
7. Chastity

PRIDE — Blue shark

Seven Wonders of the World — Pyramid of Giza Hanging Gardens Temple Artemis at Ephesus Statue
of Zeus at Olympia Mausoleum of Maussollos Collosus of Rhodes Lighthouse of Alexandria

PRIDE — comes before a fall

2007

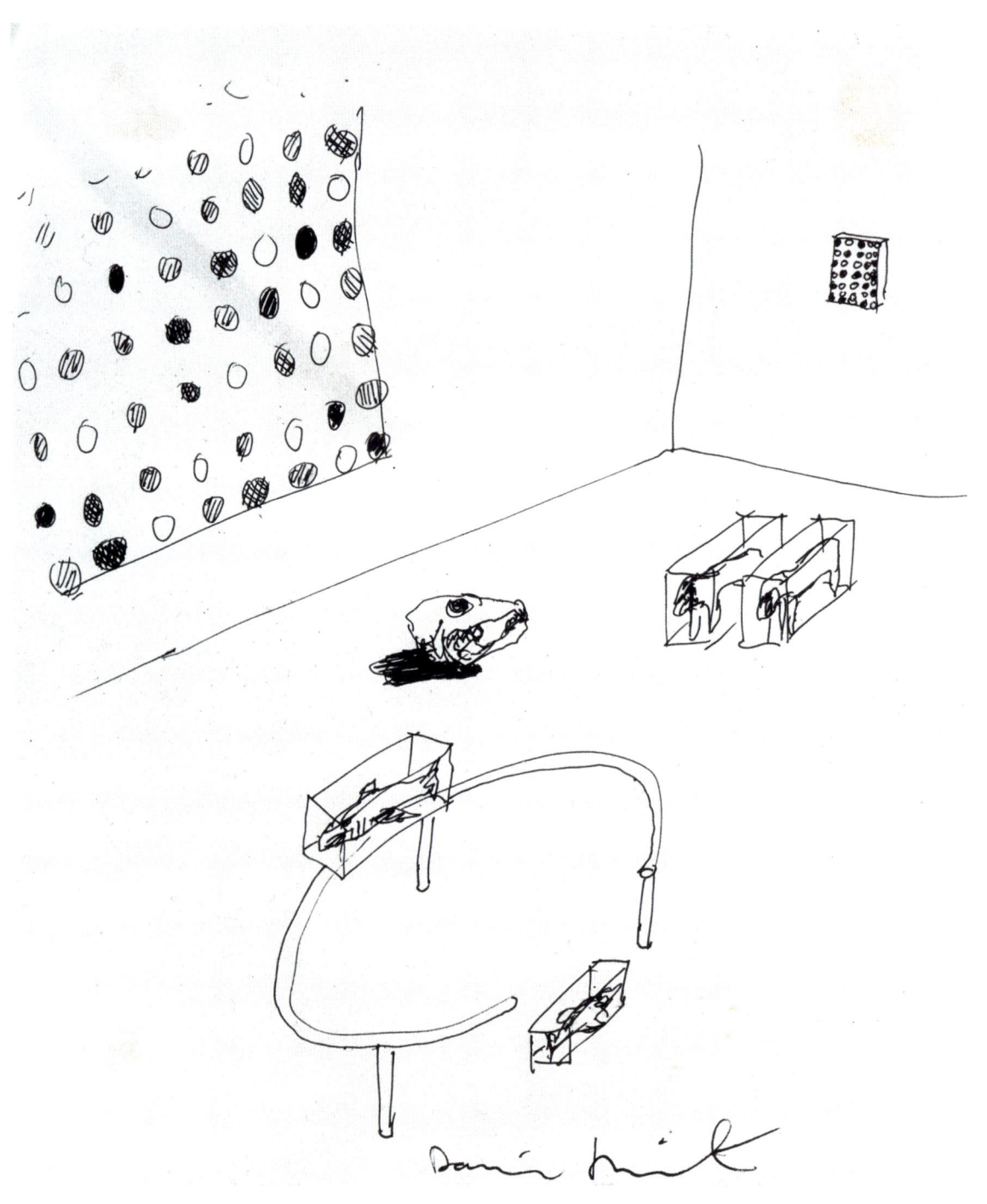

Installation Drawing, 1993 | Tinte auf Papier | Ink on paper | 25 × 21 cm

Two Similar Swimming Forms in Endless Flight/Motion, 1993
Tinte auf Papier | Ink on paper | 27 × 21 cm

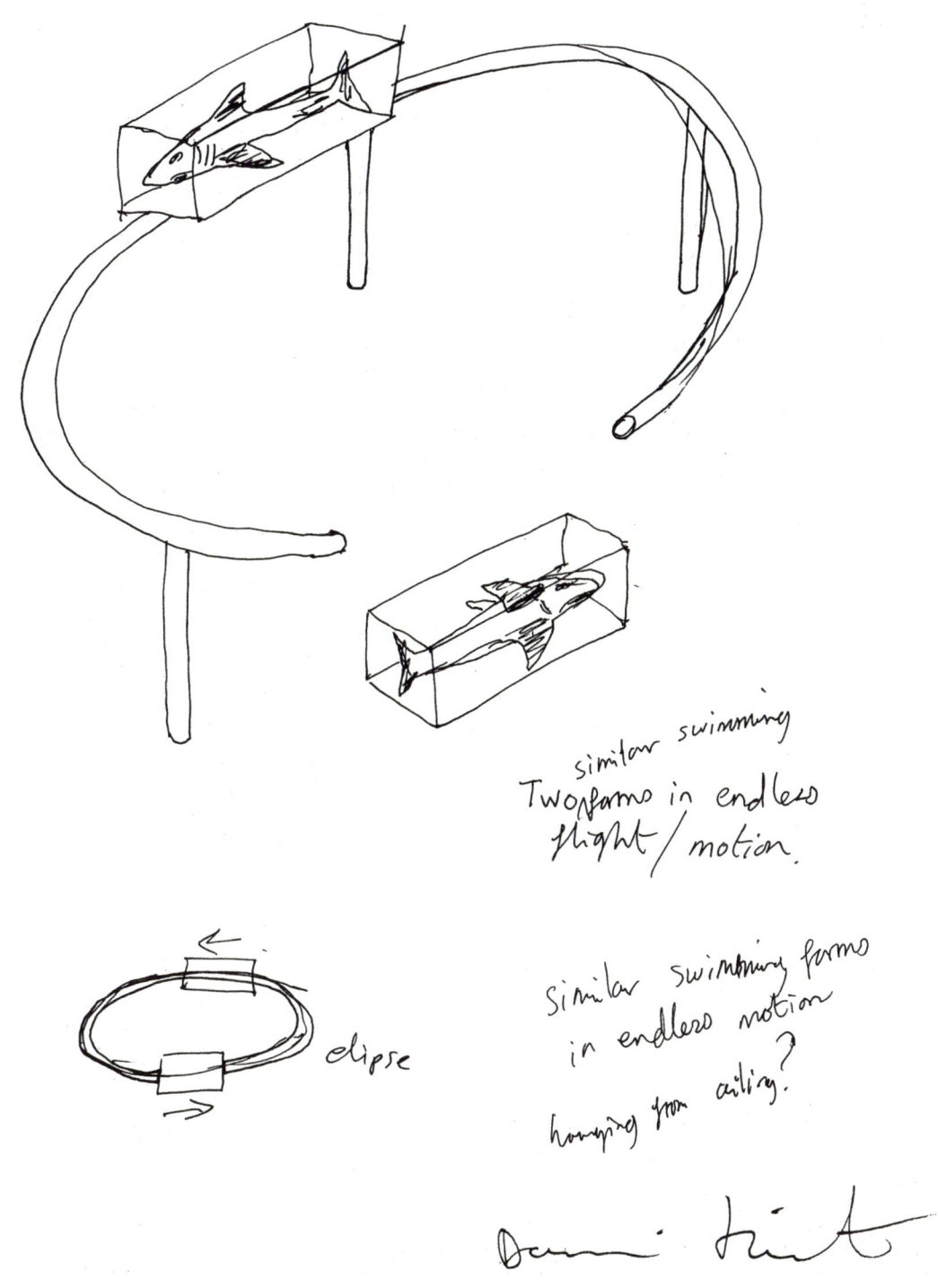

similar swimming
Two forms in endless
flight / motion.

elipse

Similar swimming forms
in endless motion
hanging from ceiling?

FOLGENDE SEITEN | FOLLOWING PAGES: Two Similar Swimming Forms in Infinite Flight, 1993
Acryl, bemaltes Aluminium, Haie und Formaldehydlösung | Acrylic, painted aluminium,
sharks, and formaldehyde solution | 83 × 274 × 285 cm

69

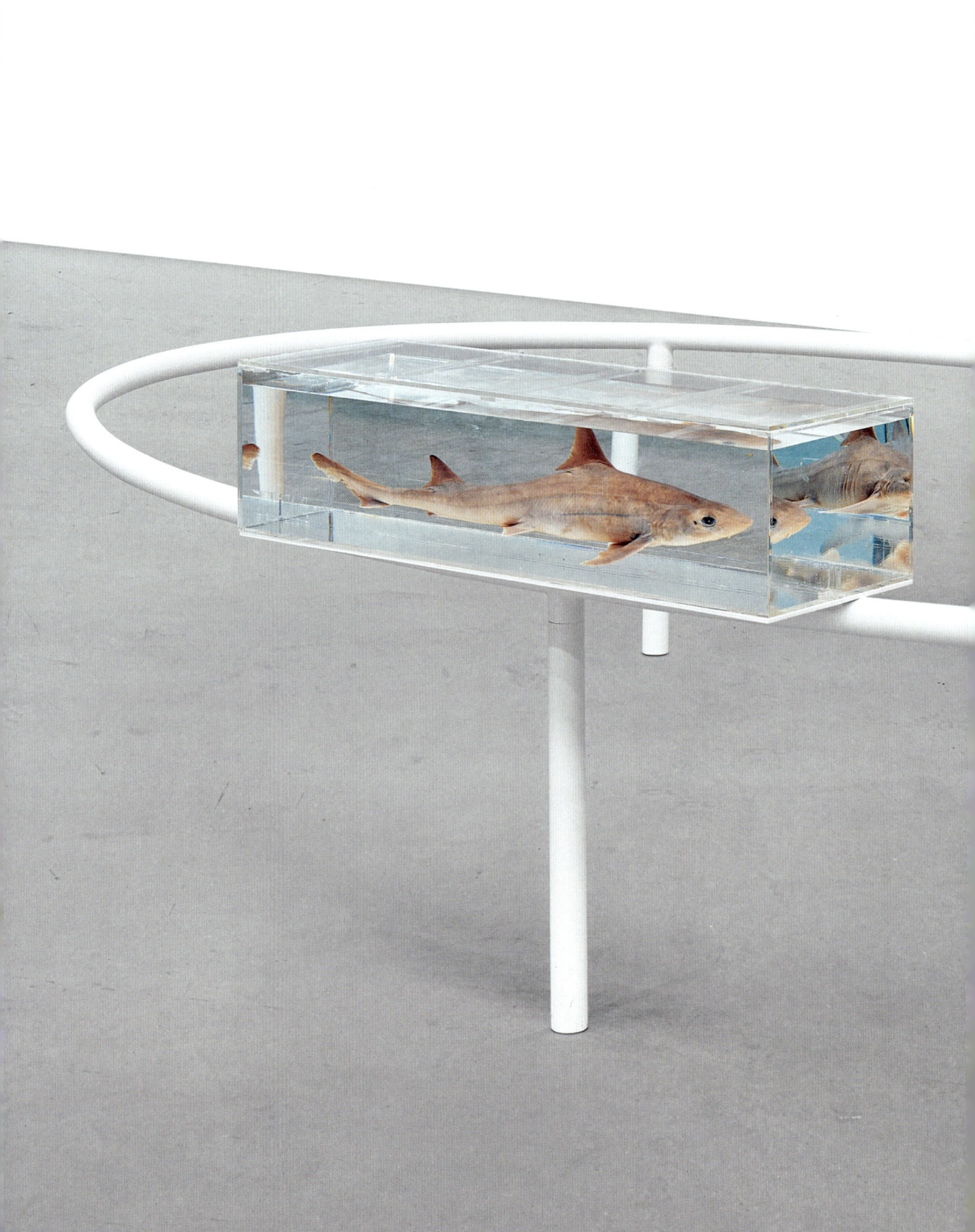

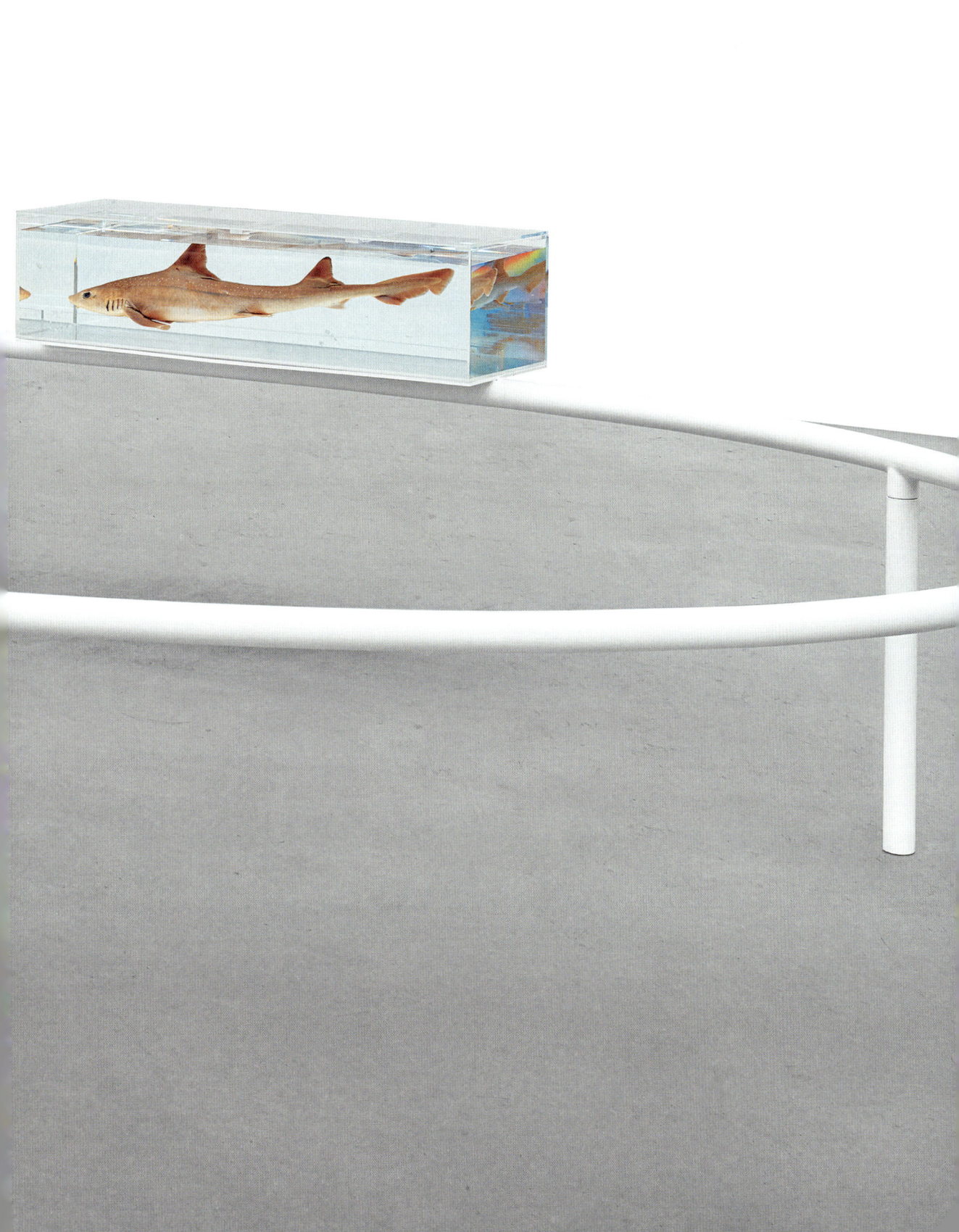

'Death Explained'

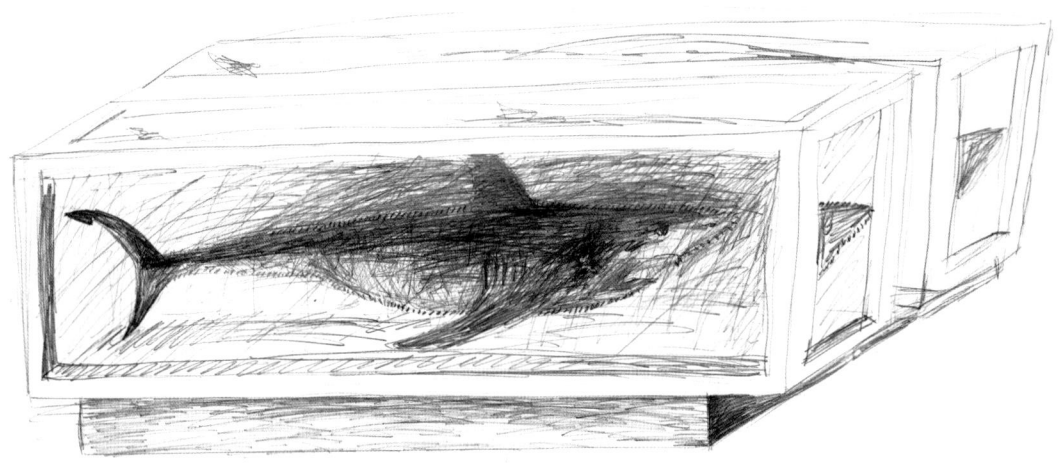

Death Explained, 2006 ⏐ Bleistift auf Karton ⏐ Pencil on card ⏐ 57 × 87 cm

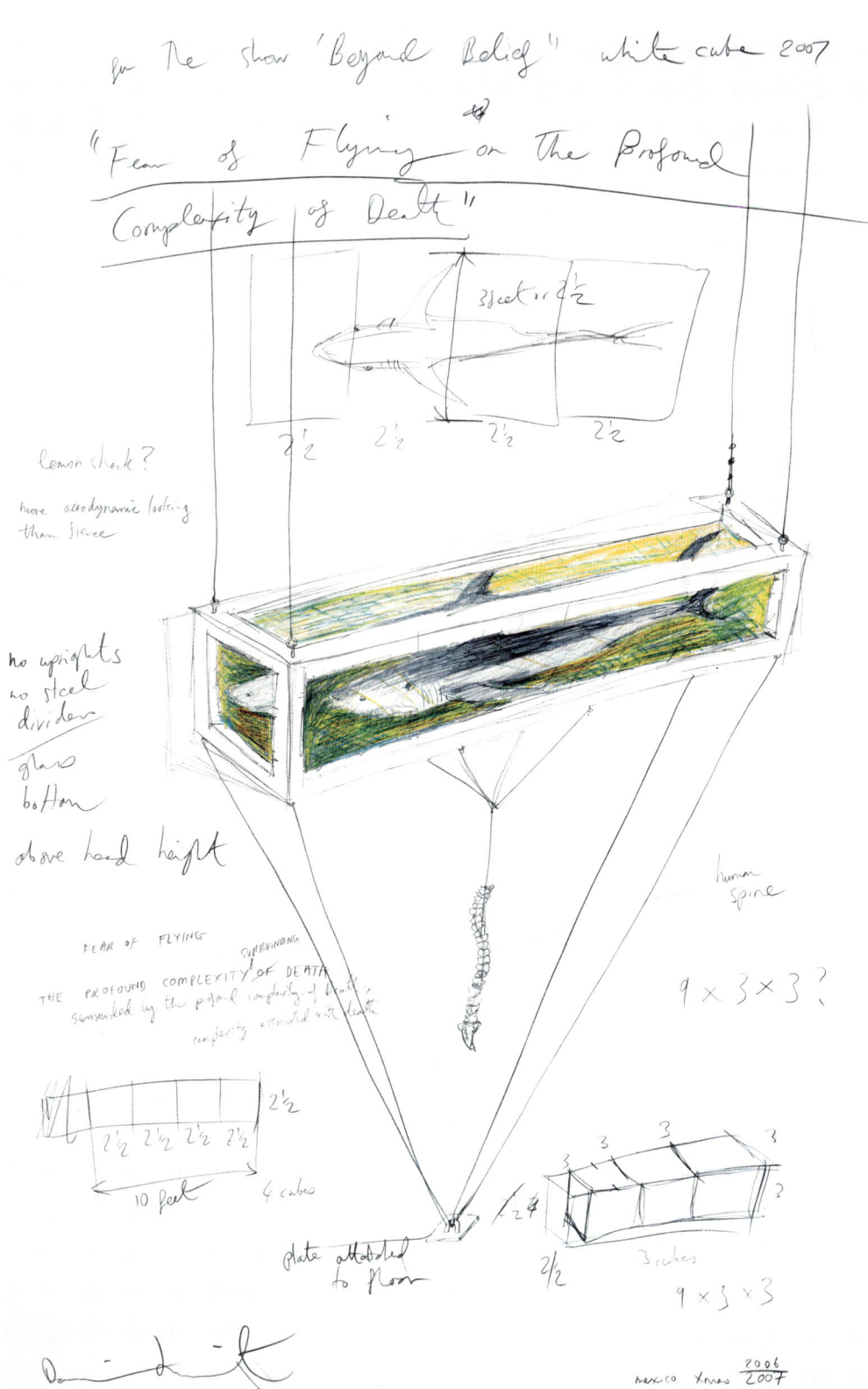

Fear of Flying or the Profound Complexity of Death, 2006–2007
Bleistift und Buntstift auf Papier | Pencil and coloured pencil on paper | 87 × 57 cm

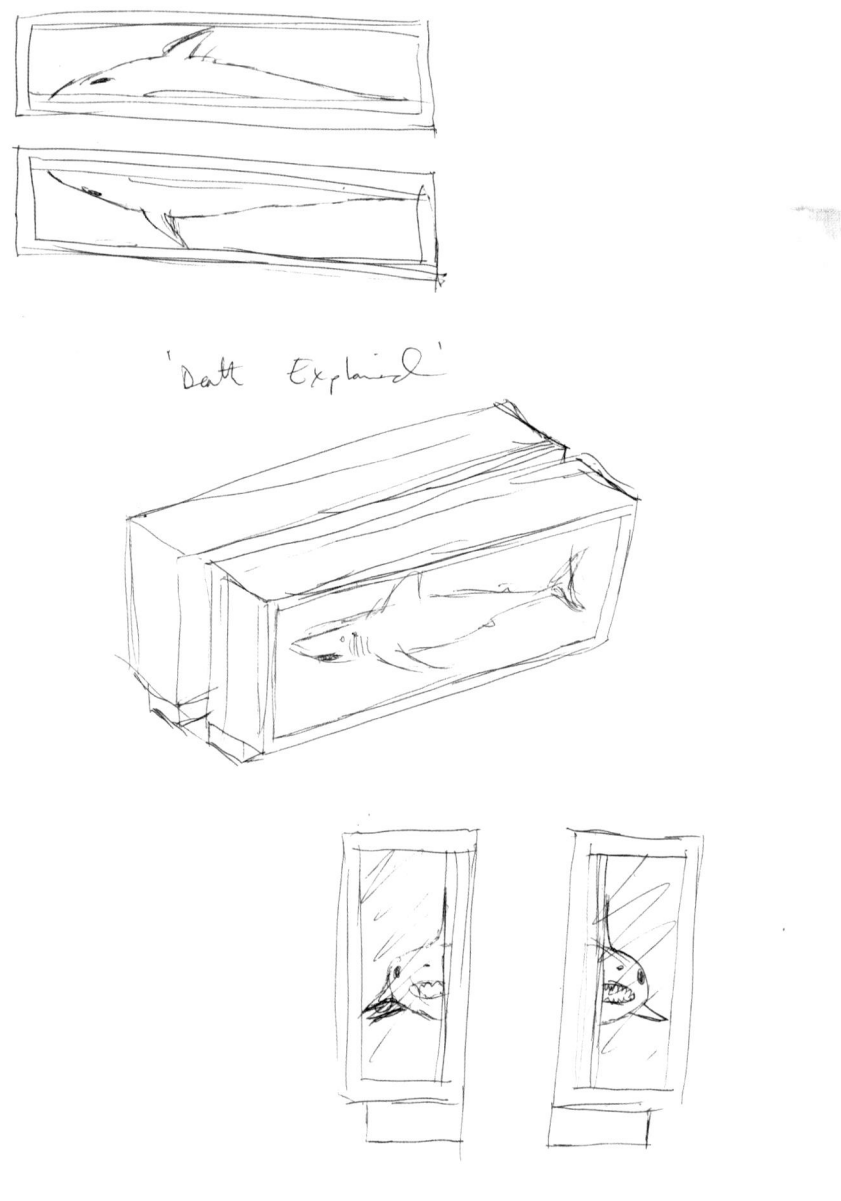

'Death Explained'

Death Explained (Three Views), 2006 | Tinte auf Papier | Ink on paper | 72 × 50 cm

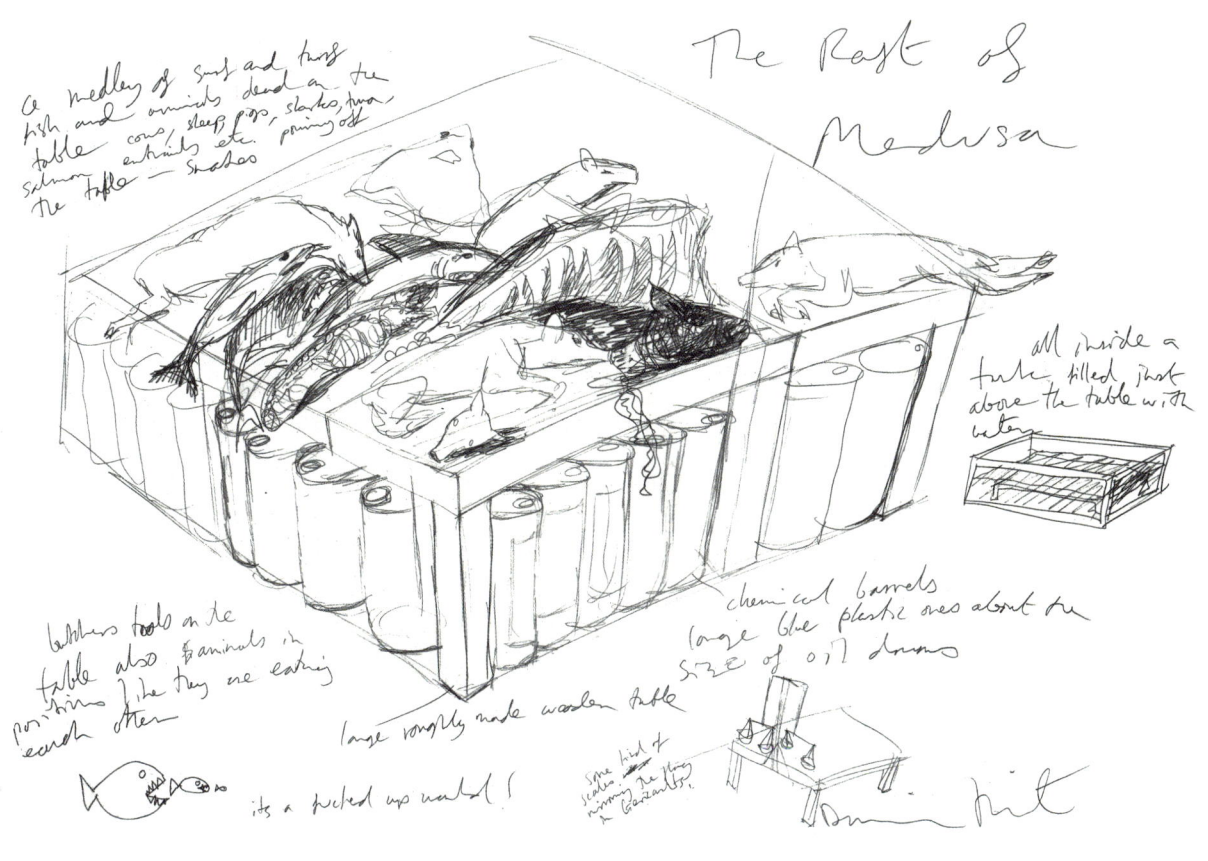

The Raft of Medusa, 2002 | Bleistift auf Papier | Pencil on paper | 75 × 110 cm

FOLGENDE SEITEN | FOLLOWING PAGES: *Away from the Flock,* 1994 | Glas, bemalter Stahl, Silikon, Acryl,
Kunststoffkabelbinder, Lamm und Formaldehydlösung | Glass, painted steel, silicone, acrylic,
plastic cable ties, lamb, and formaldehyde solution | 96 × 149 × 51 cm

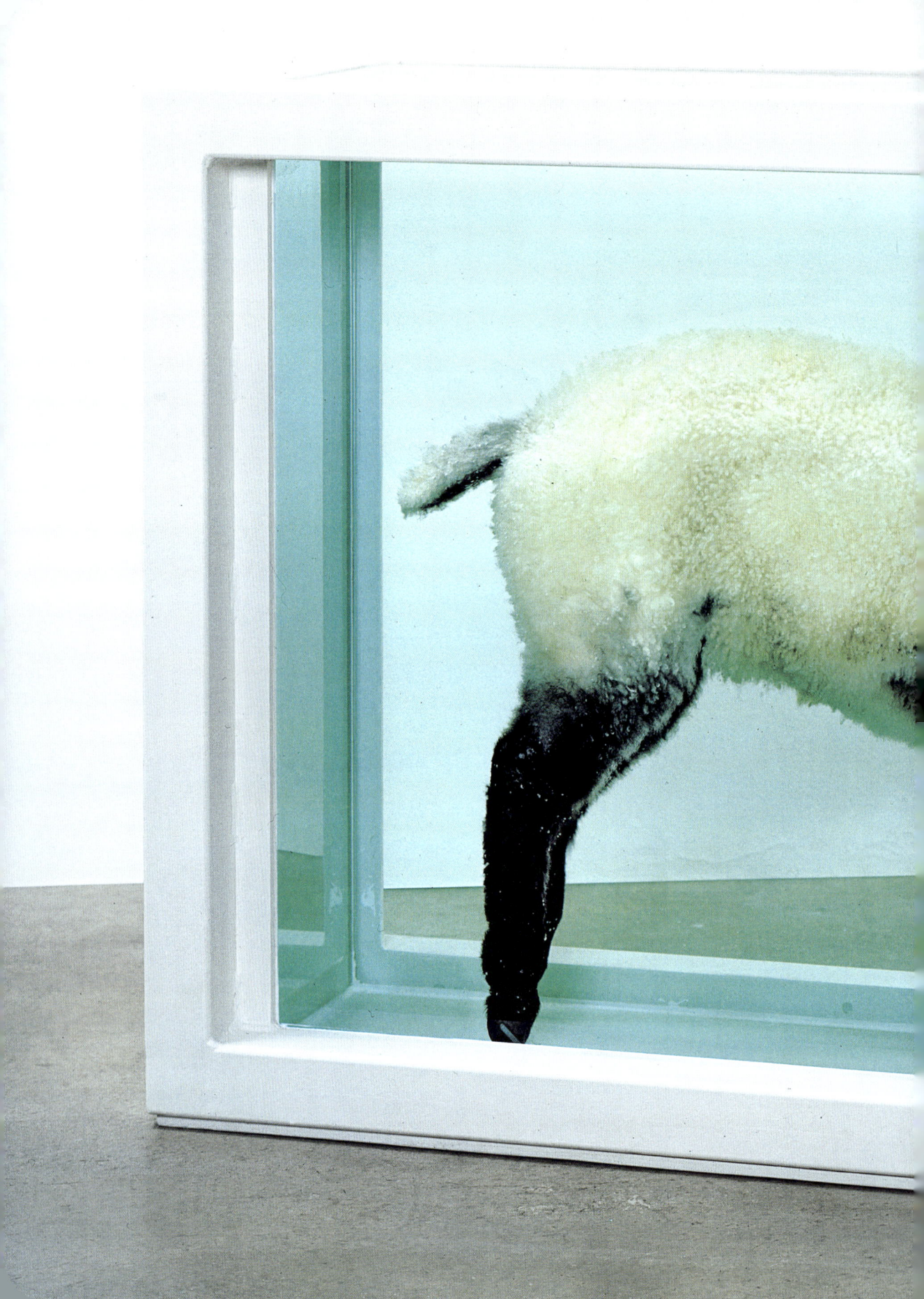

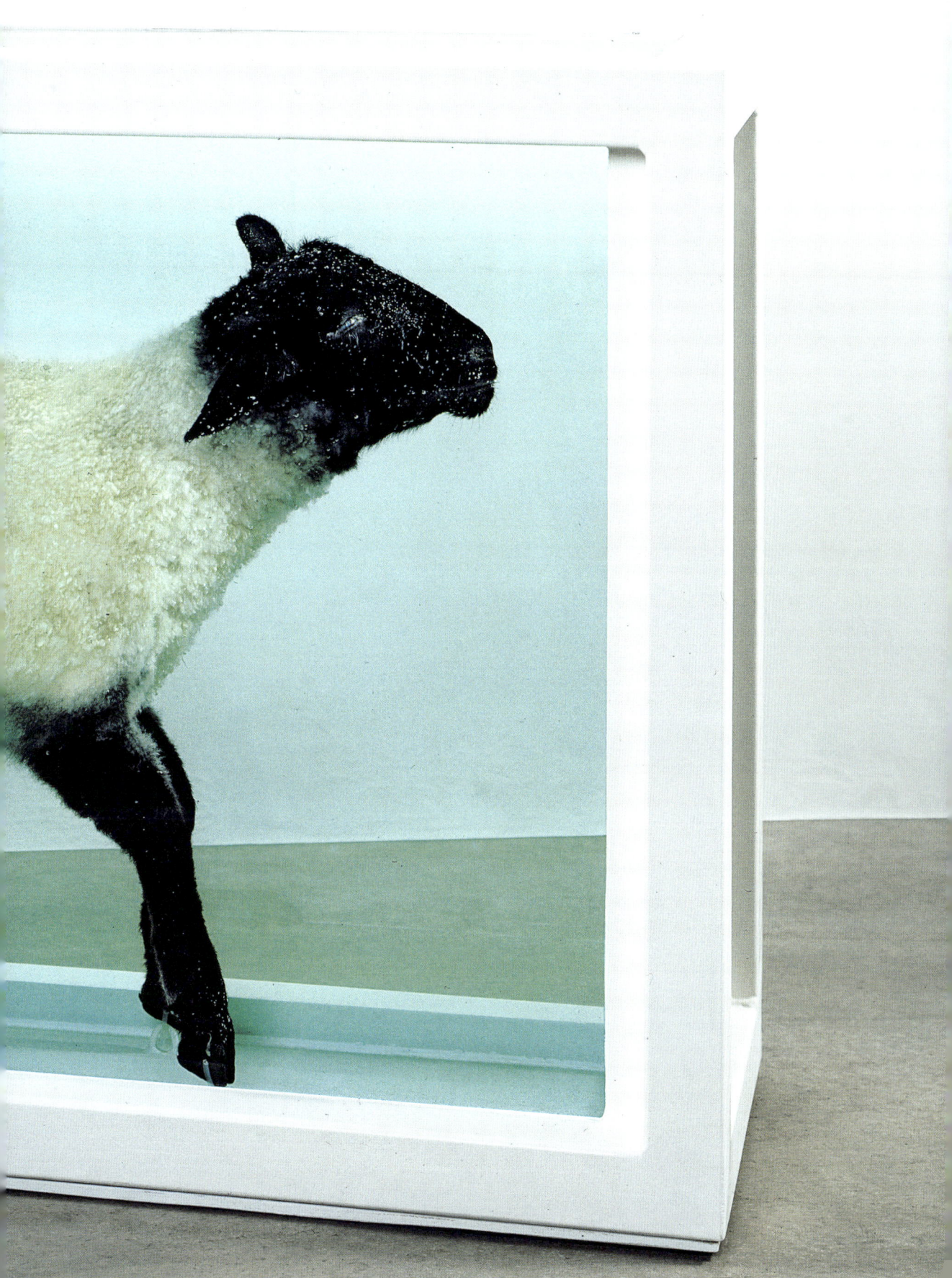

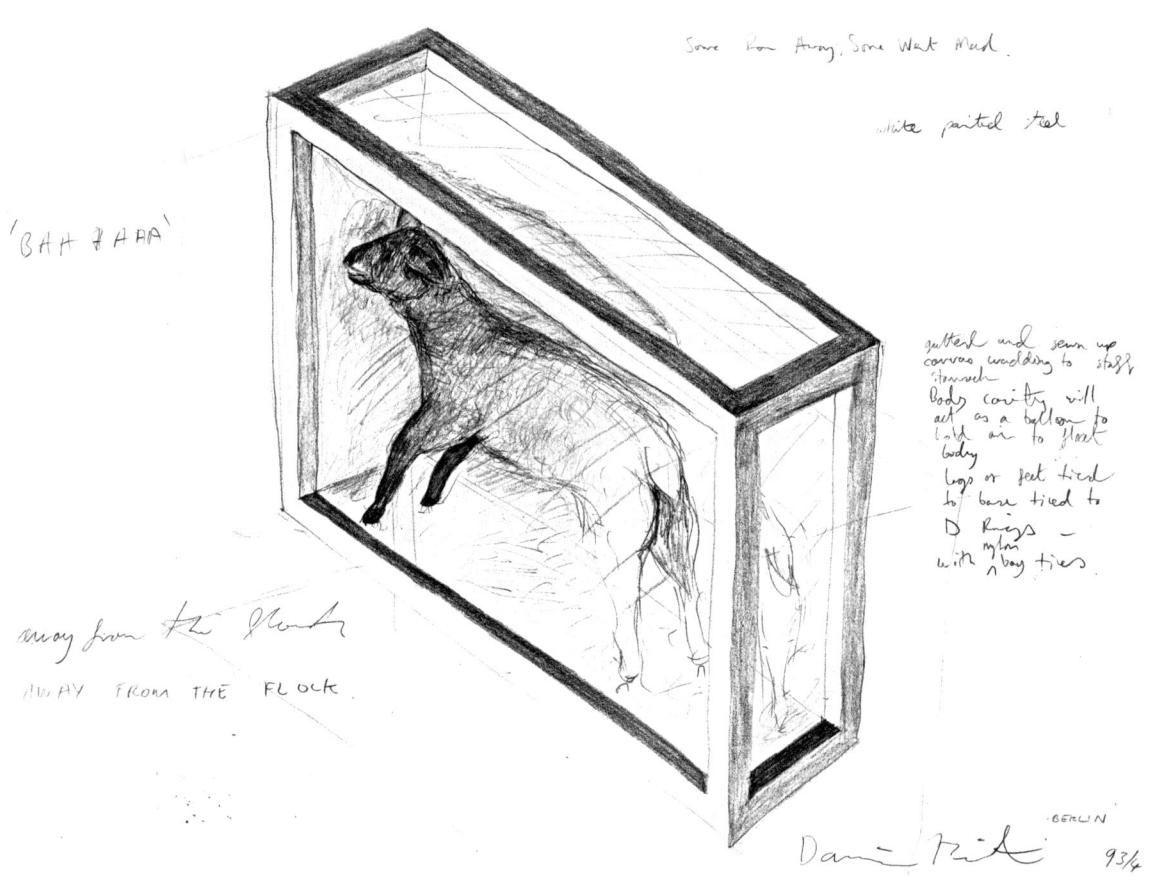

Some Run Away, Some Went Mad.

white painted steel

'BAH BAAA'

gutted and sewn up
canvas wadding to stuff
stomach
Body cavity will
act as a balloon to
hold air to float
body
Legs or feet tied
to base tied to
D Rings —
with nylon bag ties

away from the flock
AWAY FROM THE FLOCK

Damien Hirst

BERLIN
93/4

Away from the Flock, 1994 | Bleistift auf Papier | Pencil on paper | 50 × 73 cm

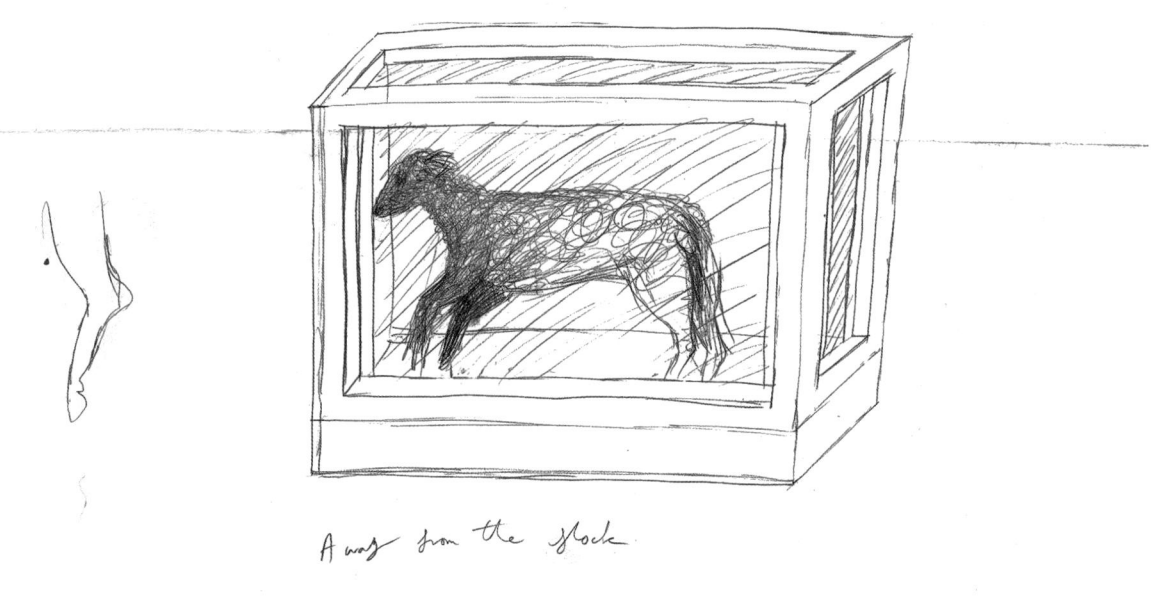

Away from the flock.

I Damien Hirst.

Untitled (Away from the Flock), 2001 | Bleistift auf Papier | Pencil on paper | 75 × 110 cm

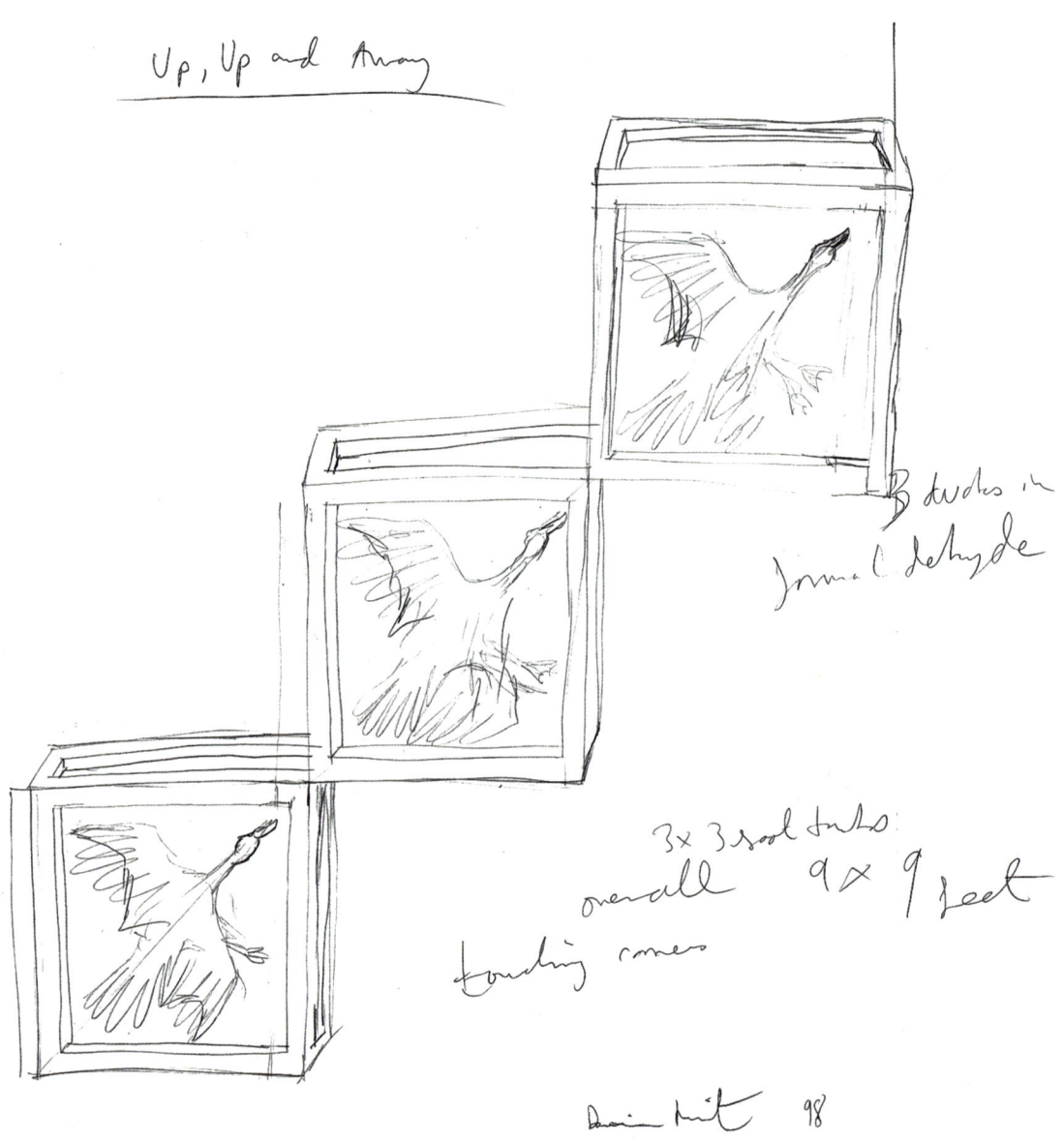

Up, Up and Away, 1998 | Bleistift und Klebeband auf Papier | Pencil and adhesive tape on paper | 90 × 95 cm

Up, Up and Away, 1997 | Glas, lackierter Stahl, Silikon, Acryl, Monofilament, Enten
und Formaldehydlösung | Glass, painted steel, silicone, acrylic, monofilament, ducks,
and formaldehyde solution | Drei Teile, je: | Three parts, each: 90 × 90 × 31 cm

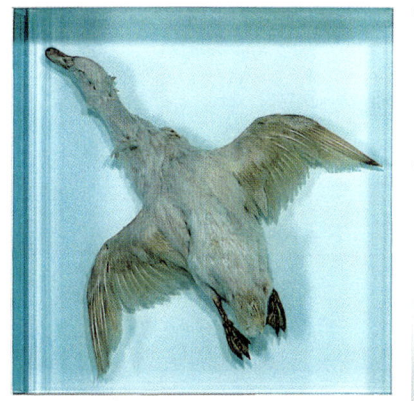
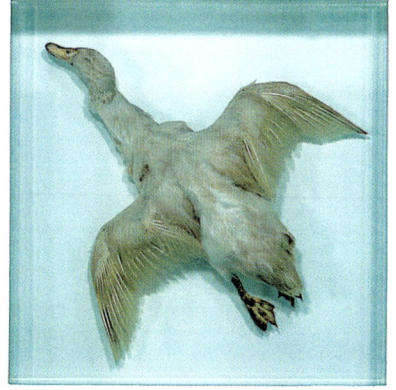
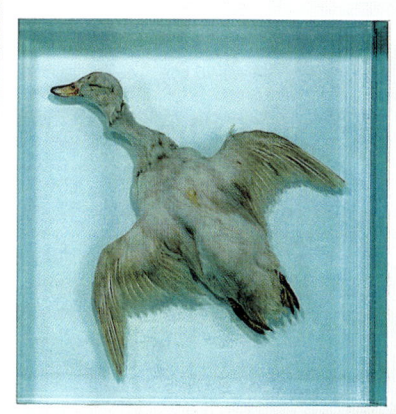

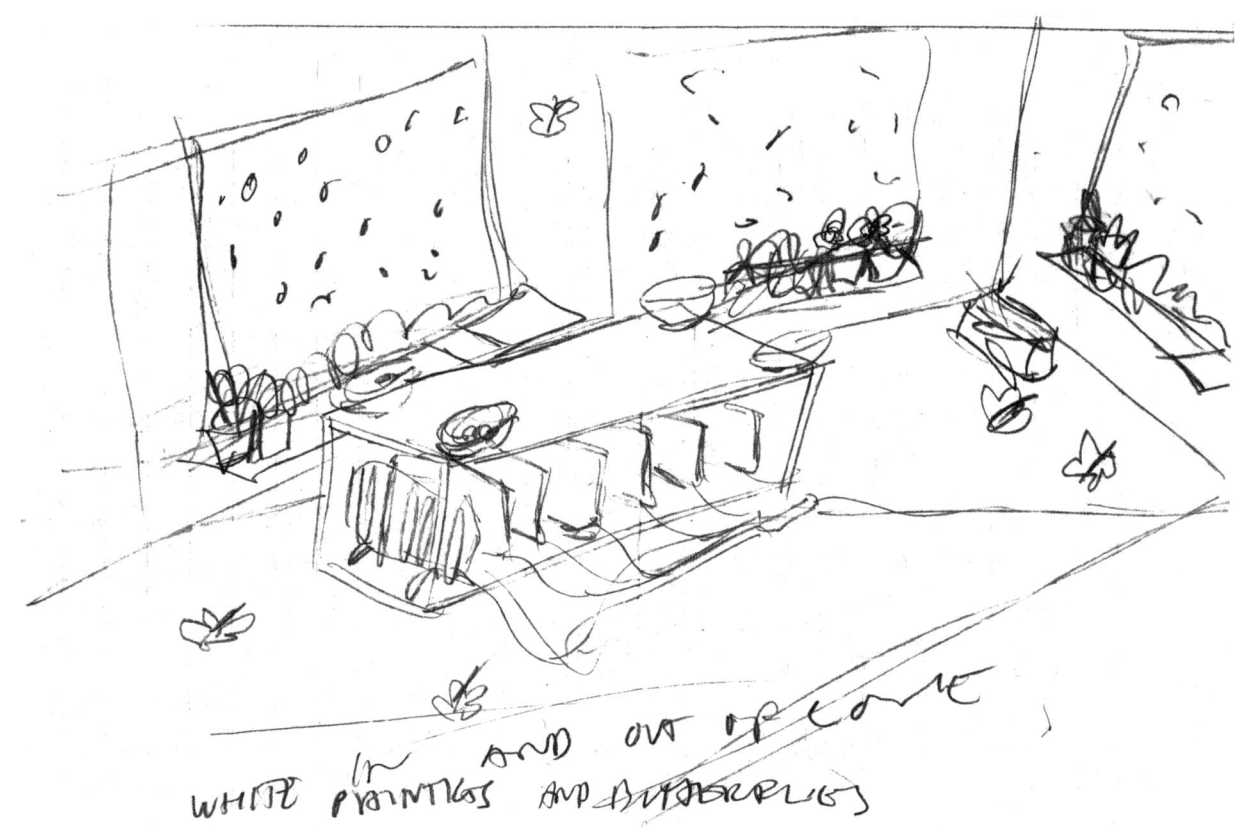

IN AND OUT OF LOVE

WHITE PAINTINGS AND BUTTERFLIES

In and Out of Love (White Paintings and Butterflies), 1991 | Bleistift auf Papier | Pencil on paper | 15 × 23 cm

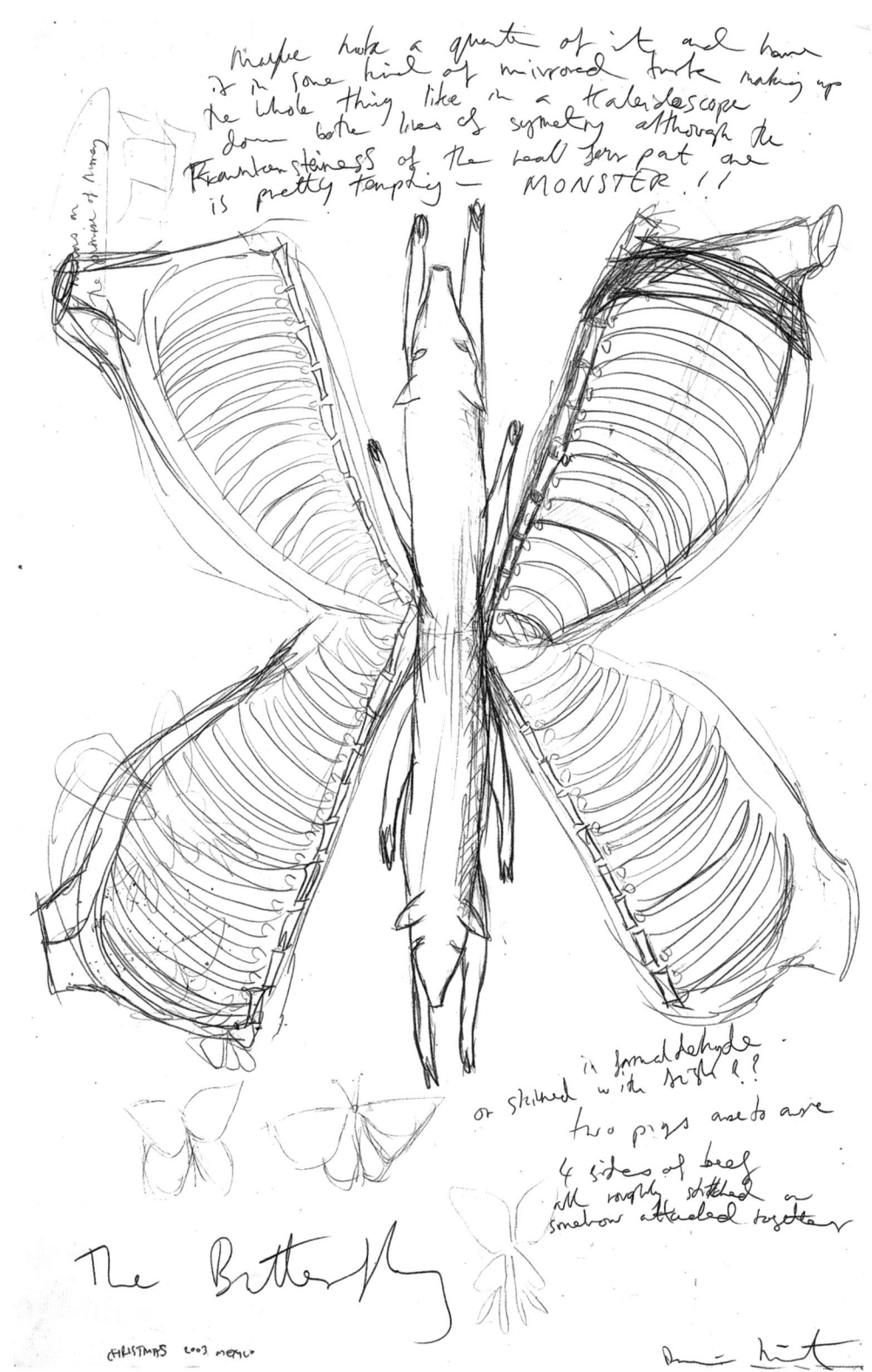

The Butterfly, 2003 | Pencil on paper | Bleistift auf Papier | 102 × 66 cm

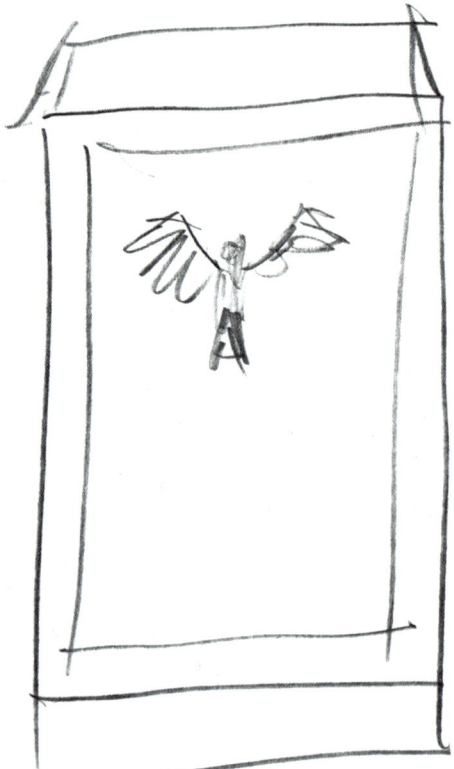

The Incomplete Truth

2 bloomsbury place   london   wc1a 2qa   tel +44 20 7637 3994   fax +44 20 7637 3995   e-mail enquiries@science.ltd.uk

The Incomplete Truth, 2006 | Bleistift auf Papier | Pencil on paper | 23 × 16 cm

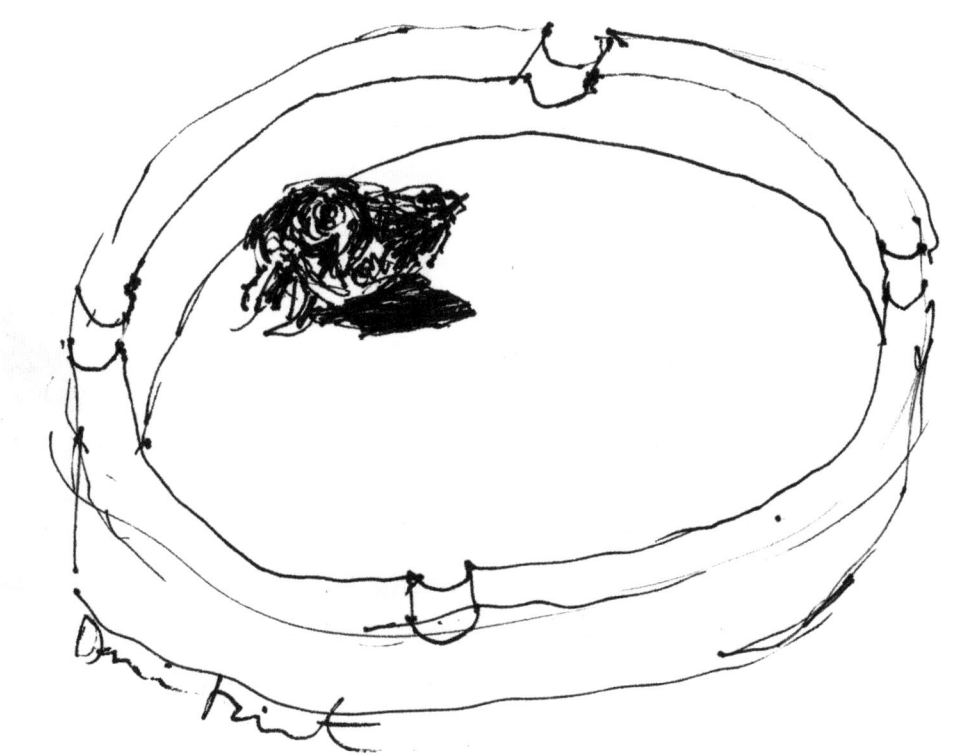

Ashtray Head, 1993 | Tinte auf Papier | Ink on paper | 11 × 16 cm

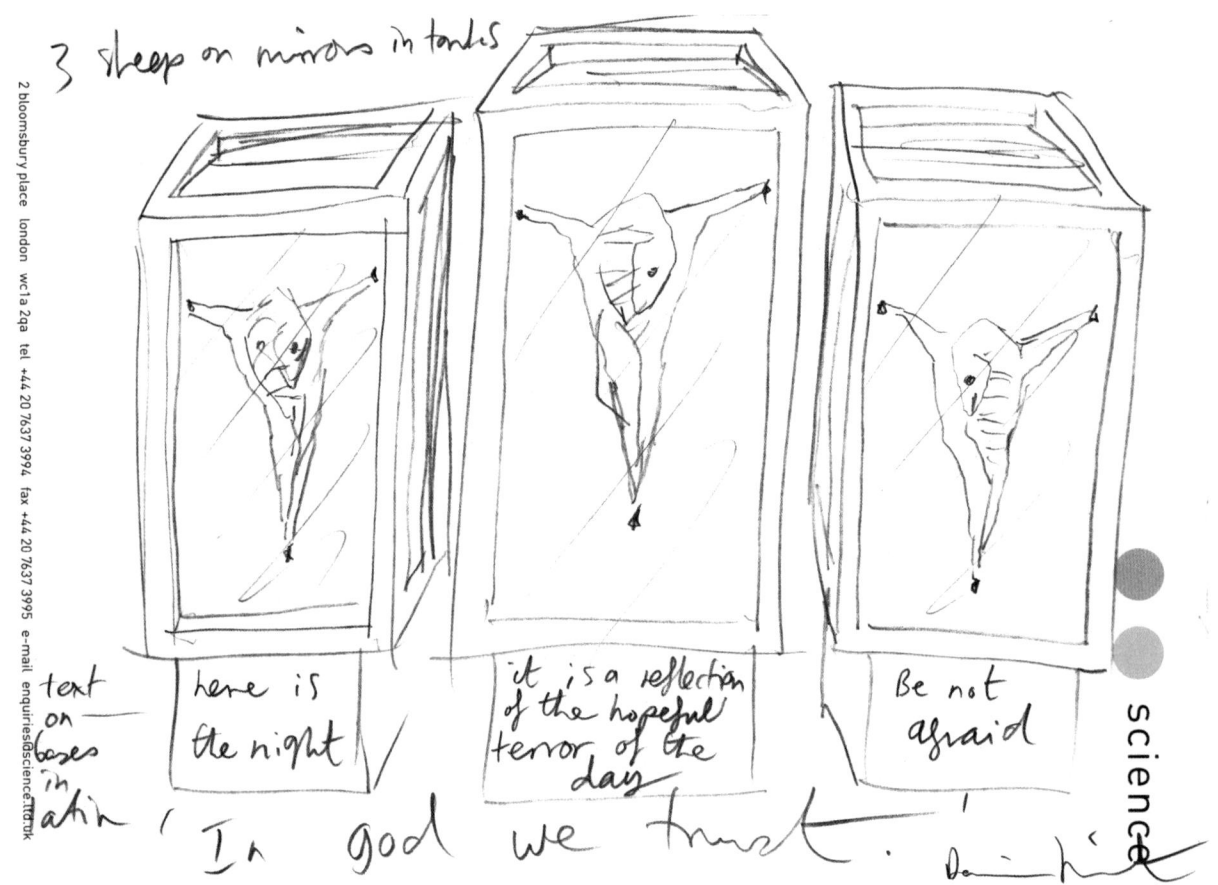

3 sheep on mirrors in tanks

here is
the night

it is a reflection
of the hopeful
terror of the
day

Be not
afraid

text
on
bases
in
latin

'In god we trust.'

2 bloomsbury place london wc1a 2qa tel +44 20 7637 3994 fax +44 20 7637 3995 e-mail enquiries@scienceltd.uk

science

In God We Trust, 2006 | Bleistift auf Papier | Pencil on paper | 16 × 23 cm

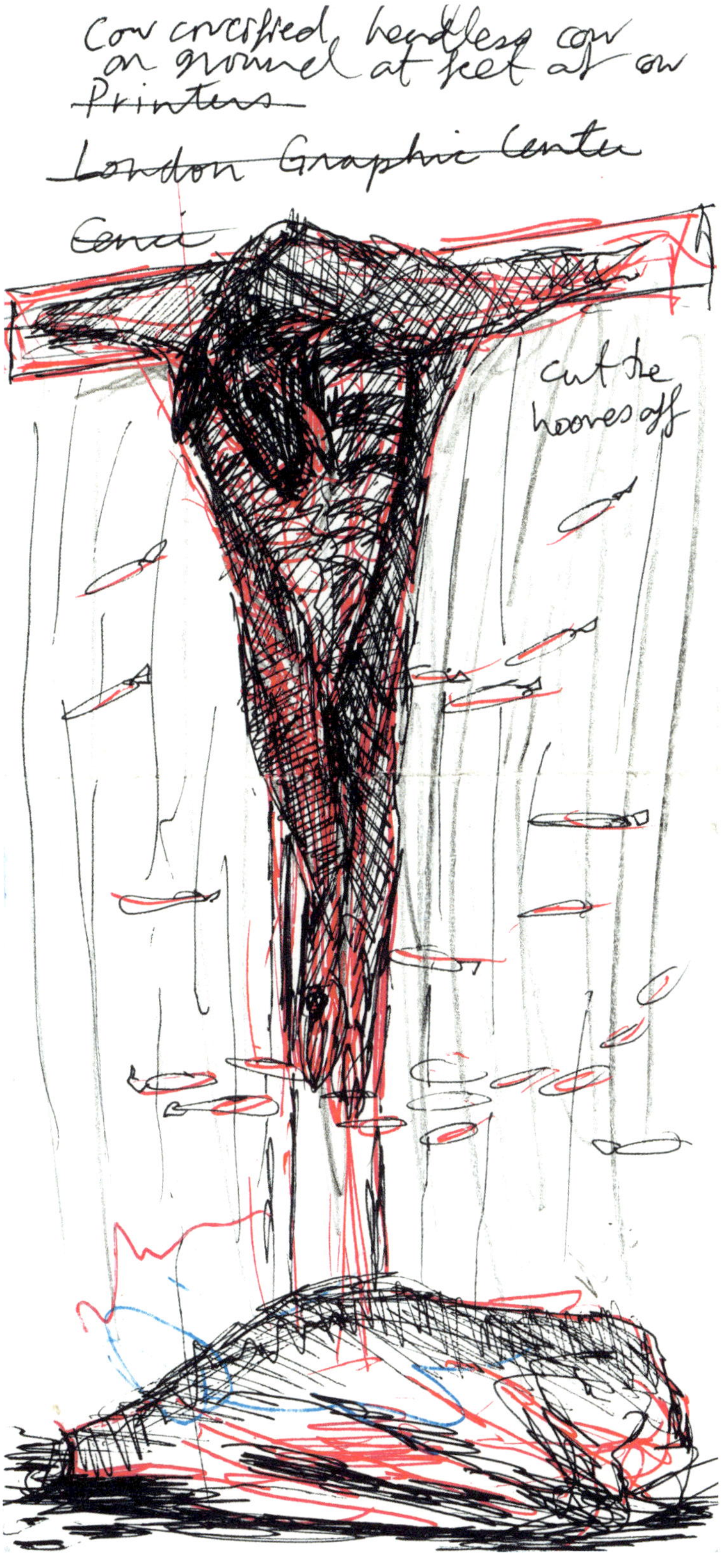

Cow crucified, headless cow
on ground at feet of cow
Printers

London Graphic Center

Cenci

cut the
hooves off

Cow Crucified, 2001 | Tinte und Bleistift auf Papier | Ink and pencil on paper | 21 × 10 cm

Crucified Cow, 2003 | Mischtechnik | Mixed media | 246 × 185 × 34 cm

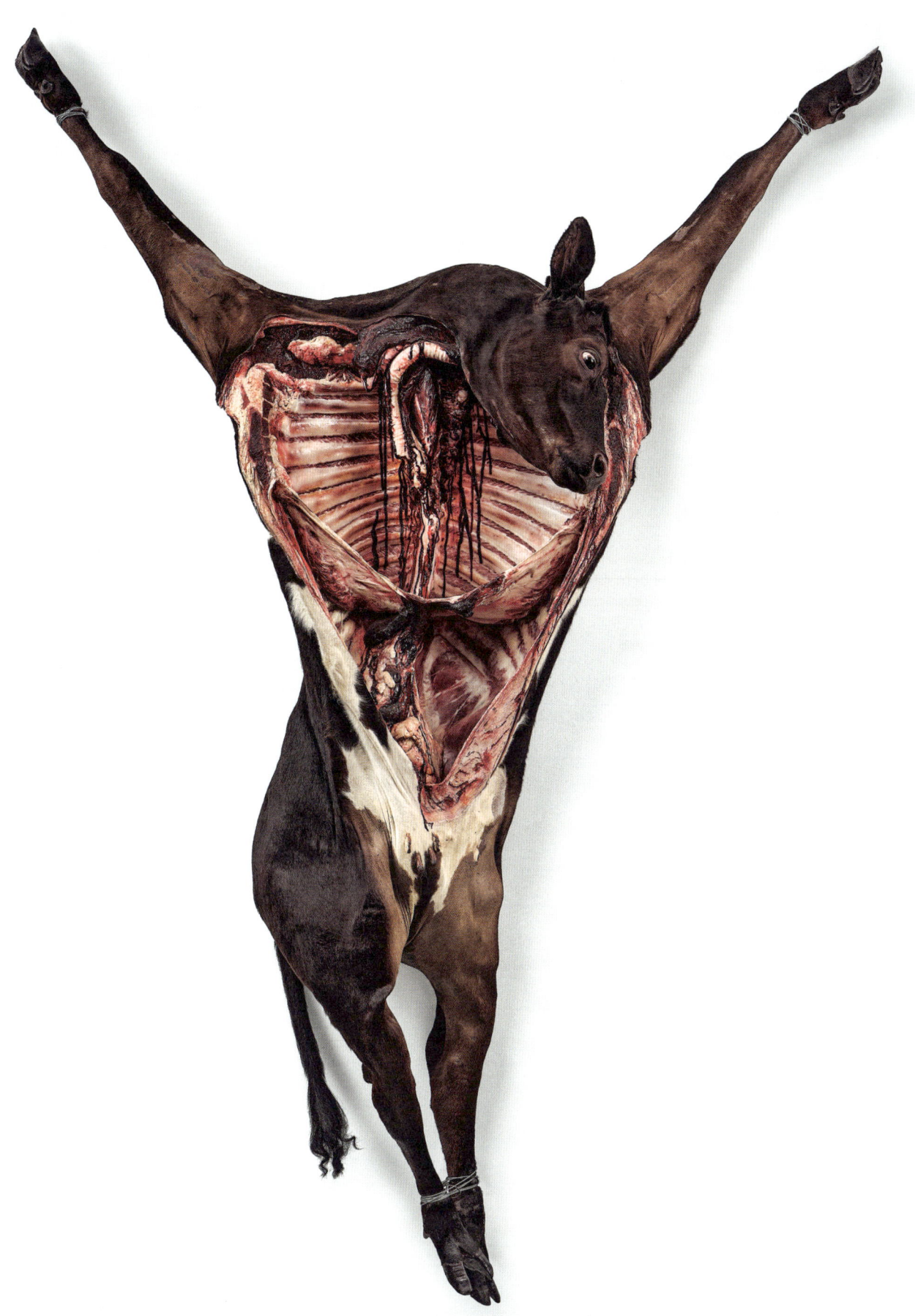

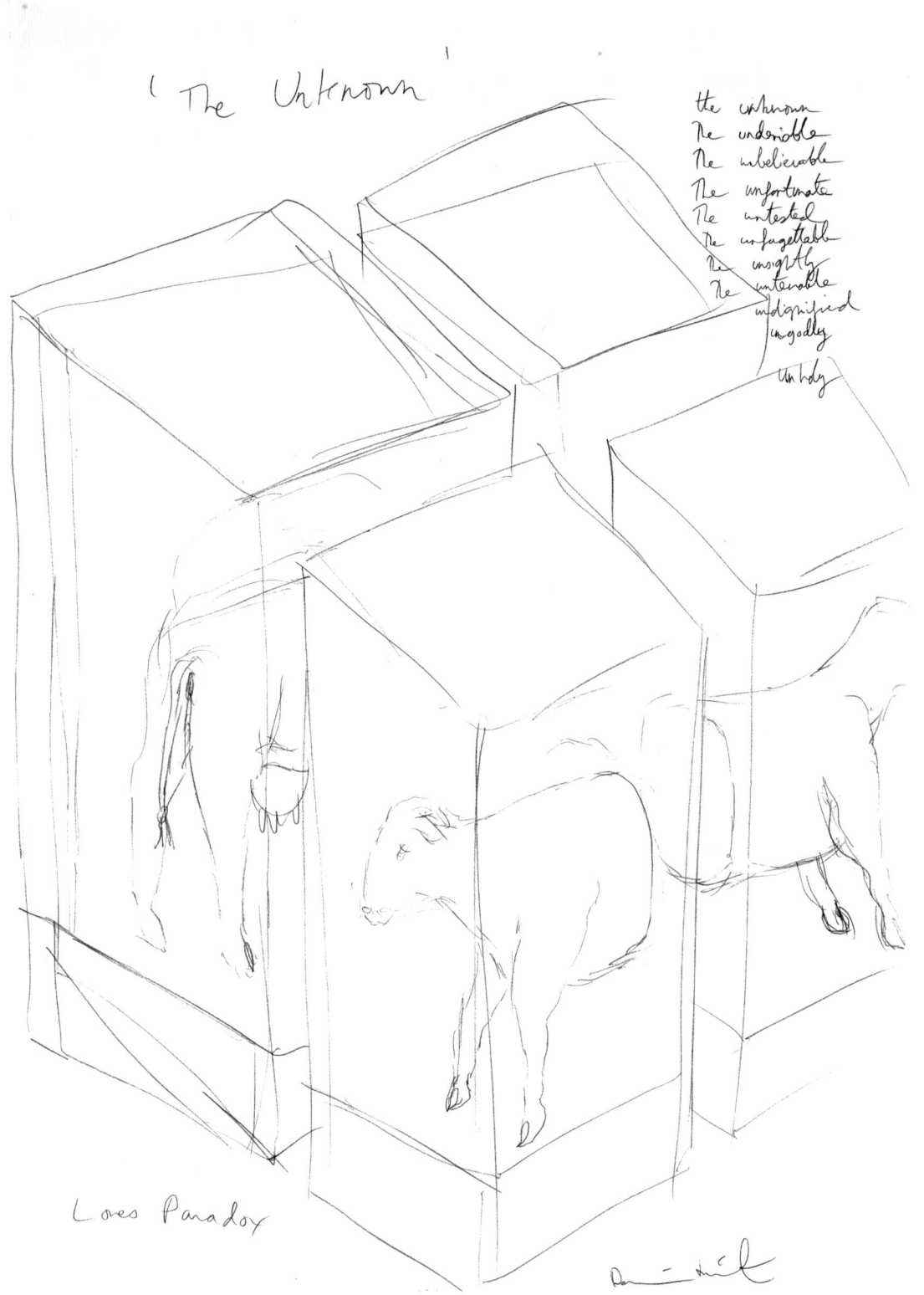

'The Unknown'

the unknown
The undeniable
The unbelievable
The unfortunate
The untested
The unforgettable
The unsightly
The untenable
    undignified
    ungodly

    unholy

Loves Paradox

The Unknown/Love's Paradox, 2006 | Bleistift auf Papier | Pencil on paper | 100 × 72 cm

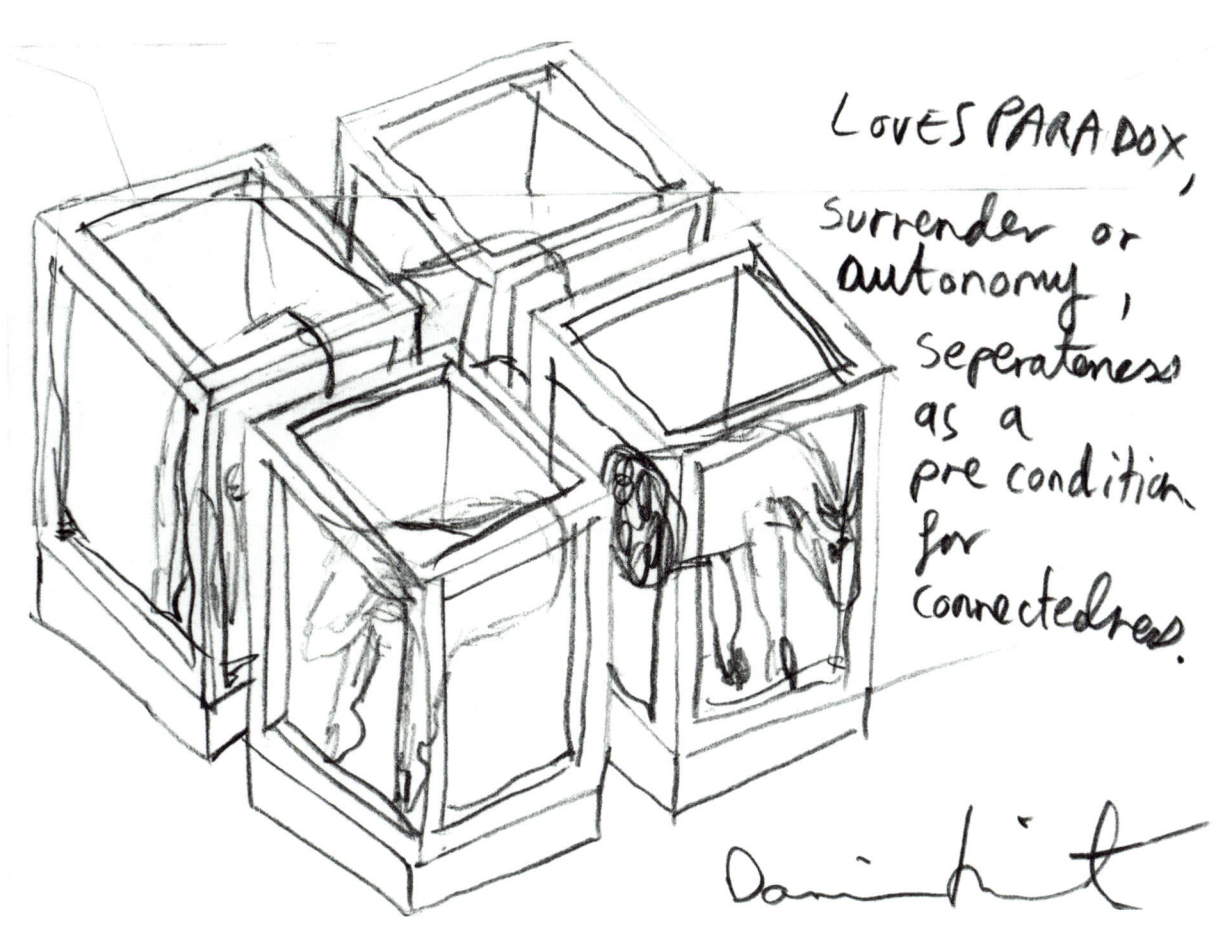

LoveS PARADOX,
Surrender or
autonomy,
Seperateness
as a
pre condition
for
connectedness.

Love's Paradox, Surrender or Autonomy, Separateness as a Precondition for Connectedness, 2006
Bleistift auf Papier | Pencil on paper | 11 × 16 cm

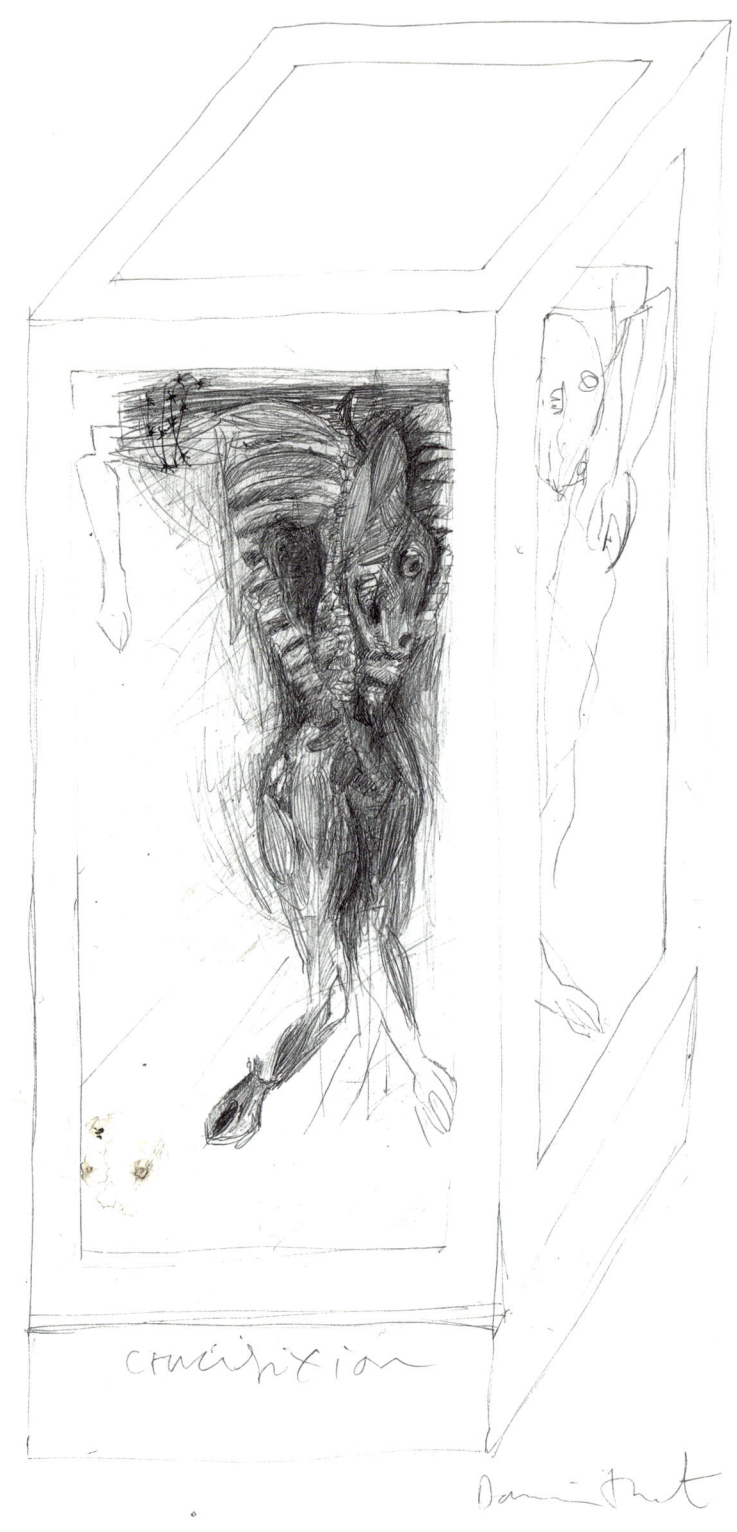

crucifixion

Crucifixion, 1998 | Bleistift auf Papier | Pencil on paper | 94 × 69 cm

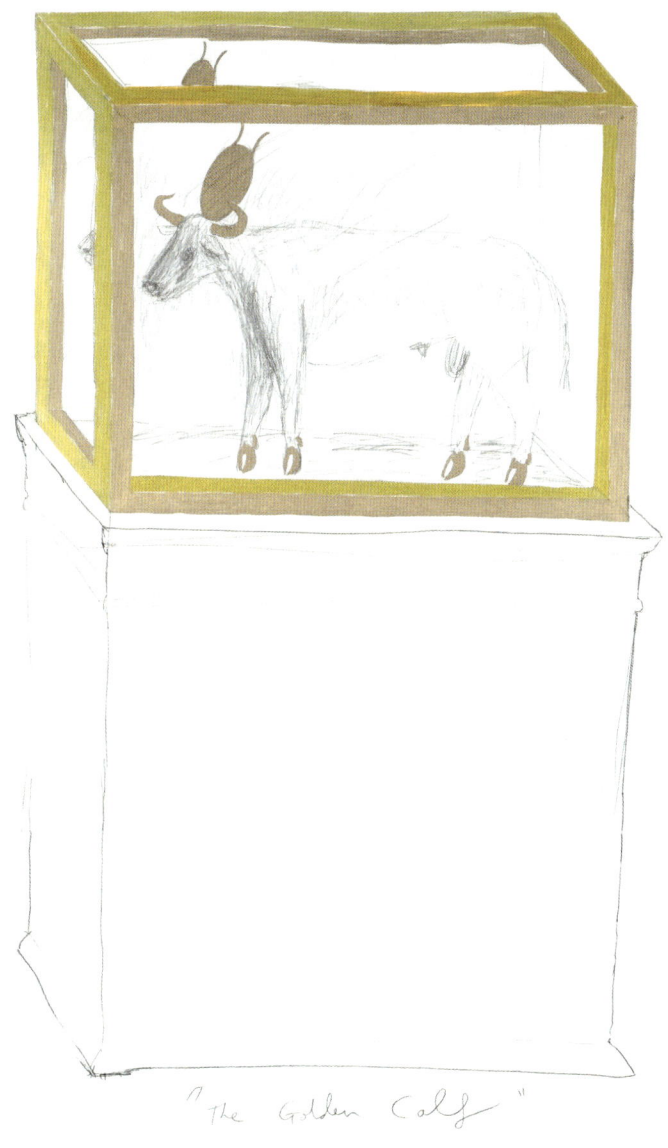

"The Golden Calf"

2008

Some Comfort Gained from the Acceptance of the Inherent Lies in Everything – New Configuration Drawing, 2006 | Bleistift auf Karton | Pencil on card | 23 × 19 cm

So the piece comes with two bases and can be shown in a long line as before or as here in two parts

it can be in two sections with one cow in each section gained from the interval lies

new configuration for Some comfort acceptance of the in everything... in two sections with 6 pieces in each

in one piece or two pieces and with or without plinths.

95

"The Dream"

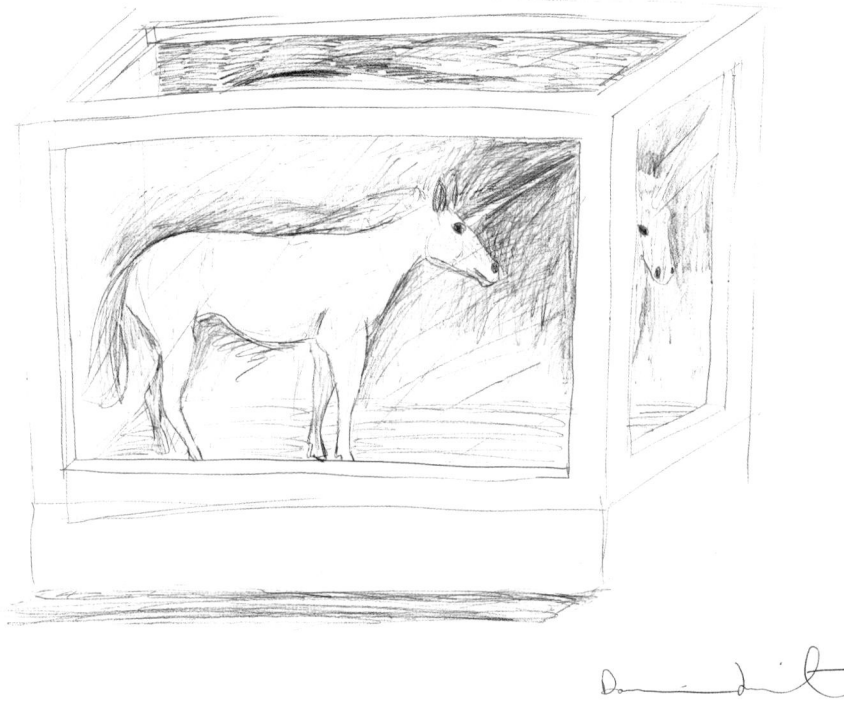

2008

The Dream Drawing, 2008 | Bleistift auf Papier | Pencil on paper | 84 × 118 cm

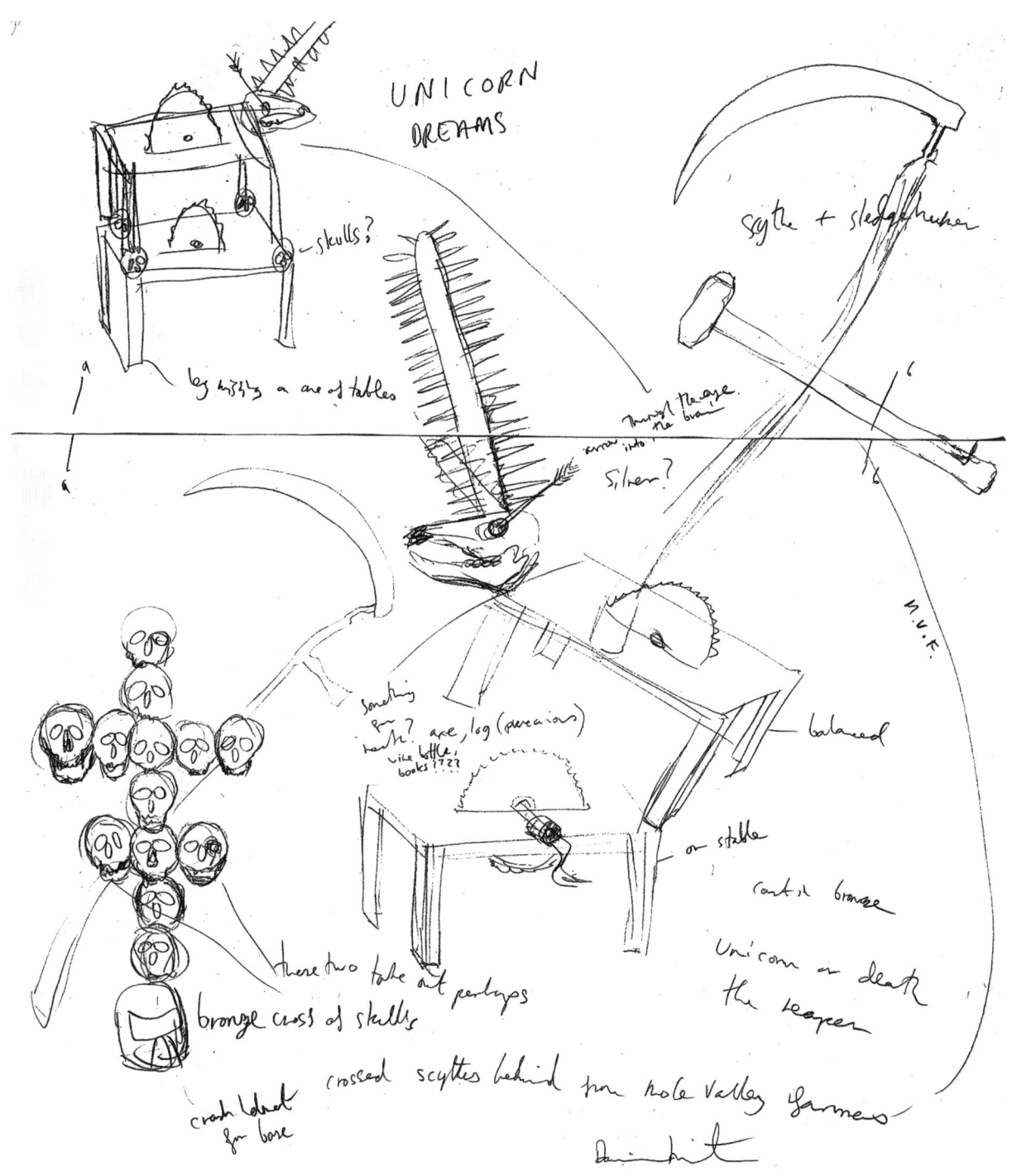

UNICORN
DREAMS

scythe + sledgehammer

—skulls?

by using a are of tables

arrow into the brain.

Through the brain.

Silver?

M.U.F.

balanced

something
from
teeth? axe, log (precautions)
wine bottle,
books ??

or stable

cast in bronze

Unicorn or death
the reaper

these two take out perhaps

bronze cross of skulls

crossed scythes behind from Mole Valley Farmers

crash helmet
for base

Damien Hirst

Unicorn Dreams, 2006 | Bleistift auf Papier | Pencil on paper | 65 × 59 cm

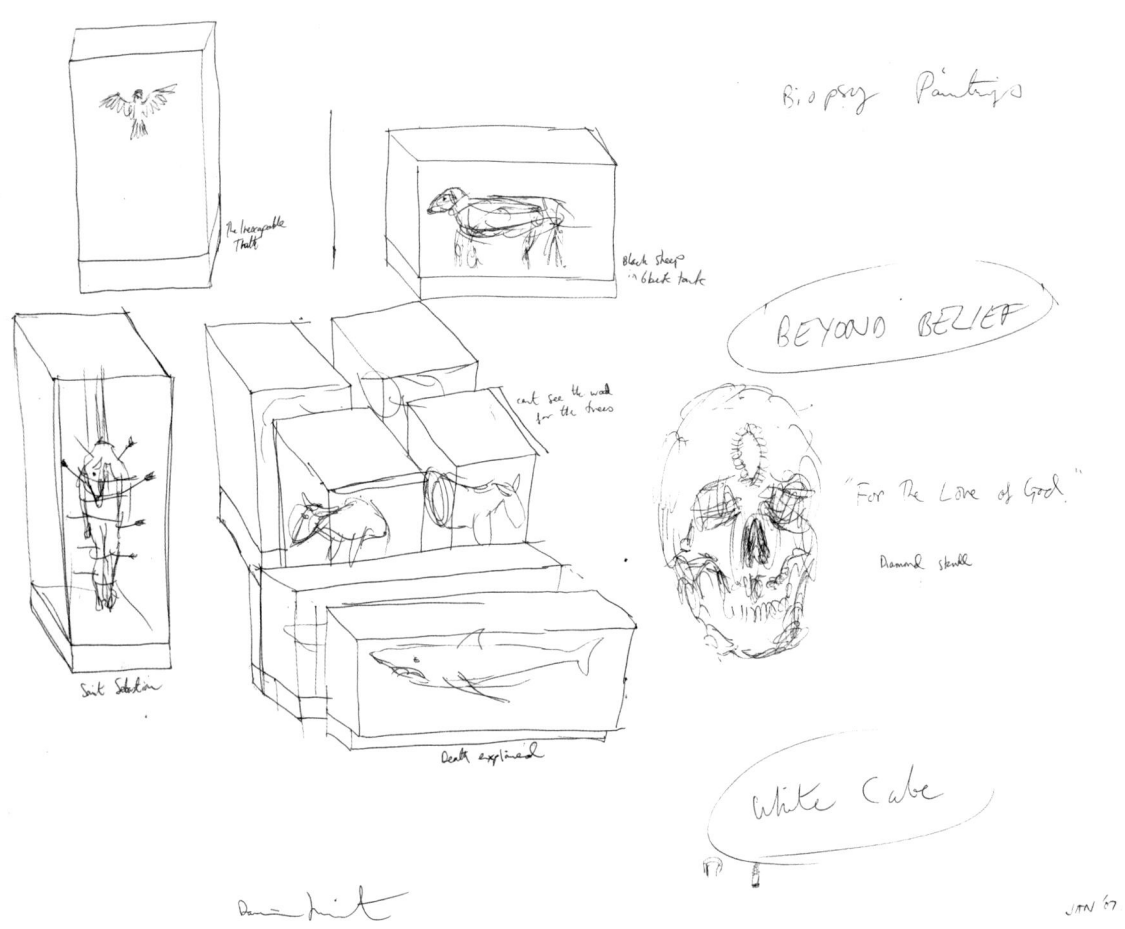

Biopsy Paintings

The Incorruptible Truth

Black Sheep in black tank

BEYOND BELIEF

can't see the wood for the trees

"For The Love of God."

Diamond Skull

Suit Solution

Death explained

White Cube

Damien Hirst

JAN '07

Beyond Belief Sketches, 2007 | Tinte auf Papier | Ink on paper | 72 × 101 cm

Beyond Belief (For the Love of God/Death Explained), 2006
Bleistift auf Papier | Pencil on paper | 72 × 101 cm

„Ich habe mir einfach überlegt, was kann
ich maximal erfinden, um den Sieg über
den Tod zu markieren. [...] Da dachte ich
mir: Du musst einen perfekten Schädel
mit perfekten Diamanten überziehen."

'I asked myself: what is the ultimate
way to pit yourself against death? [...]
I thought to myself: you have to cover
a perfect skull with perfect diamonds.'

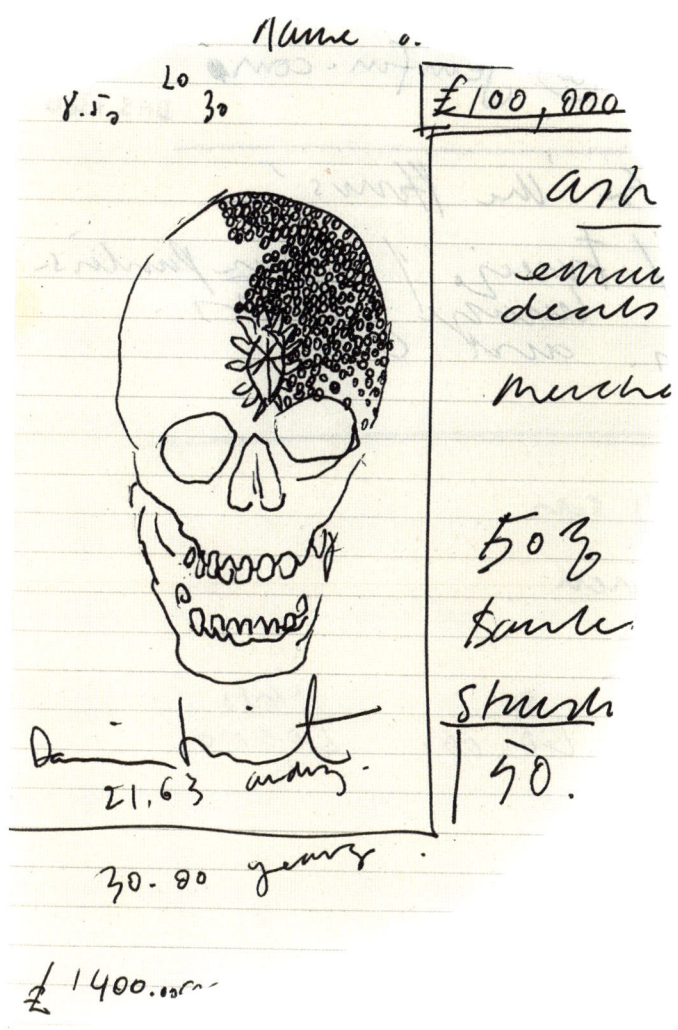

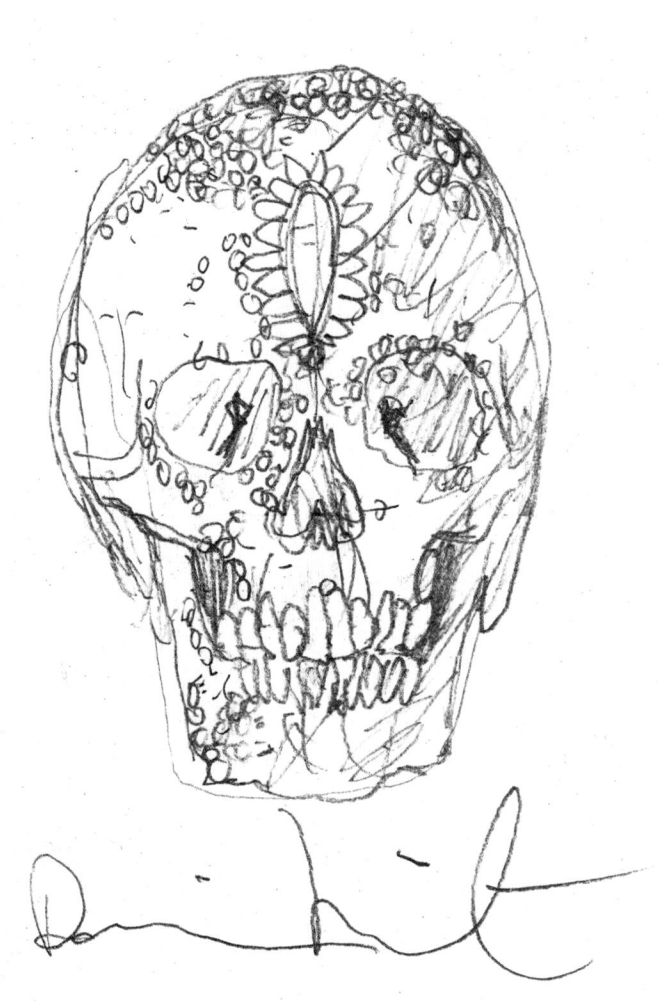

For the Love of God, 2007 | Bleistift auf Papier | Pencil on paper | 12 × 9 cm

For The Love Of God

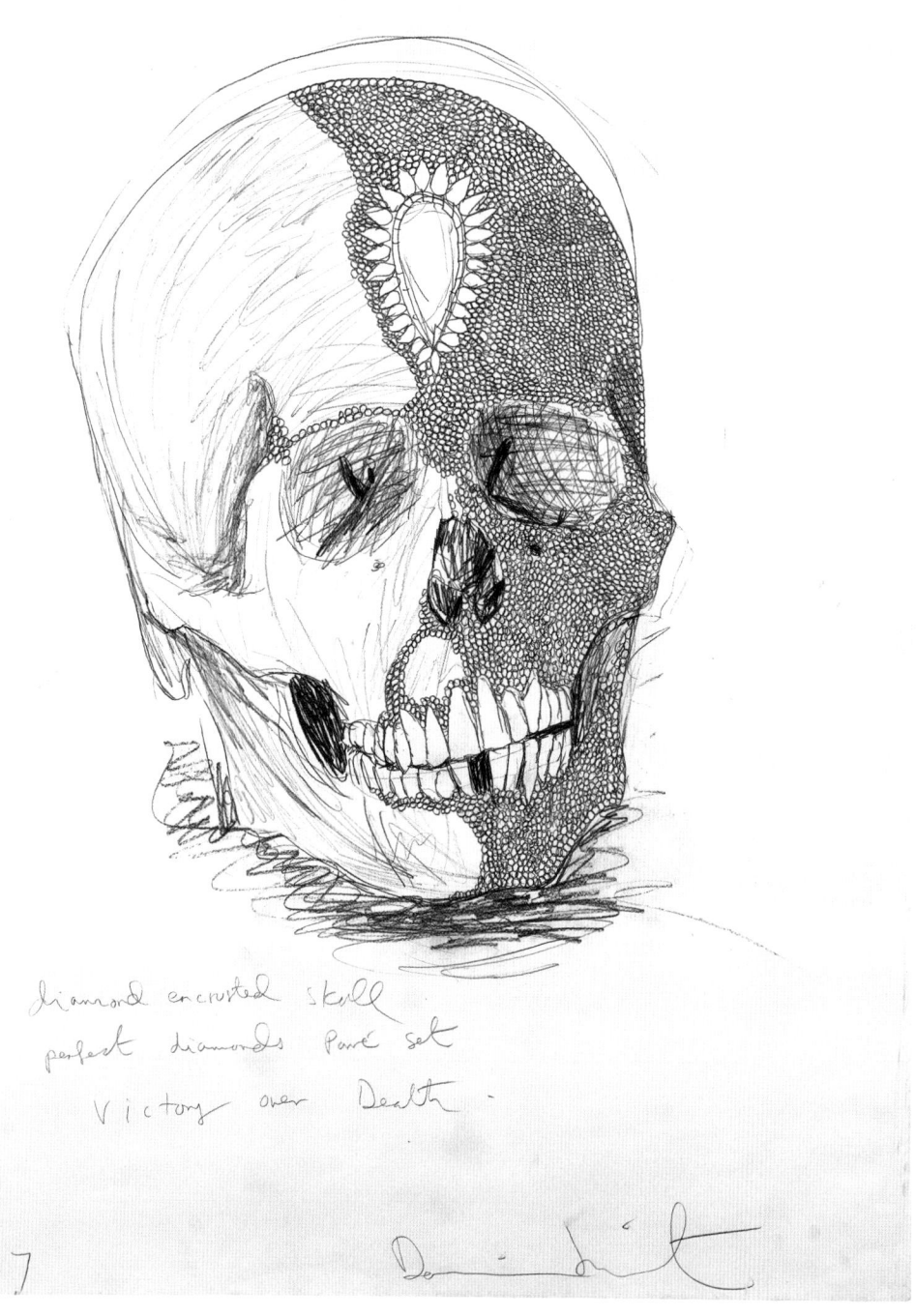

diamond encrusted skull
perfect diamonds Part set
Victory over Death.

2007

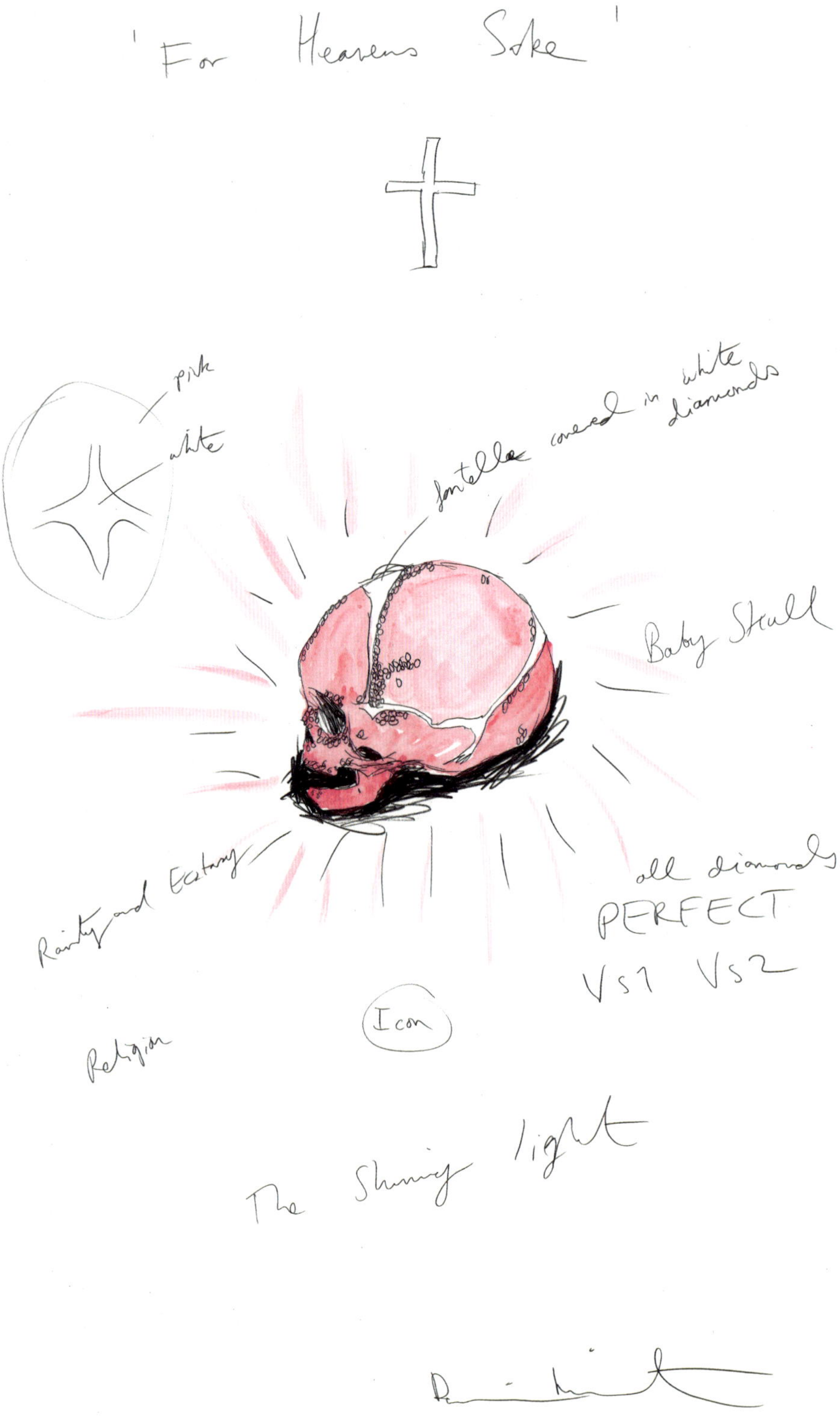

'For Heavens Sake'

✝

pink

white

fontelles covered in white diamonds

Baby Skull

Rarity and Ecstasy

all diamonds
PERFECT
VS1 VS2

Religion

Icon

The Shining light

The Shining Light Drawing, 2008 | Bleistift und Tinte auf Papier | Pencil and ink on paper | 119 × 84 cm

'For Heavens Sake'

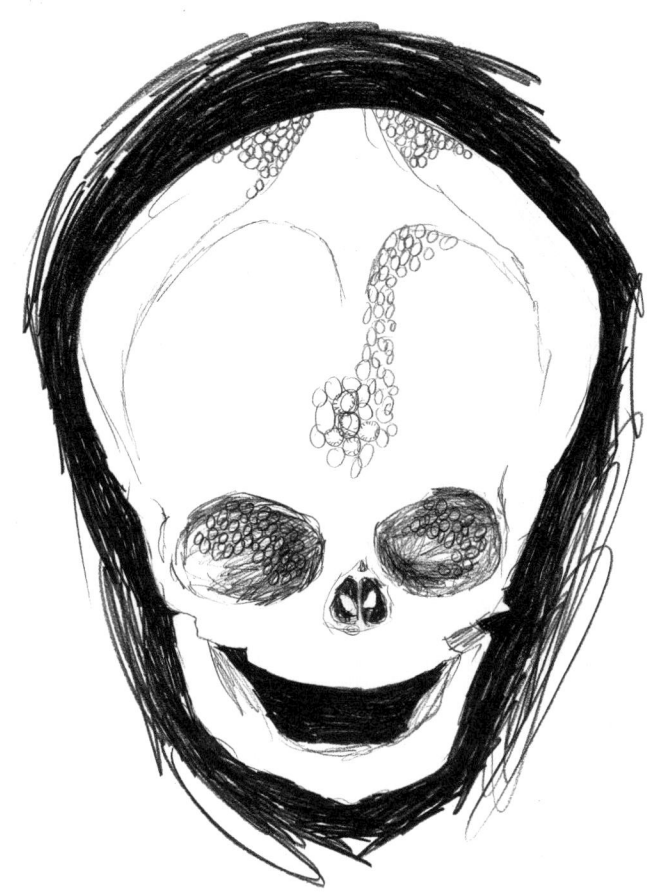

For Heaven's Sake Drawing (I), 2008 | Bleistift auf Papier | Pencil on paper | 76 × 56 cm

For Heaven's Sake, 2008 | Platin, rosa und weiße Diamanten |
Platinum, pink and white diamonds | 9 × 9 × 10 cm

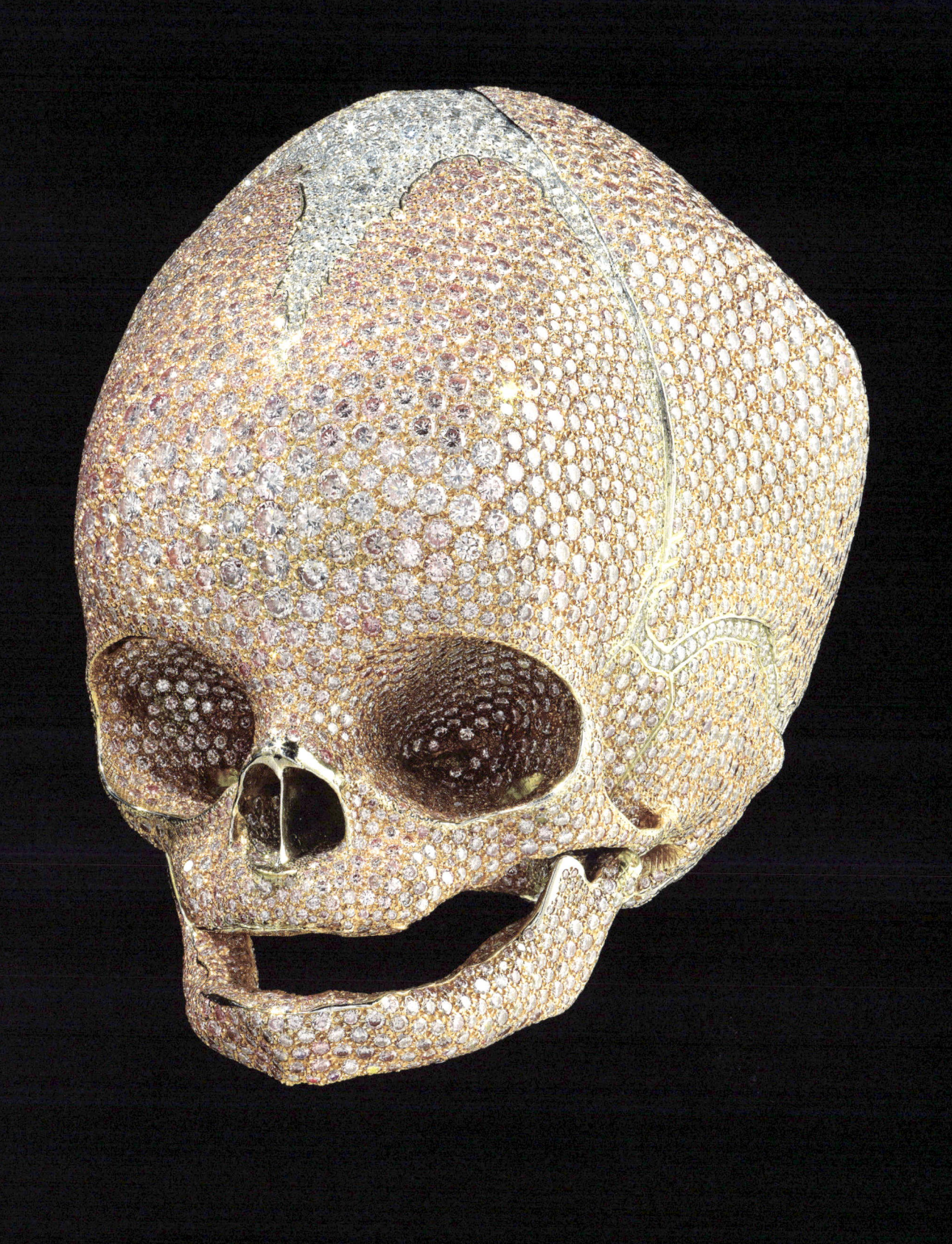

„Die meisten meiner Ideen entstehen
aus dem Wunsch heraus, ein Gefühl
zu beschreiben."

'Most of my ideas come from the
desire to describe a feeling.'

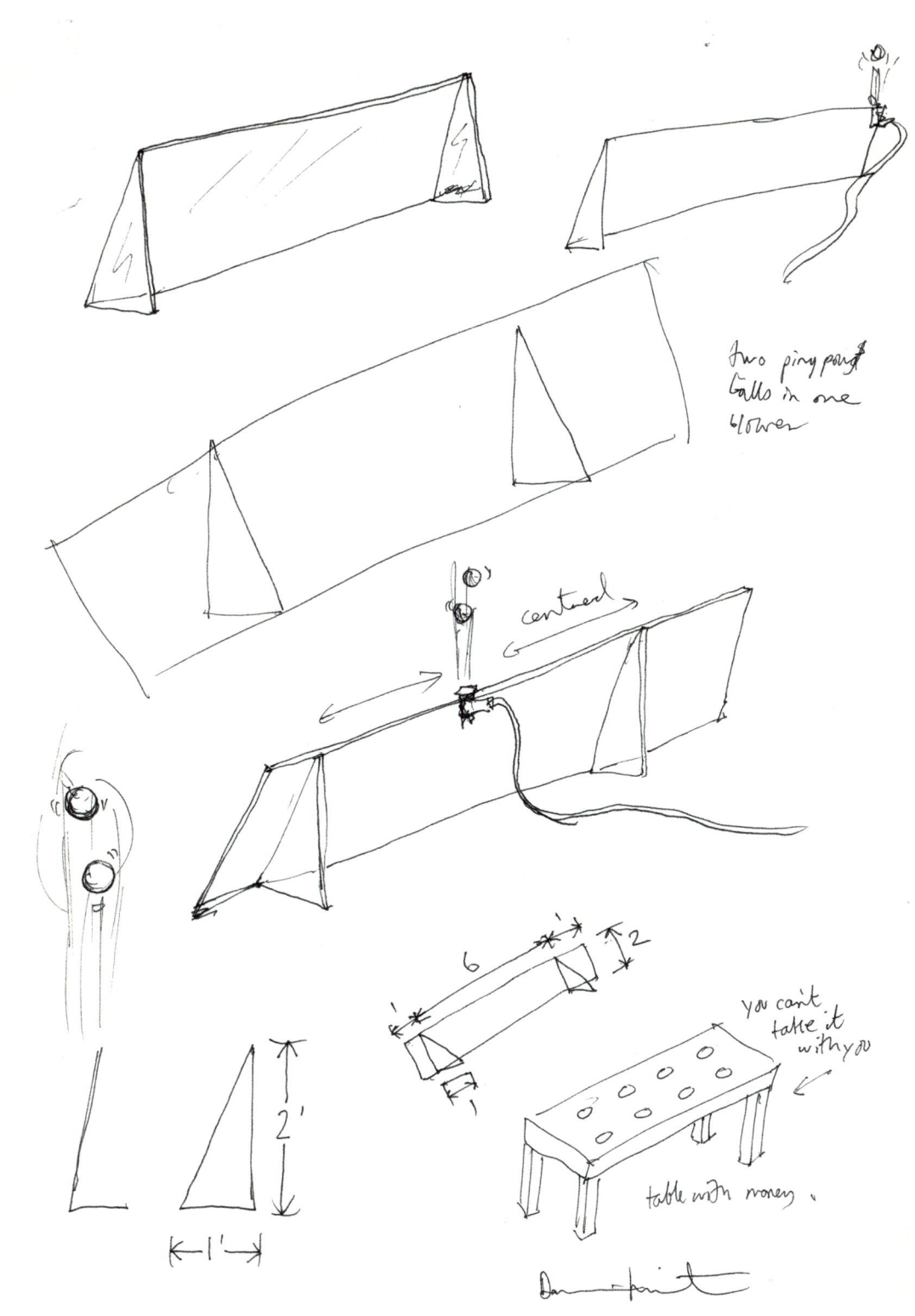

Two ping pong balls in one blower

centeal

6   2

you can't take it with you

table with money .

I Want to Spend the Rest of My Life Everywhere, with Everyone, One to One, Always, Forever, Now, 1991 | Tinte auf Papier | Ink on paper | 31 × 23 cm

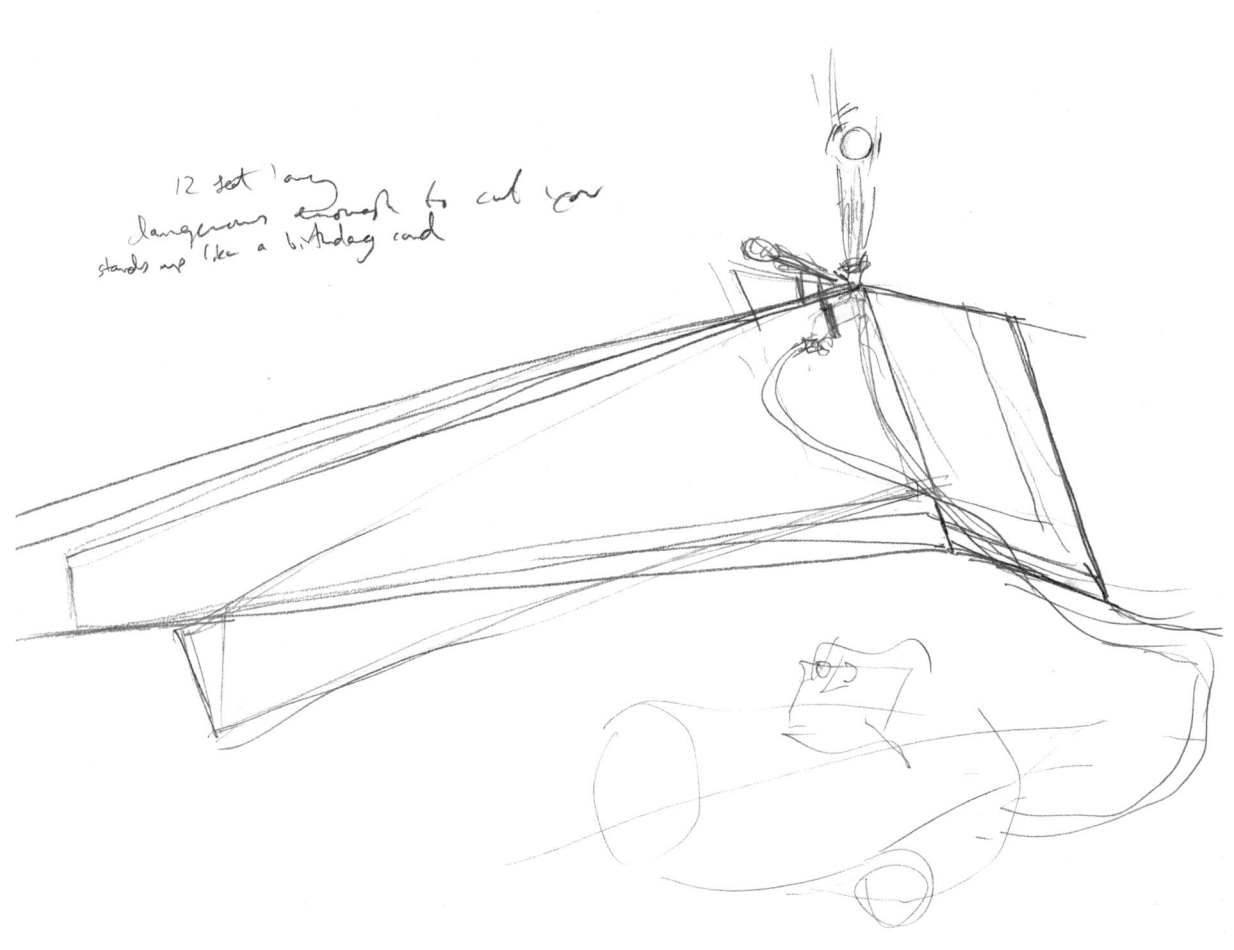

12 feet long
dangerous enough to cut you
stands up like a birthday card

12 Feet Long, 1991 | Bleistift auf Papier | Pencil on paper | 30 × 40 cm

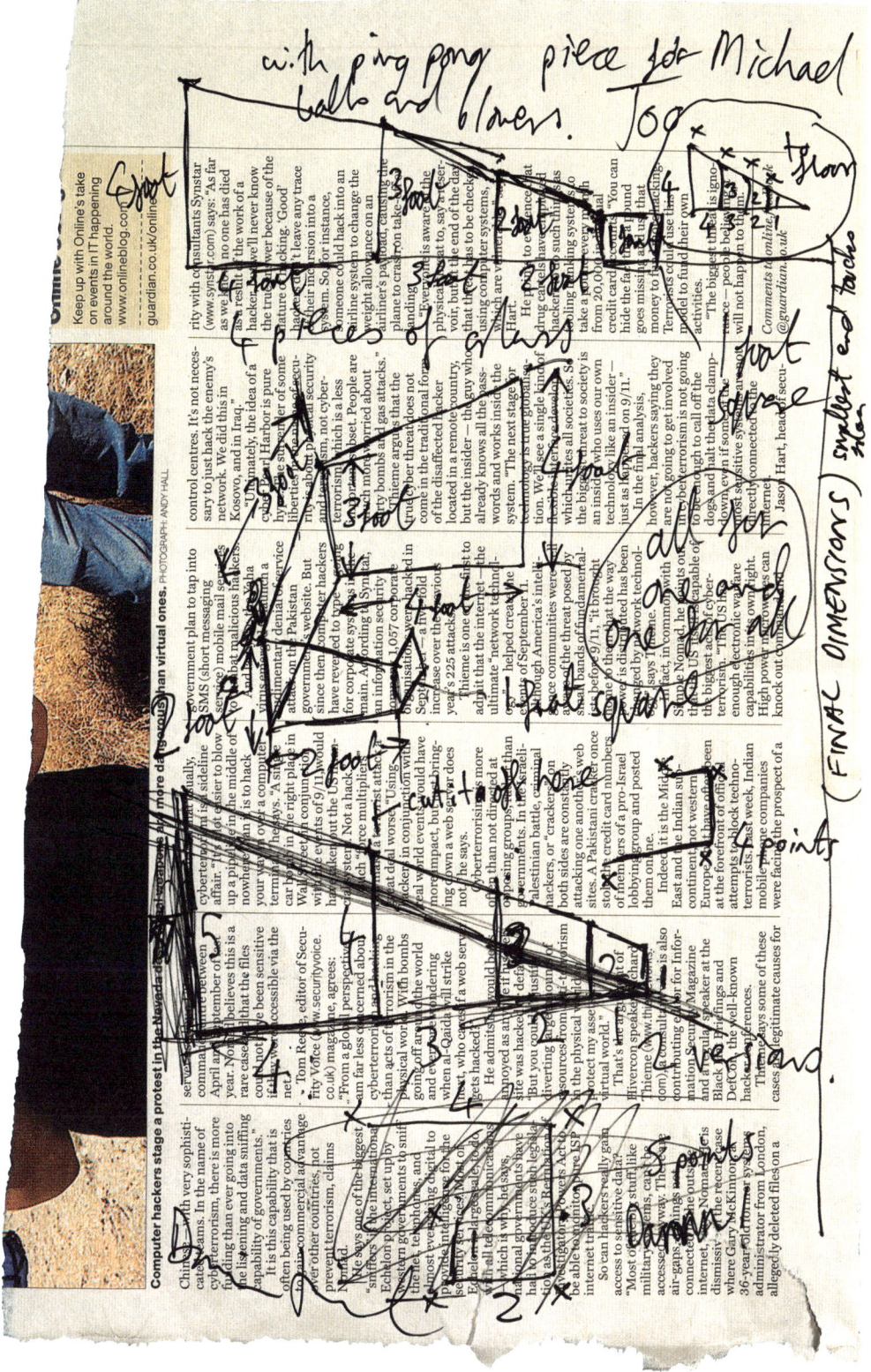

we've got style — invisible vessels glass vessels in a white cabinet.

glass

7 feet □

2 ping pong balls

falling in and out of love the
making up and breaking up.
We keep falling in and out of love.
making friends and falling out.
I keep making up and falling out.

(articulated)
some safety from some solidity beneath the surface of something things
the skeleton piece — something solid beneath the
surface
some solidity beneath the surface of things
the solidity beneath the surface (of things)
some safety from solidity at the centre of things some spaces
some safety from the some solidity beneath the surface of things!
some safety from some solidity beneath the surface of several objects.

We've Got Style, 1993 | Tinte auf Papier | Ink on paper | 26 × 21 cm

WHAT GOES UP MUST COME DOWN.

41·1·272·1086
Dieter.

ping pong ball

HAIR
DRYER

← To
Plug

as close as possible
to glass

Silicone (to hold
hair dryer
vertical)

ping pong ball floats in air jet.
from hair dryer

FROM DAMIEN HIRST

What Goes Up Must Come Down, 1994 | Tinte auf Papier | Ink on paper | 30 × 21 cm

What Goes Up Must Come Down, 1994 | Plexiglas, Föhn und Tischtennisball |
Plexiglass, hairdryer, and ping pong ball | 30 × 30 cm Durchmesser | diameter

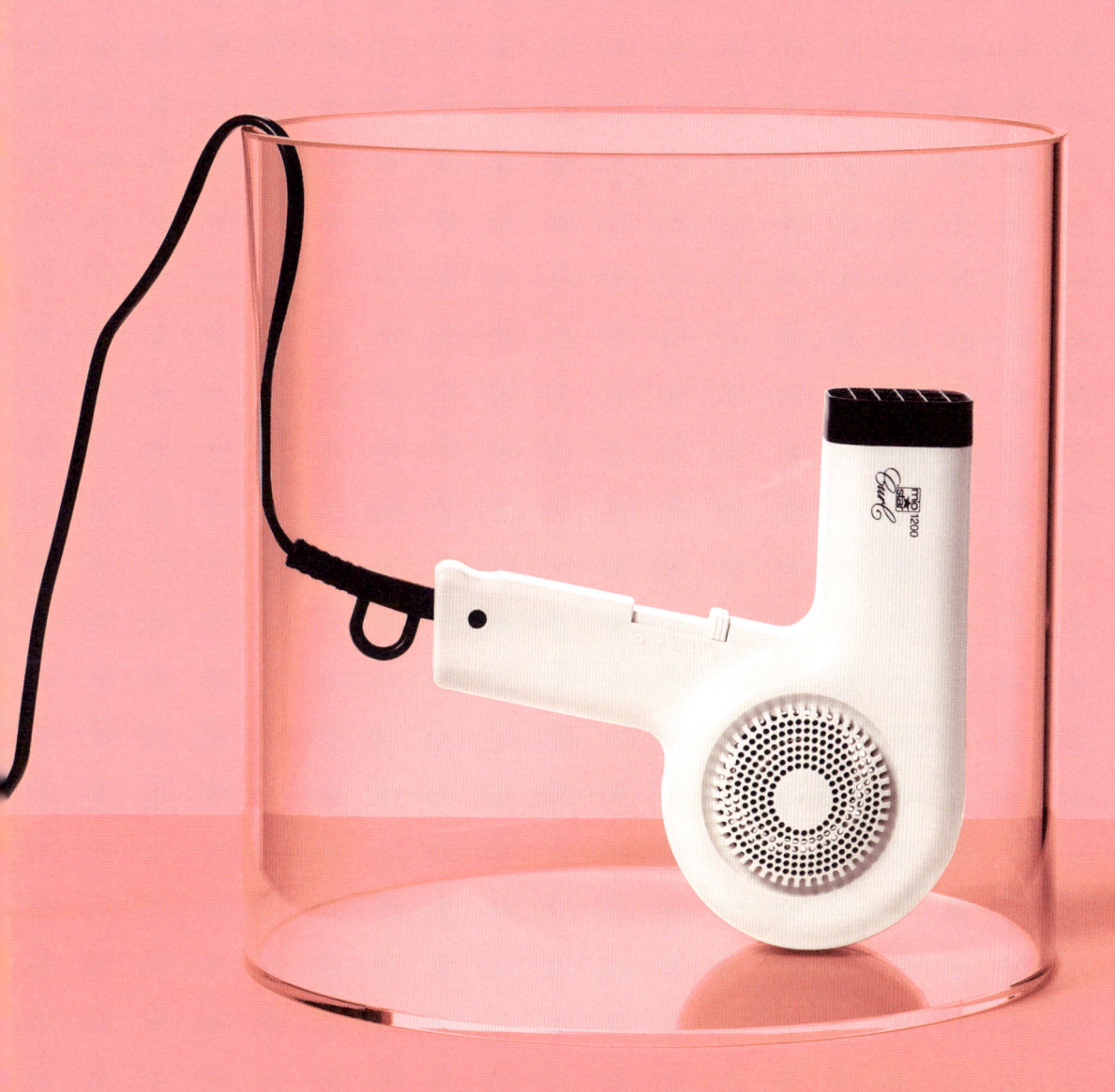

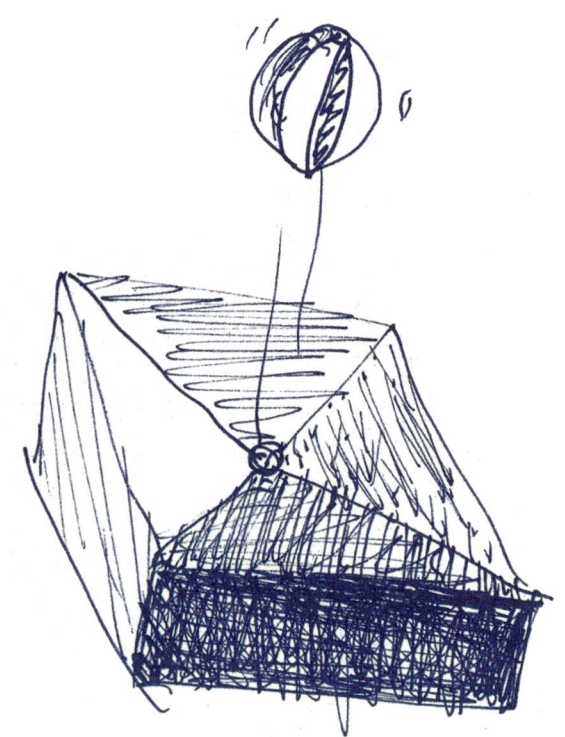

Loving in a World of Desire, 1995 | Tinte auf Papier | Ink on paper | 20 × 12 cm

The last supper — a moment of Unity
The last supper — calm before the storm — a moment of Lucidity — against all odds
together as one — united we stand, divided we fall, strength in numbers,

The last supper — The fragile hearts of men   The Victory of love
The last supper — triumphant in death   The last Supper the purity of the soul
The victory of love over death

no black ball because here it more of a sense of unity, togetherness, hope — a moment
if only everything in life could be so simple — this single

THE   LAST   SUPPER —   THE   FRAGILE   HEARTS   OF   MEN

The last Supper — Fear before dying; (ping pong balls on jets of air)   no black ball

MEXICO CALIENTE 03.

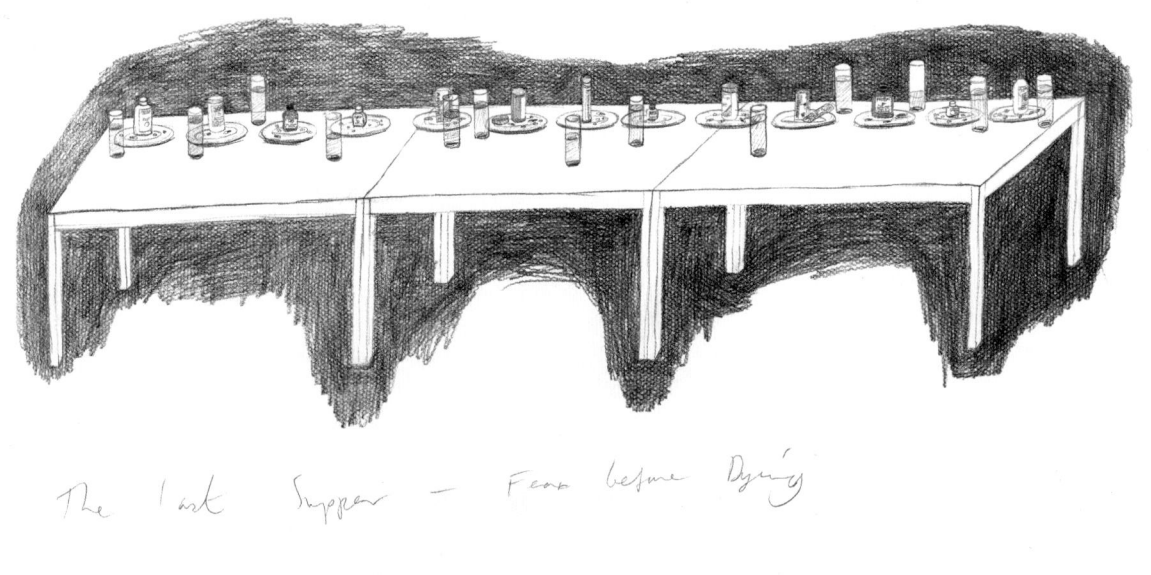

'Fear of Dying'

The Last Supper — Fear before Dying

The Last Supper – Fear Before Dying, 2003 | Bleistift auf Papier | Pencil on paper | 50 × 65 cm

stainless steel serving platters set on top ready to carve skulls of thirteen skeletons wrapped in velvets and safety pinned and taped up & tables in total cut down to recieve glass sheets set the glass guys to bugh the hight of the long thing.s glass 7,8 or 10 feet tall

broken sheets of glass dividing the whole scene The last supper objects on the table religious artefacts ashtrays etc all sat on chairs

The Last Supper with Skeletons, 2003 | Bleistift auf Papier | Pencil on paper | 30 × 40 cm

„Wir müssen es einfach halten. Alle
können es machen, alle können schöne
Zeichnungen machen. So einfach ist
das: schöne Zeichnungen zu machen."

'We have to keep everything simple,
anyone can do it, anyone can make
beautiful drawings. It's as simple as
that: making beautiful drawings.'

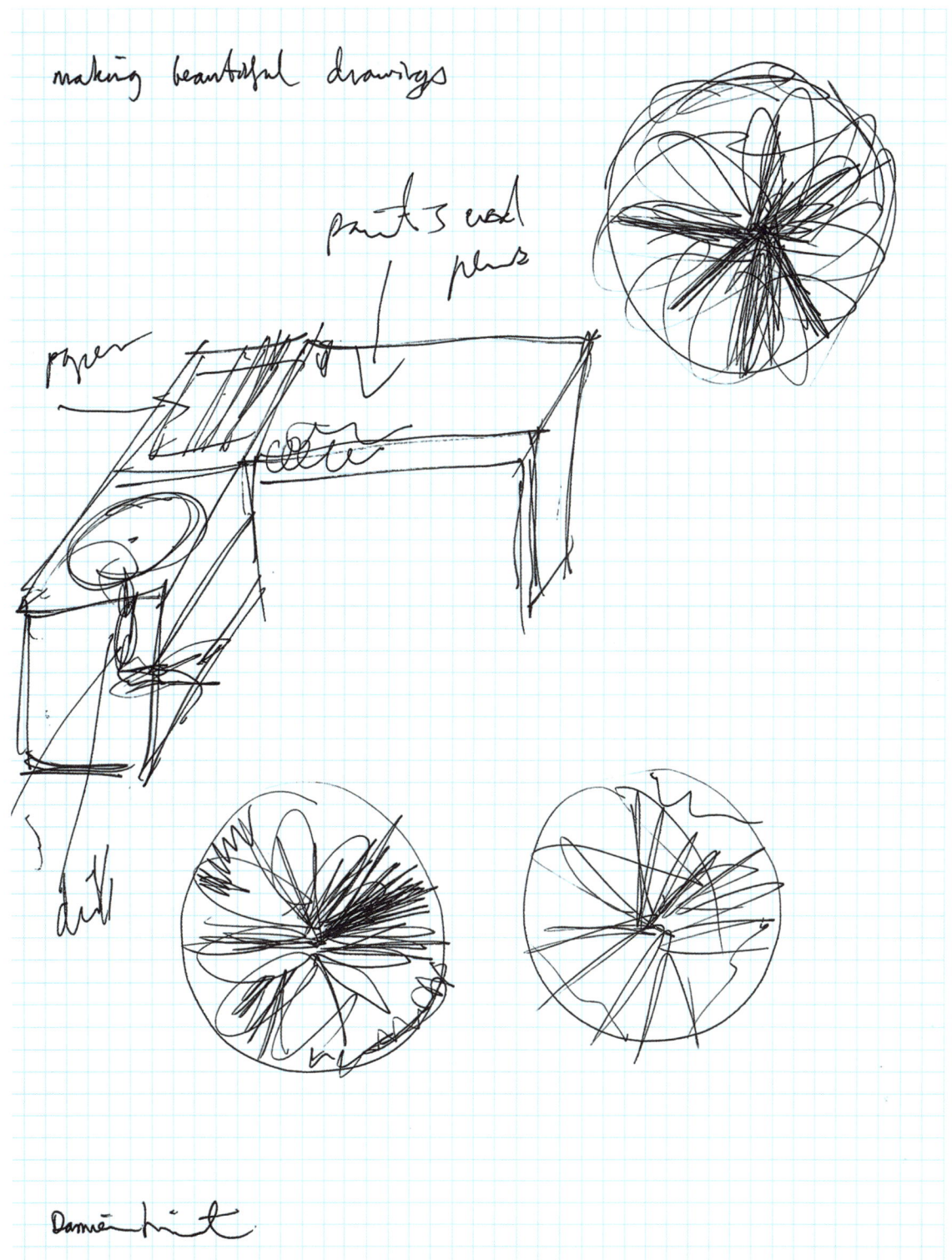

Making Beautiful Drawings, 1993 | Tinte auf Papier | Ink on paper | 27 × 21 cm

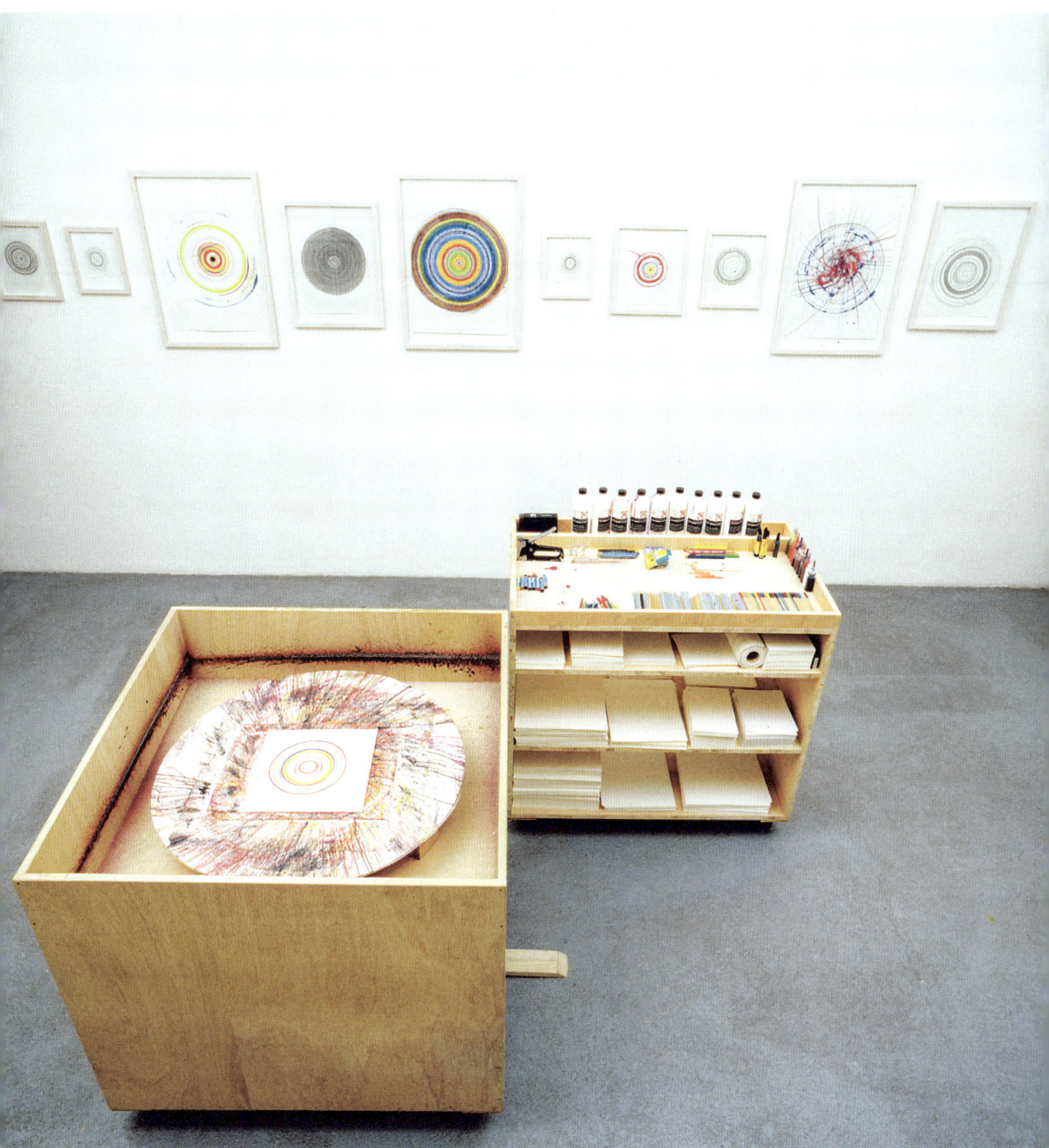

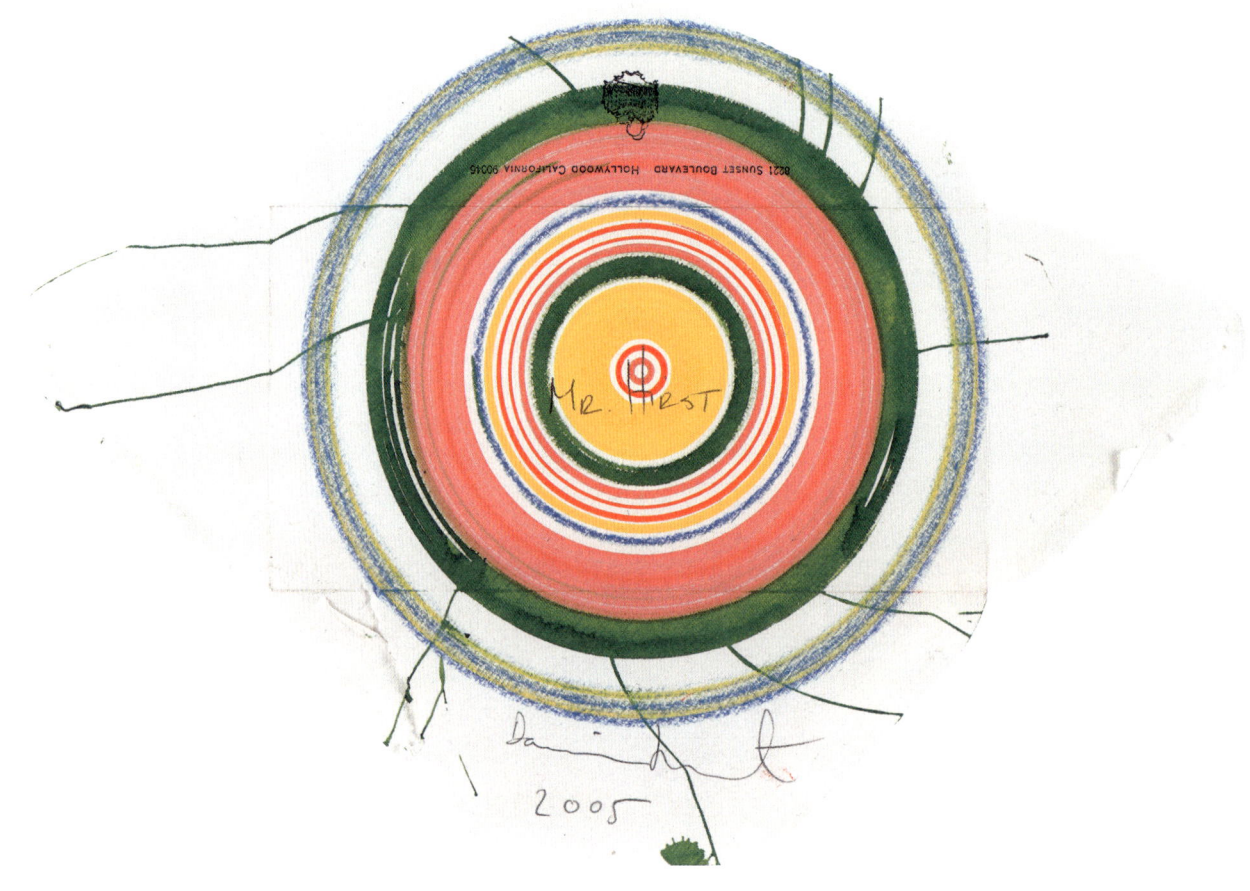

Beautiful, Crashing Head on into the Future, Drawing, 2005 | Wachsmalstift, Tinte und
Filzstift auf Papier | Crayon, ink, and felt-tip pen on paper | 23 × 32 cm

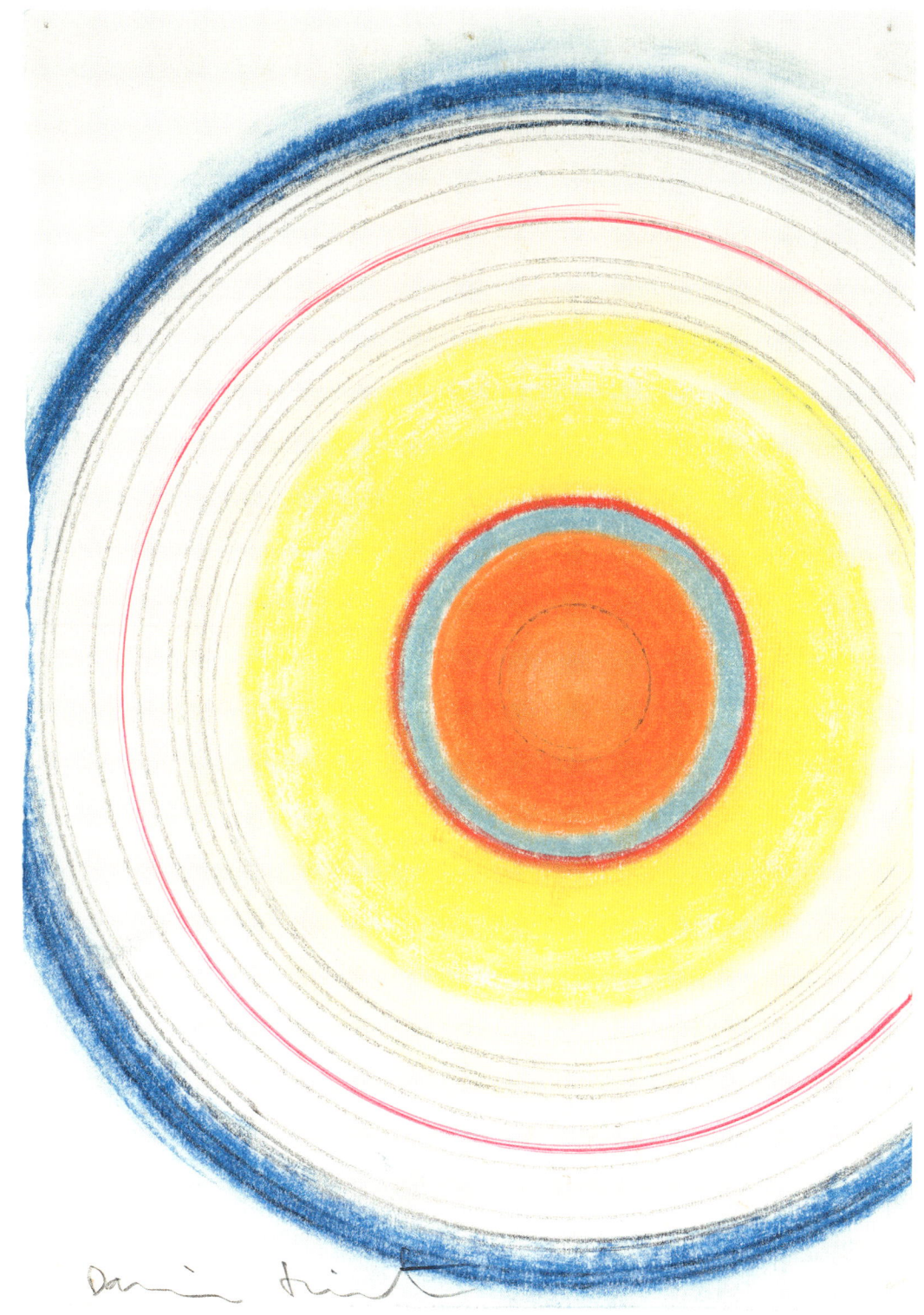

Beautiful Sunny Side Up Drawing, 2002 | Buntstift auf Papier | Coloured pencil on paper | 30 × 22 cm

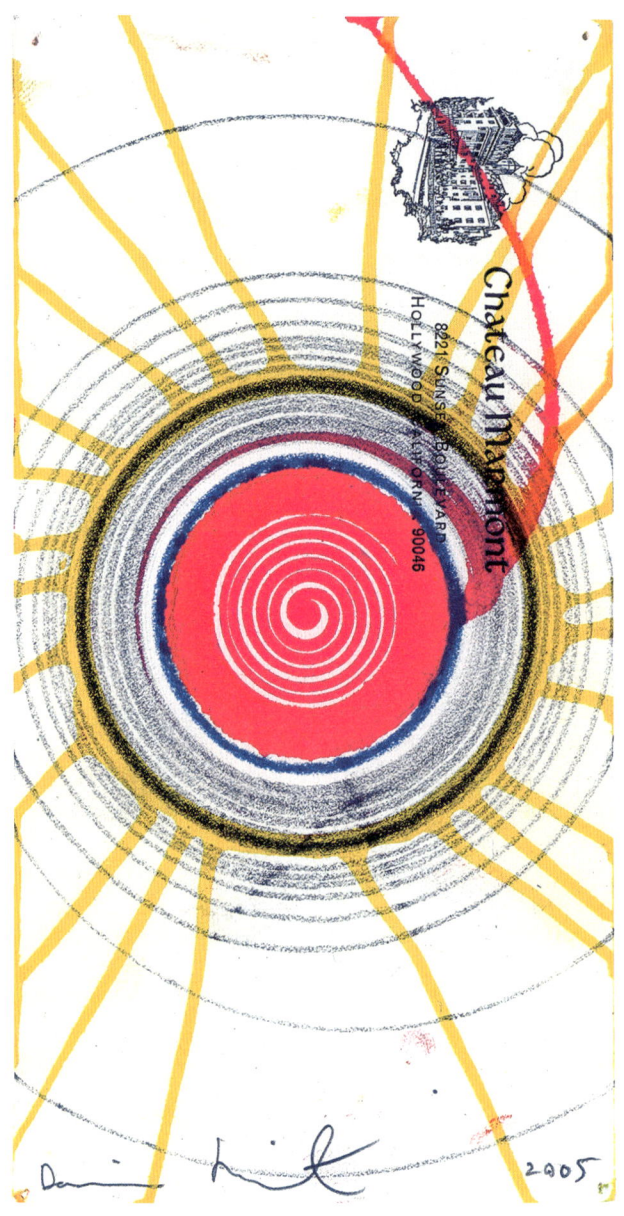

Chateau Marmont
8221 Sunset Boulevard
Hollywood, California 90046

Beautiful, Amazing Optical Hardware Drawing, 2005 | Bleistift, Tinte und Filzstift
auf Papier | Pencil, ink, and felt-tip pen on paper | 19 × 10 cm

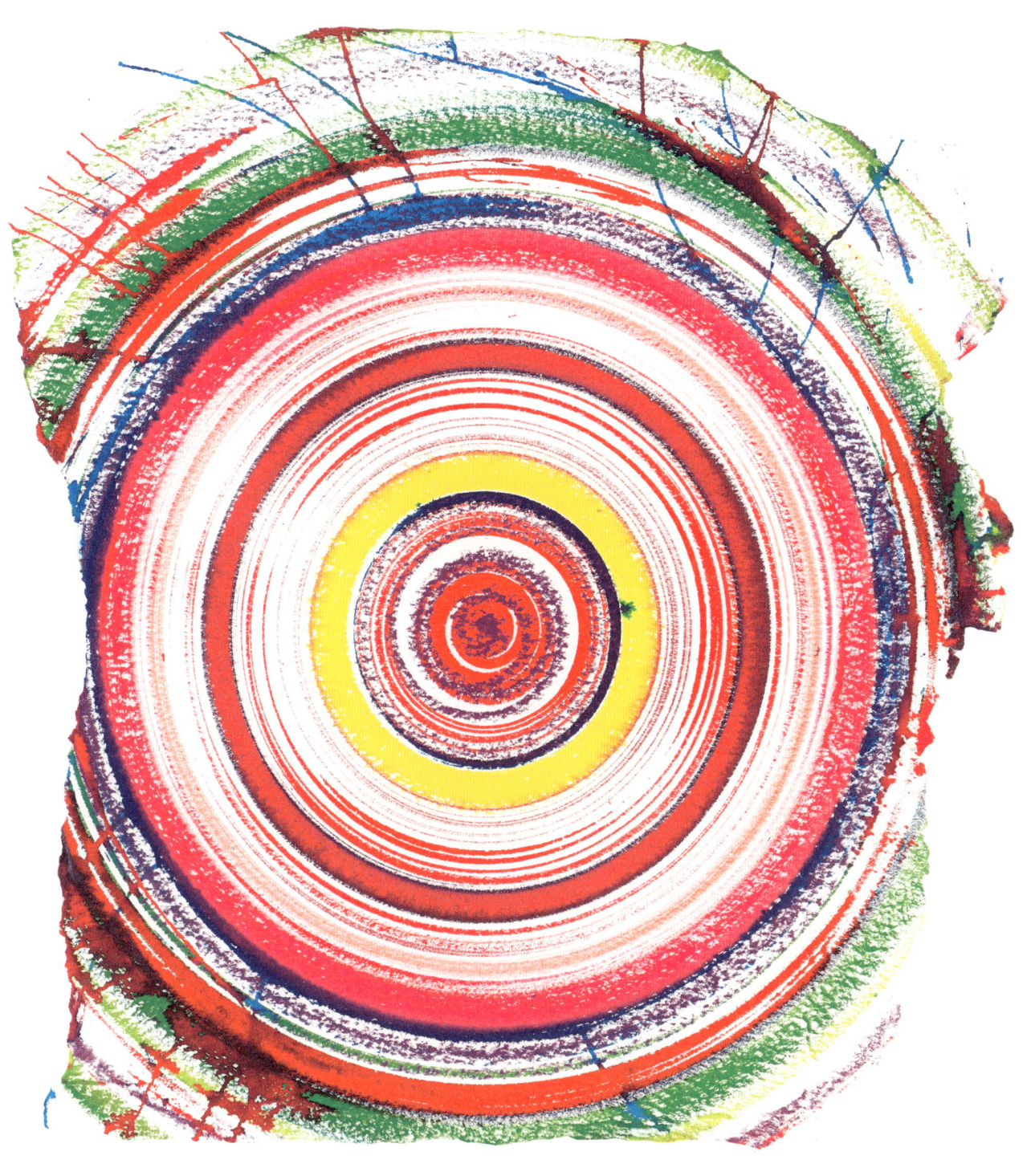

Beautiful Aztec Carnival Drawing, 2007 | Ölpastell und Acrylfarbe auf Karton |
Oil pastel and acrylic ink on card | 25 × 23 cm

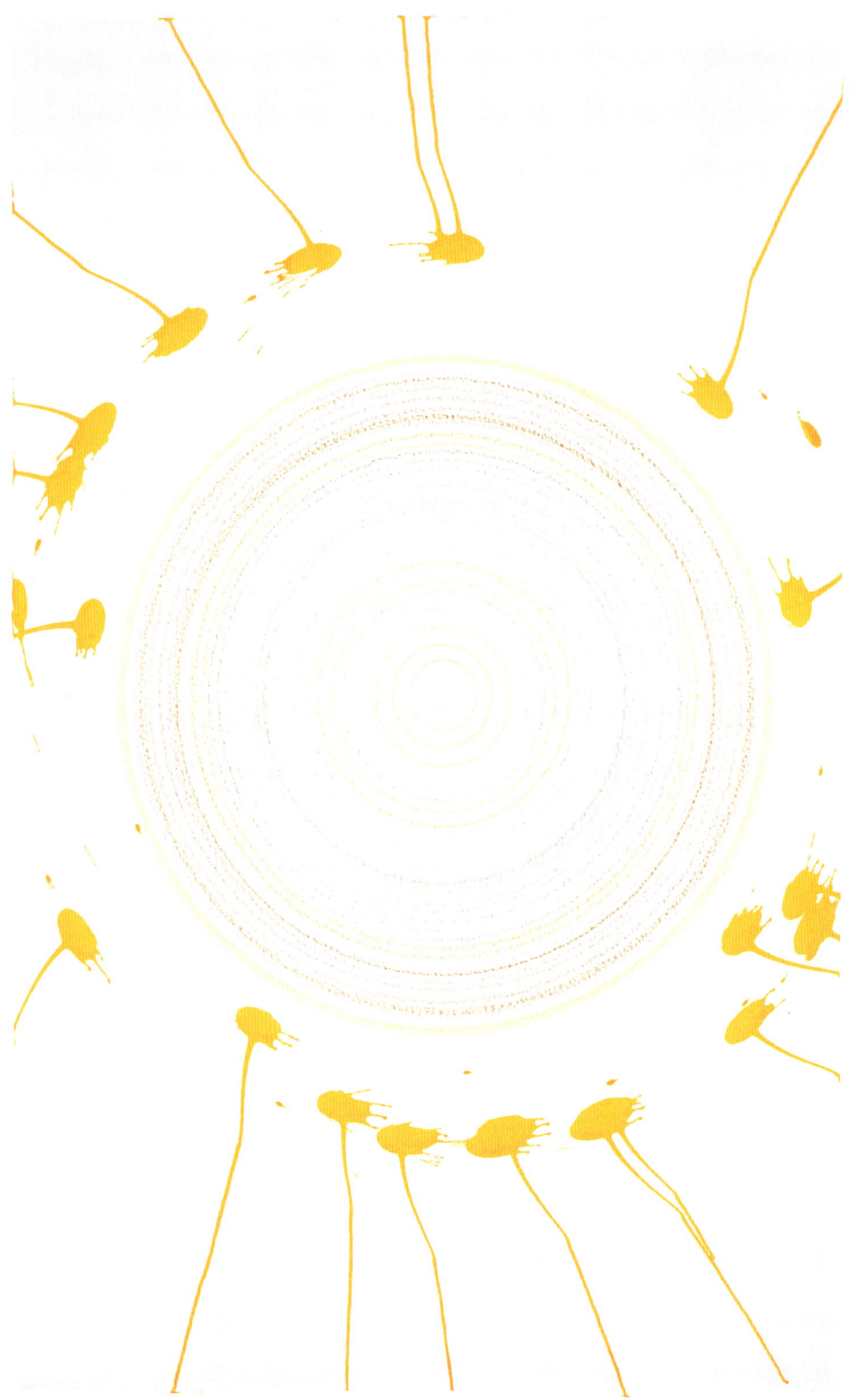

Beautiful Fertilisation Drawing, 2007 | Buntstift und Acrylfarbe auf Karton | Coloured pencil and acrylic ink on card | 48 × 30 cm

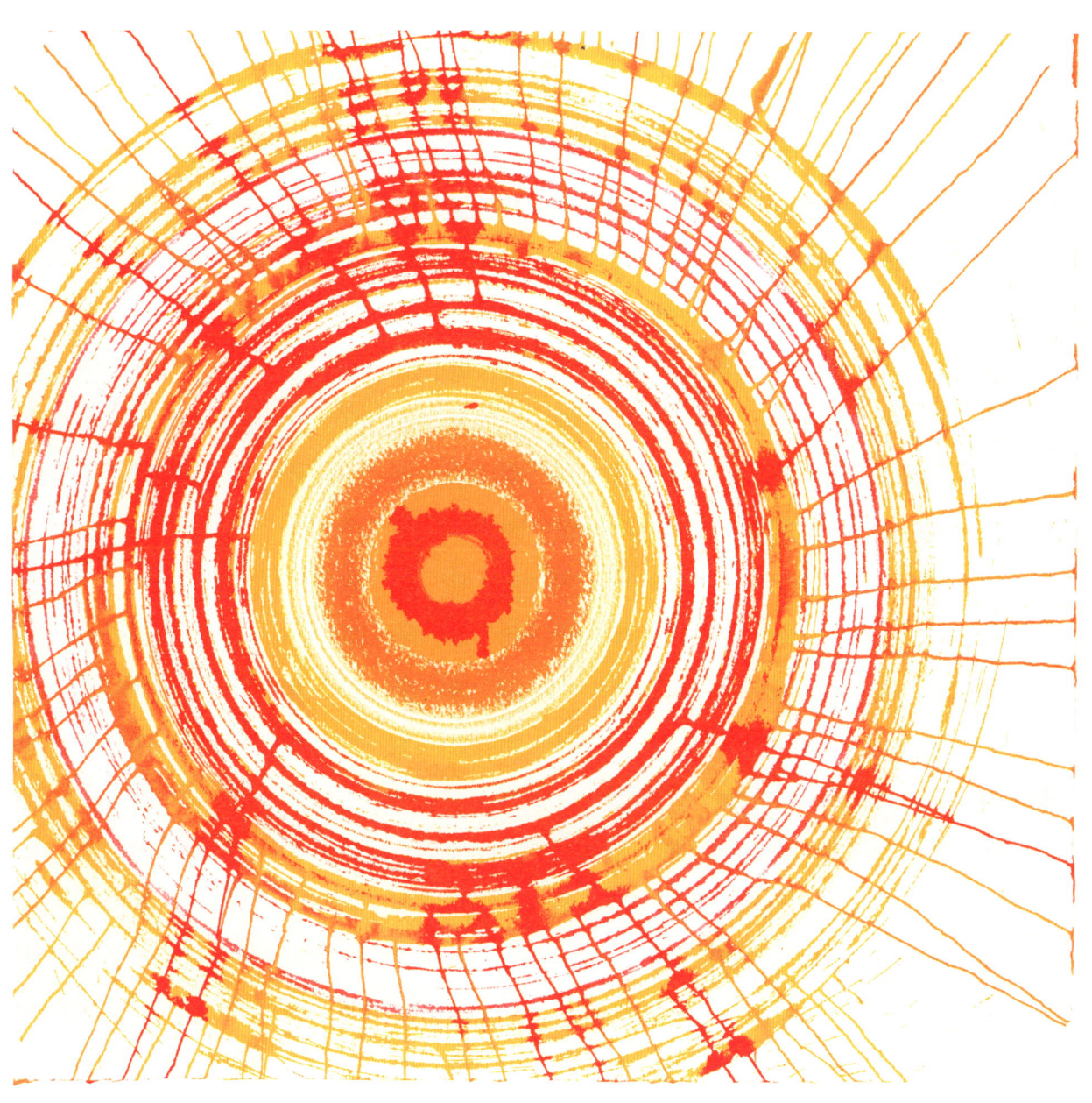

Beautiful Blast of Sunshine Drawing, 2007 | Acrylfarbe und Ölpastell auf Karton |
Acrylic ink and oil pastel on card | 29 × 30 cm

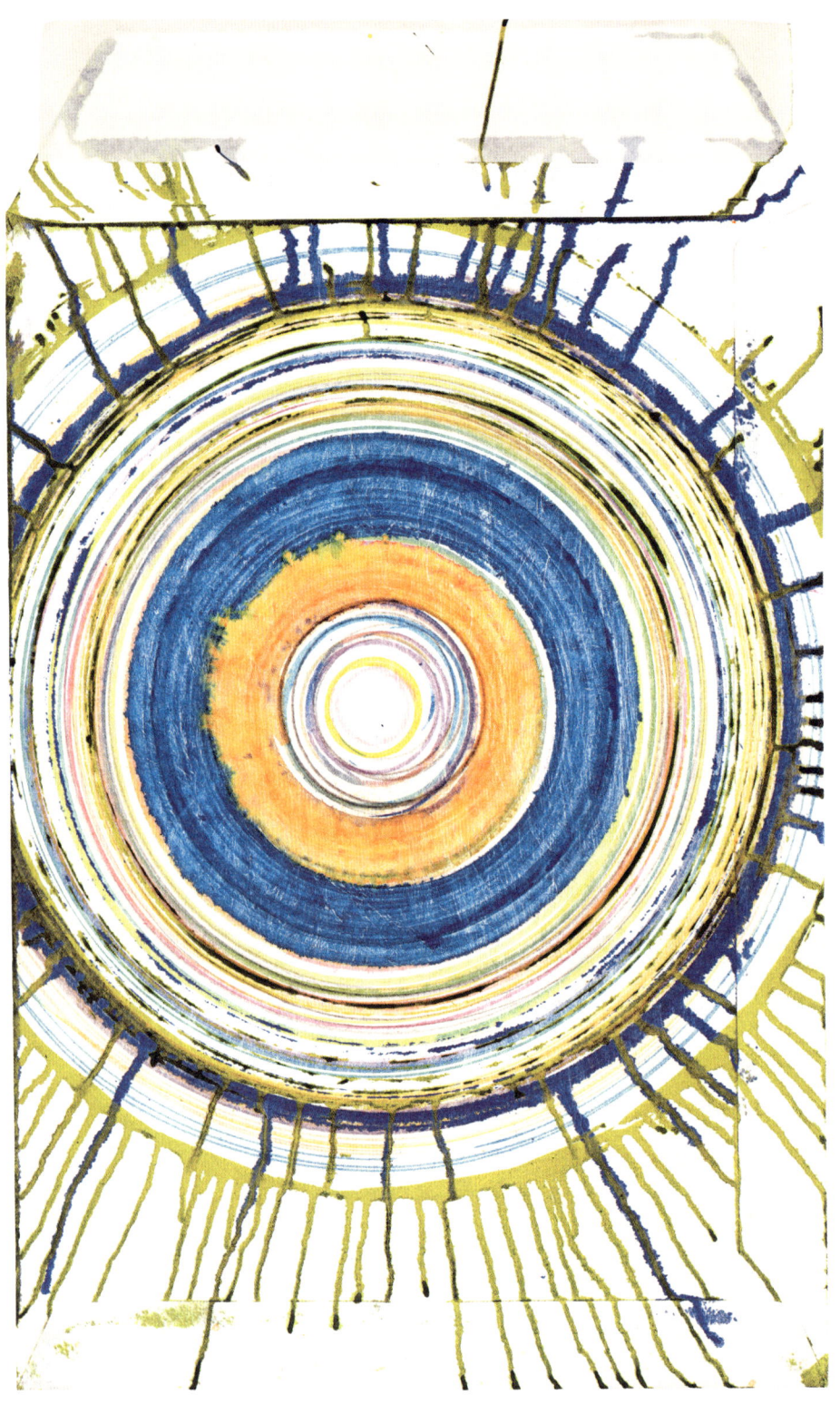

Beautiful Slithering Moss Drawing, 2007 | Filzstift, Acrylfarbe, Bleistift und Ölpastellkreide
auf Papier | Felt-tip pen, acrylic ink, pencil, and oil pastel on paper | 38 × 23 cm

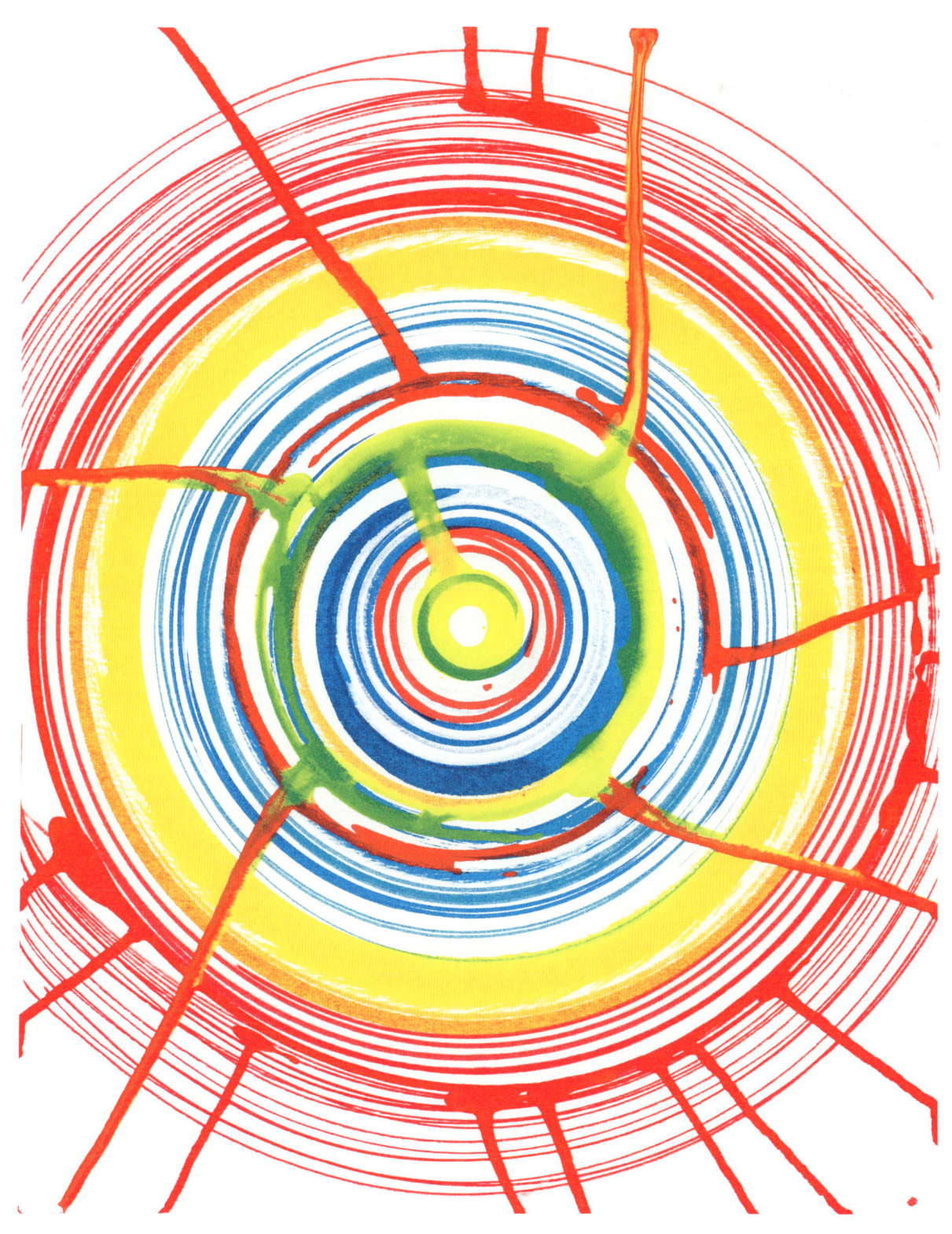

Beautiful Spinning Out of Control Drawing, 2007 | Buntstift, Acrylfarbe und Filzstift
auf Karton | Coloured pencil, acrylic ink, and felt-tip pen on card | 26 × 20 cm

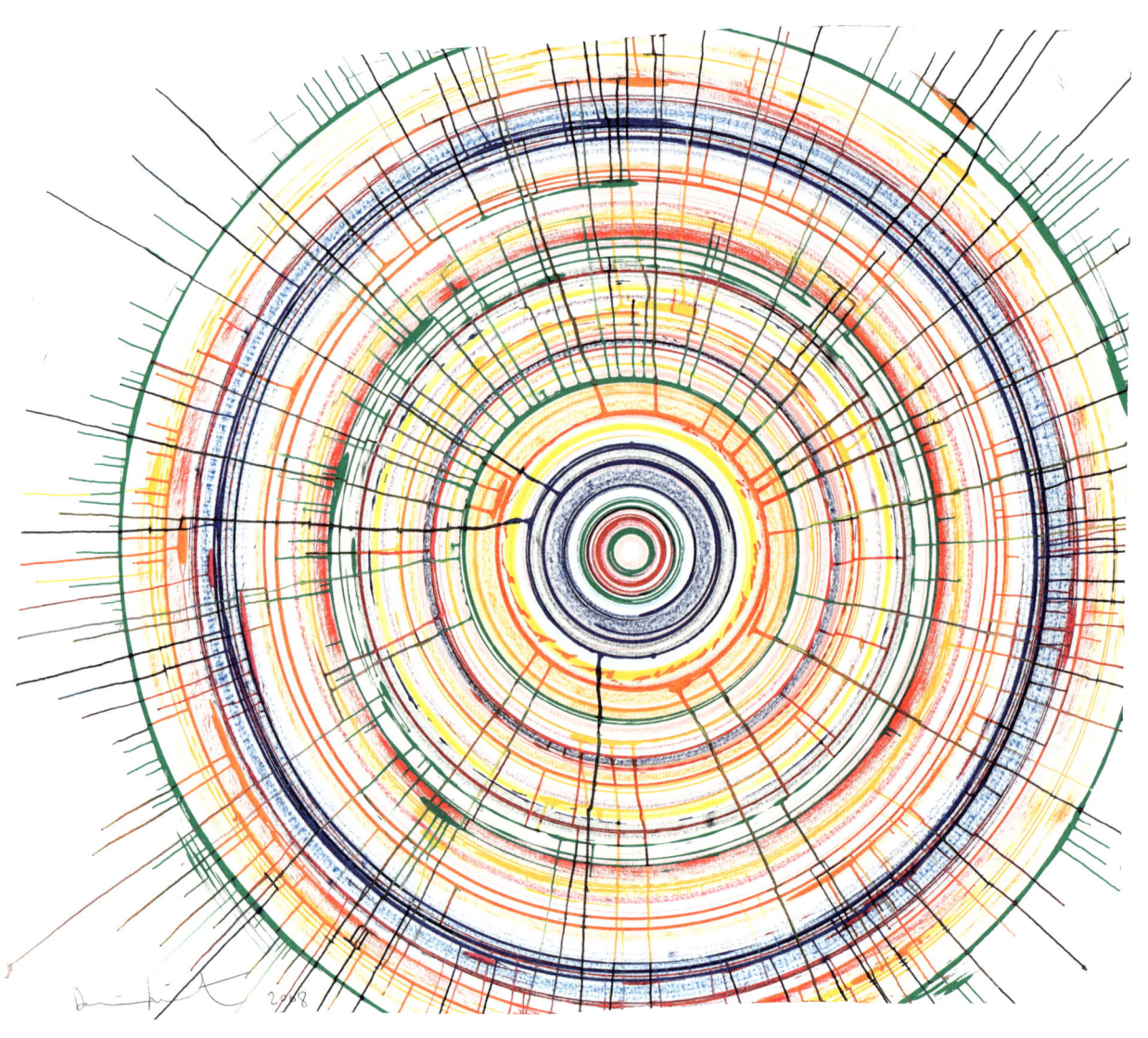

Beautiful Footloose and Fancy Free Drawing, 2008 | Tinte und
Pastell auf Papier | Ink and pastel on paper | 72 × 85 cm

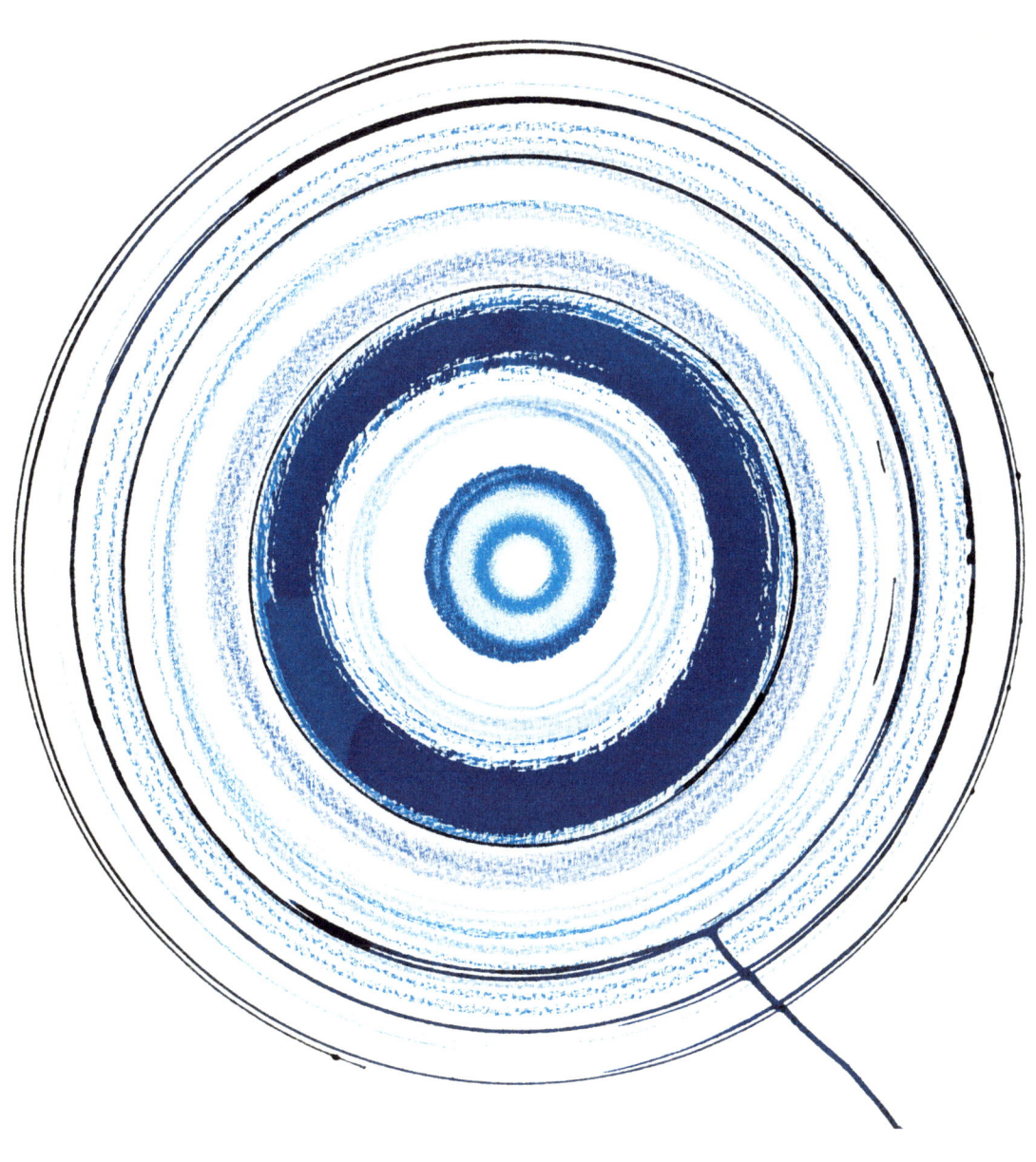

Beautiful Yo-Yo-ing Lollipop Drawing, 2007 | Ölpastell, Acrylfarbe und Filzstift
auf Karton | Oil pastel, acrylic ink, and felt-tip pen on card | 29 × 30 cm

133

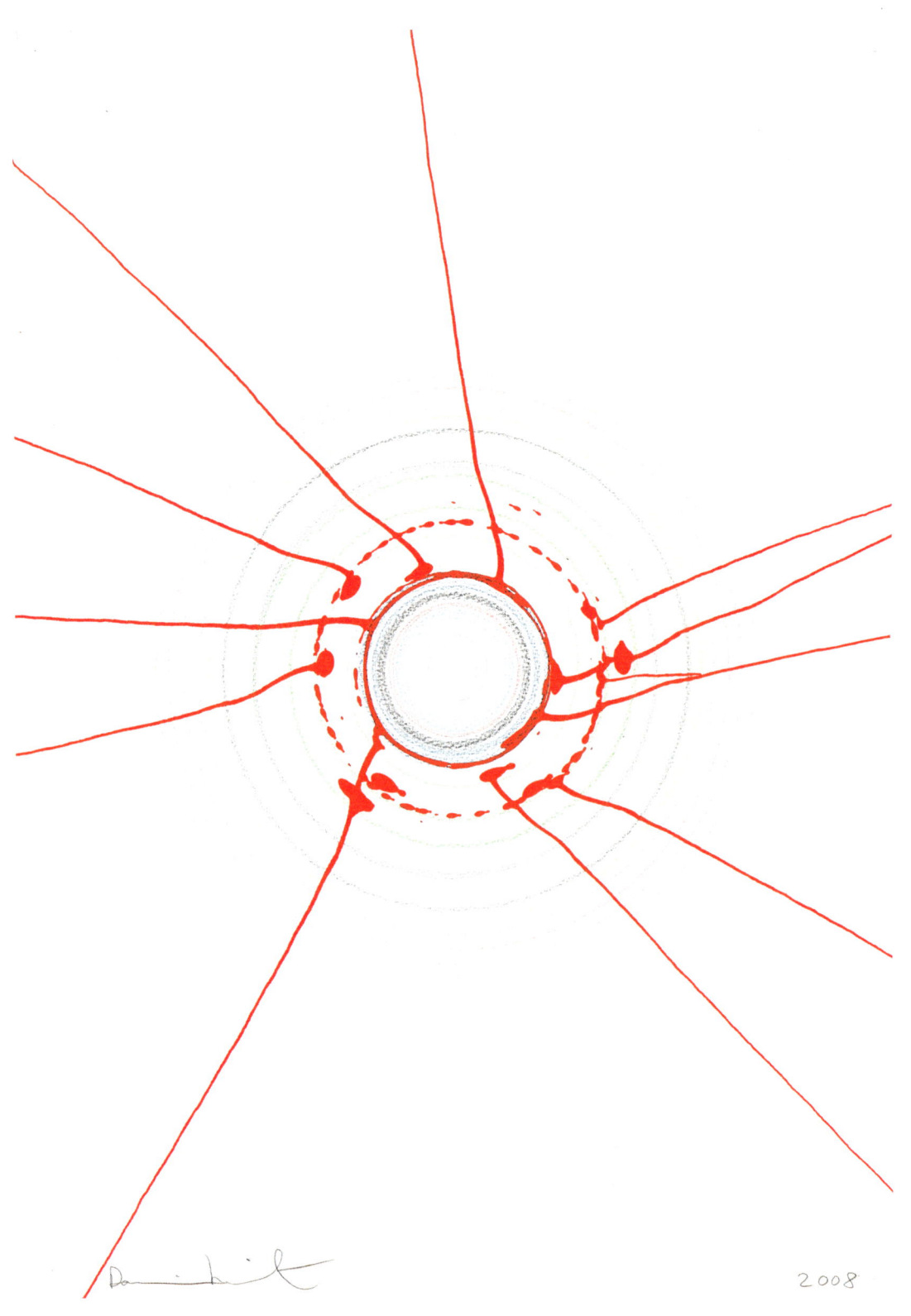

2008

Beautiful Is the Art of Beginning Drawing, 2008 | Bleistift, Tinte und
Pastell auf Papier | Pencil, ink, and pastel on paper | 60 × 43 cm

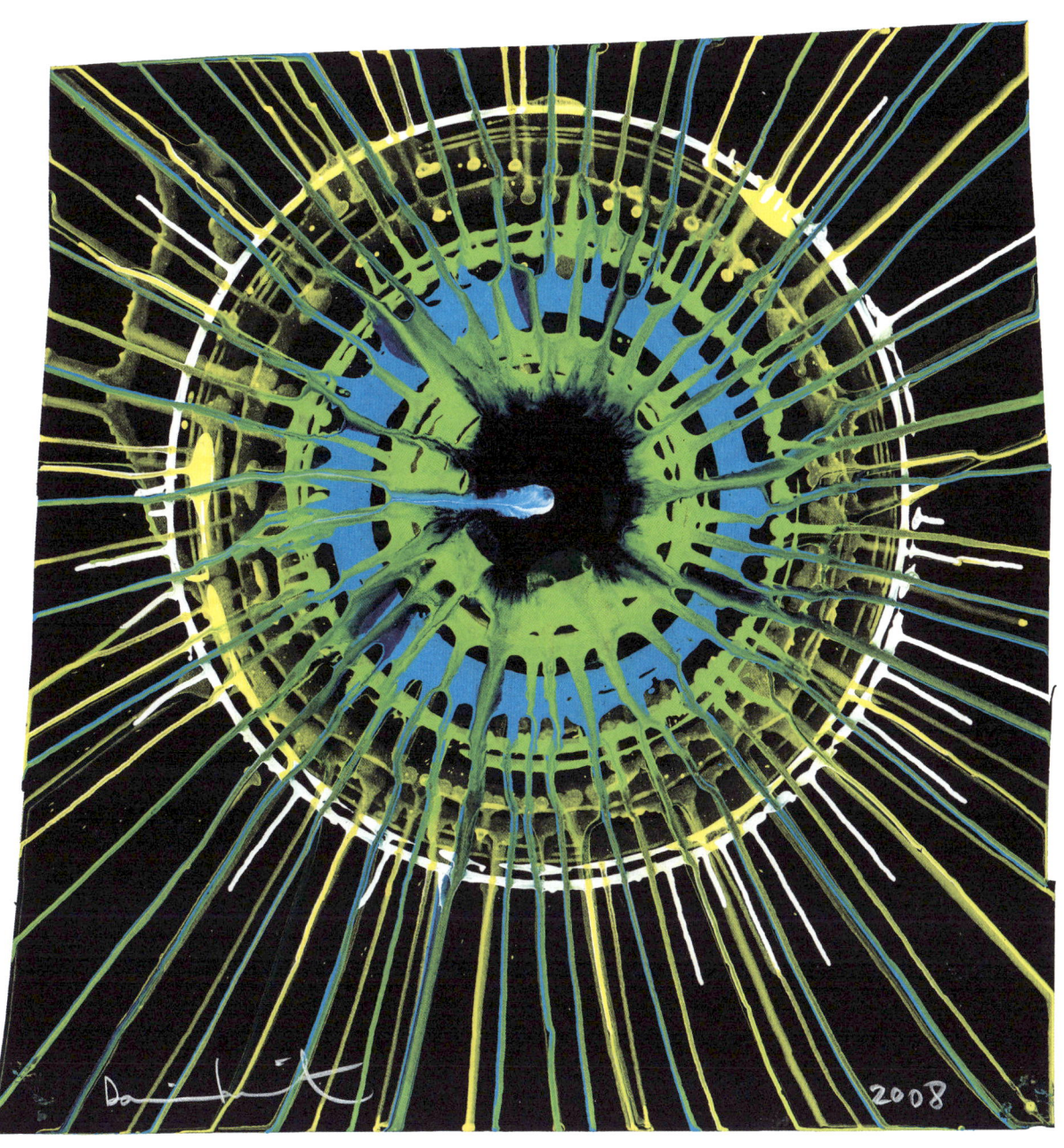

Beautiful That's No Immaculate Conception Drawing, 2008 |
Tinte auf Papier | Ink on paper | 31 × 21 cm

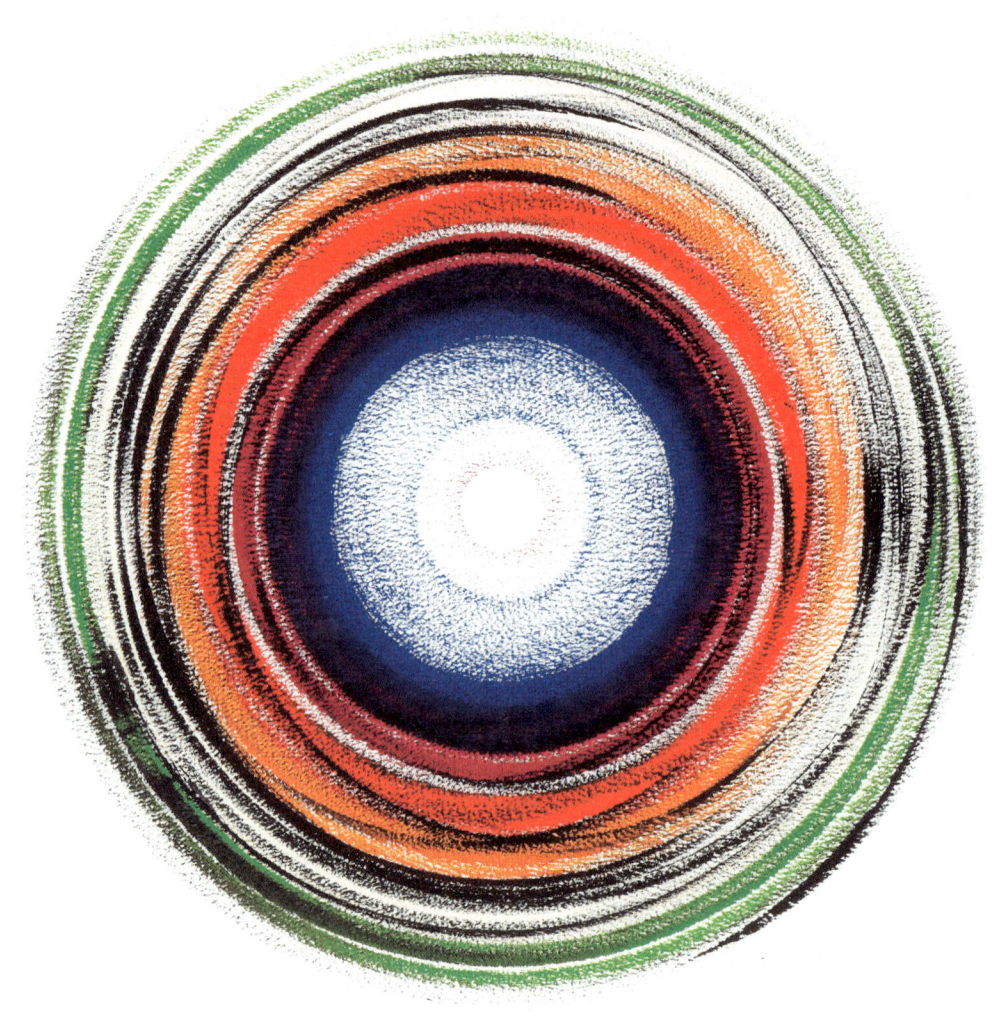

Beautiful the Future Is Unwritten Drawing, 2008 |
Acryl auf Papier | Acrylic on paper | 60 × 51 cm

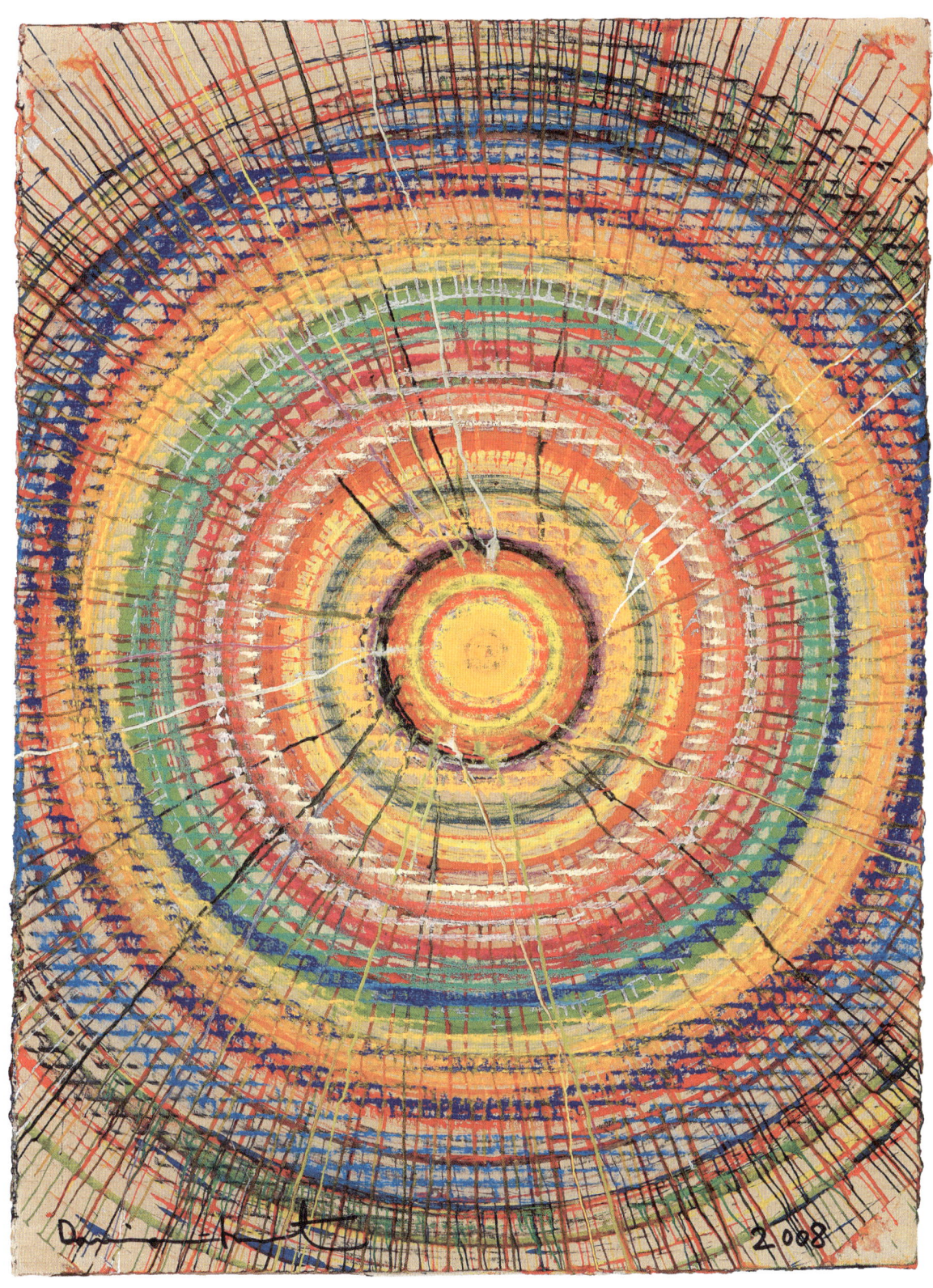

Beautiful Uproar's Your Only Music Drawing, 2008 | Tinte, Bleistift und
Pastell auf Karton | Ink, pencil, and pastel on cardboard | 60 × 45 cm

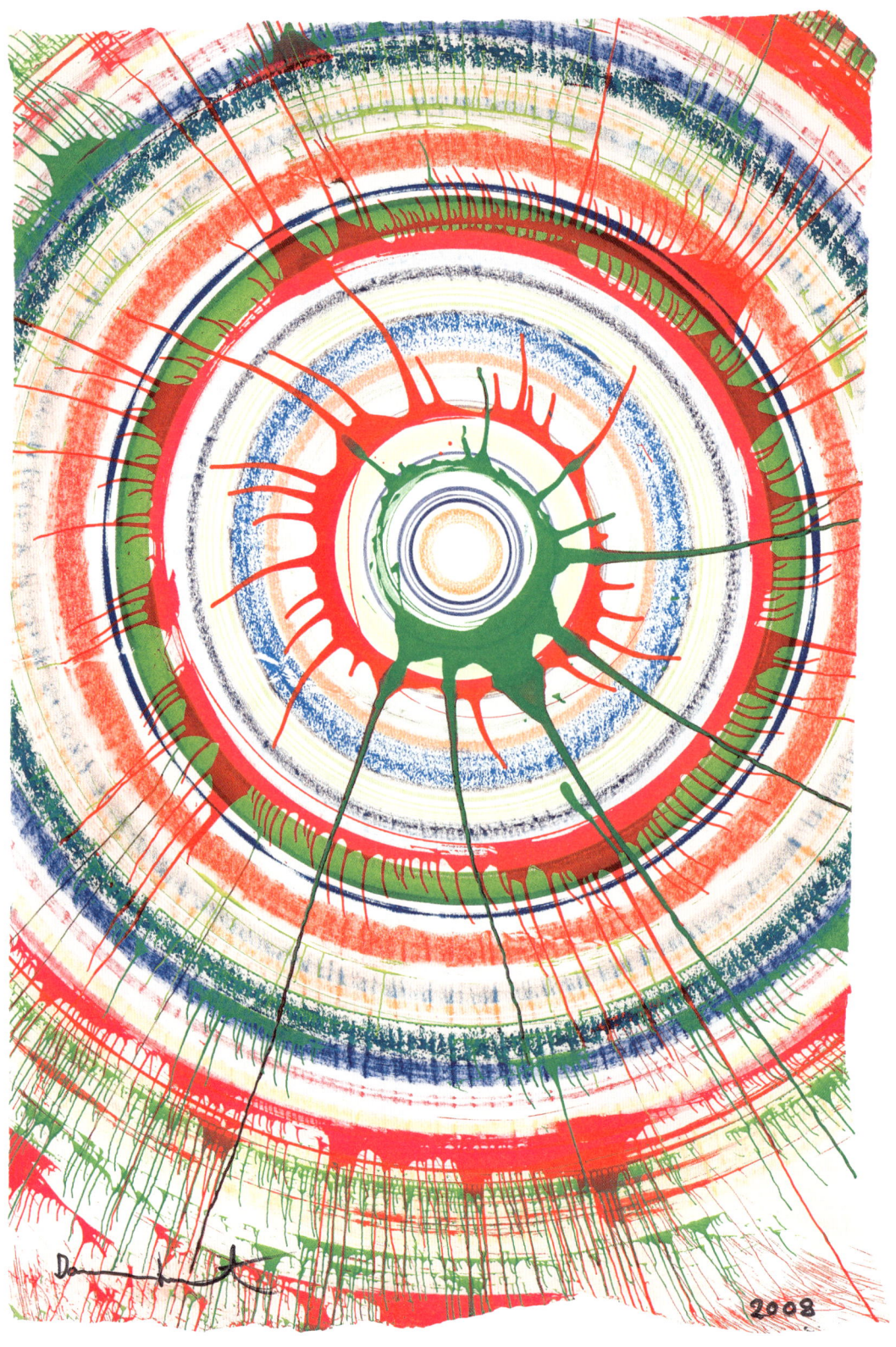

Beautiful Squish Squash Lovable Love-Bug Soup Drawing, 2008 | Tinte, Bleistift, Pastell und
Faserstift auf Papier | Ink, pencil, pastel, and fibre pen on paper | 56 × 38 cm

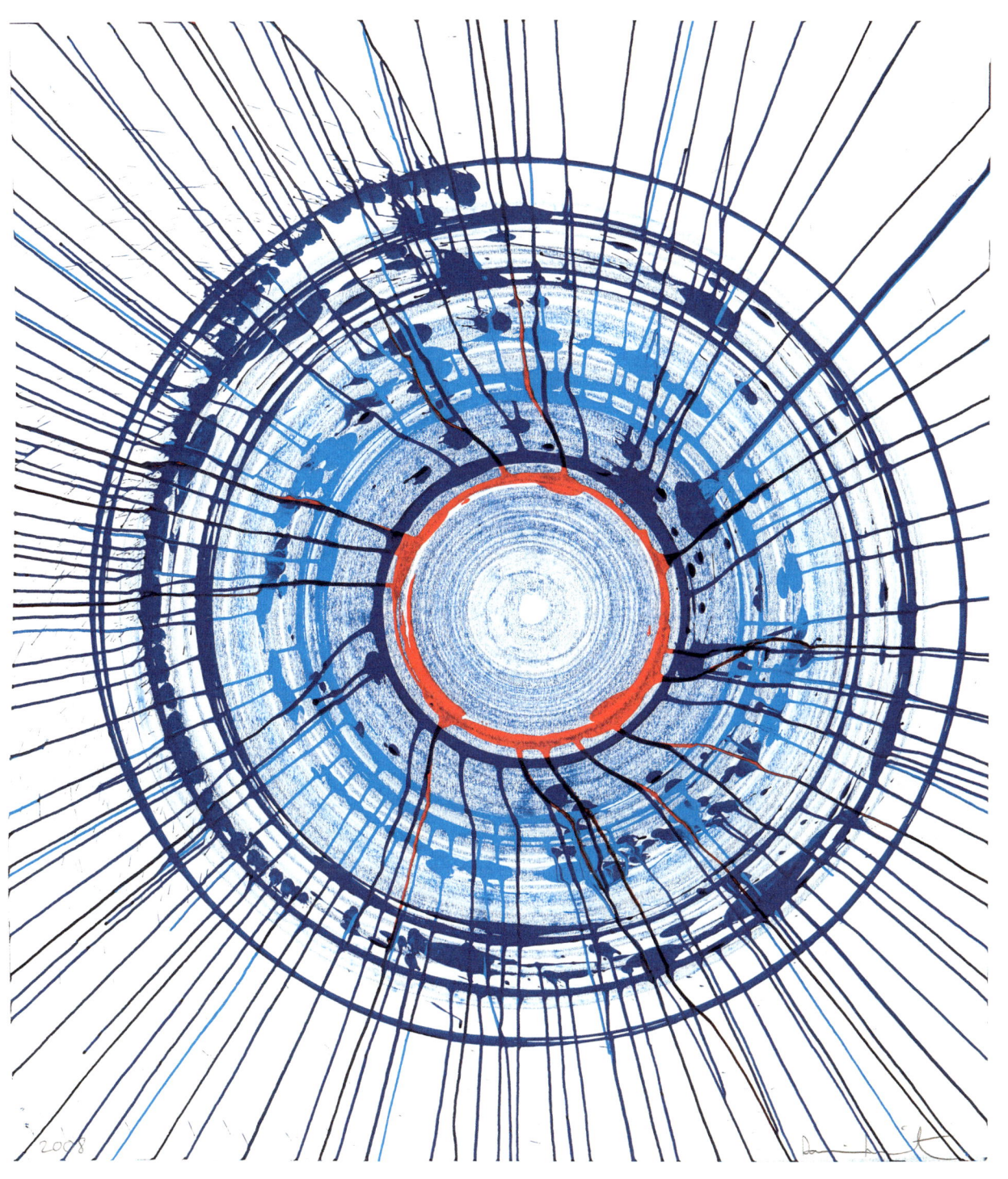

Beautiful Temporarily Lost at Sea Drawing, 2008 | Pastell und
Tinte auf Papier | Pastel and ink on paper | 47 × 42 cm

Ein Gespräch zwischen Damien Hirst und Ralph Gleis

Ralph Gleis: Bei unserem ersten Besuch in deinem Atelier erwähntest du, dass deine Werke immer auf Papier beginnen und dass das Zeichnen für dich einem Denkprozess ähnelt. Wie kann man sich deine Arbeitsweise in dieser Hinsicht vorstellen? Hast du immer ein Notizbuch bei dir, um deine Ideen festzuhalten? Was bedeutet es für dich, diese Zeichnungen allein zu erstellen, während du bei deinen Objekten und Installationen mit einem Team zusammenarbeitest?

Damien Hirst: Ja, ich habe immer Notizbücher oder Papier und Bleistifte und Kugelschreiber dabei. Alles beginnt immer mit einer Idee. Bleistift und Papier sind immer noch die beste Möglichkeit, komplexe Ideen kostengünstig zu erkunden, und damit können viele Dinge auch auf wirtschaftliche Weise erarbeitet werden, ohne viel Geld für die Herstellung teurer Glas- und Stahltanks auszugeben, die die falsche Größe haben könnten und ohne vorheriges Austüfteln teuer wären. Als Künstler fühle ich mich immer allein, und die Assistentinnen und Assistenten sind nur eine Möglichkeit, meine Ideen zu verwirklichen, so wie mir auch ein Notizbuch dabei hilft.

RG | Inwieweit denkst du bei den Zeichnungen bereits darüber nach, das Werk in eine Skulptur umzusetzen? Spielt die Logistik bei der Herstellung größerer Werke eine Rolle, wenn du Zeichnungen als Denkhilfe verwendest?

DH | Ja, in vielerlei Hinsicht denke ich, dass Kritzeleien zu Skizzen werden können, die zu Zeichnungen werden, die dann wiederum zu technischen Zeichnungen werden, aus denen man tatsächlich Dinge herstellen kann, aber in den Zeichnungen geht es oft eher um die Ideen als um die endgültige Skulptur. Häufig sind Zeichnungen Ideen, die nicht zu Skulpturen werden. Das größte Problem bei der Bildhauerei

A Conversation between Damien Hirst and Ralph Gleis

Ralph Gleis: During our first visit to your studio, you mentioned that your works always begin on paper and that drawing for you is akin to a thought process. How can we imagine your working method in this regard? Do you always carry a notebook to capture your ideas? What does it mean to you to create these drawings alone, while collaborating with a team for your objects and installations?

Damien Hirst: Yeah, I always have notebooks or bits of paper and pencils and pens on me. Everything always starts with an idea. Pencil and paper is still the best way to explore complex ideas cheaply, also it's really a good way to economically work a lot of things out without spending loads of money on making expensive glass and steel tanks that could be the wrong size and costly without some advance working out. I always feel alone as an artist and the assistants are just a way to realise my ideas the same way a notebook helps.

RG | In the drawings, to what extent are you already thinking about translating the work into a sculpture? Do the logistics of making larger-scale work come into play when using drawing as a way of thinking?

DH | Yeah, in many ways I think doodles can become sketches and sketches become drawings which can then become technical drawings to actually fabricate things from, but the drawings are often about the ideas rather than the final sculpture; drawings are often drawings of ideas that sometimes don't become sculptures. The biggest thing to deal with in sculpture is gravity and of course in a drawing there is no gravity which makes working things out a lot easier.

ist die Schwerkraft, und in einer Zeichnung gibt es
natürlich keine Schwerkraft, was die Arbeit erheblich
erleichtert. Ich sehe eine Zeichnung genauso als
Kunstwerk an wie ein Gemälde oder eine Skulptur.

RG | Deine Zeichnungen gehen oft mit Text einher.
Beeinflusst der Text die Zeichnung oder umgekehrt?

DH | Sie beeinflussen sich gegenseitig; Worte und
Bilder sind mir sehr wichtig. Ich habe eine lange Liste
von Skulpturen ohne Titel und eine noch längere Liste
von Titeln ohne Skulpturen. Ich genieße es wirklich,
clevere sprachliche Möglichkeiten zu finden, um etwas
Visuelles zu beschreiben.

RG | Leben, Tod und Vergänglichkeit standen schon
immer im Mittelpunkt deiner künstlerischen
Erkundungen. Durch die ikonische Verwendung von
Symbolen wie Totenköpfen, Schmetterlingen oder
medizinischen Gegenständen führst du das Vanitas-
thema ins Feld und erinnerst uns an die Zerbrech-
lichkeit und Vergänglichkeit der menschlichen Existenz.
Welche Rolle spielt das Zeichnen bei der
Themenfindung?

DH | Ich bin immer auf der Suche nach universellen
Triggern, und Zeichnen ist meine erste Anlaufstelle,
wenn ich eine Idee habe. Es ist eine Möglichkeit, das
zu sehen, was in meinem Kopf ist. Ich skizziere eine
Idee fast immer, bevor ich etwas anfertige. Ich liebe
Dinge, die Gefühle beschreiben. Und das beginnt
immer mit einer Zeichnung. Ich sehe keinen Unterschied zwischen einer Zeichnung, die ich selbst
angefertigt habe, und einer, die von jemandem in
meinem Team angefertigt wurde, solange die
Zeichnung zu 100 % so ist, wie sie sein soll.

RG | Für mehrere Werkgruppen, wie *The Secret Gardens
Paintings*, *Art & Artists* und *Pipe Cleaner Animals*, lässt
du deine Assistentinnen und Assistenten äußerst
akribische Zeichnungen mit Bleistift oder Farbstift
anfertigen – entweder parallel zu oder sogar nach den
Gemälden und Skulpturen. Was ist die Idee hinter

I see a drawing as an artwork, just as much as a
painting or a sculpture is.

RG | Your drawings are often accompanied by text.
Does the text inform the drawing, or vice versa?

DH | Both ways round, words and images are really
important to me. I have a big list of sculptures
without titles and a bigger list of titles without
sculptures. I really enjoy trying to find clever verbal
ways to describe visual things.

RG | Life, death, and transience have always been at
the core of your artistic exploration. Through the
iconic use of symbols such as skulls, butterflies, or
medical objects, you invoke the vanitas theme,
reminding us of the fragility and impermanence of
human existence. What role does drawing play in the
process of finding themes?

DH | I'm always looking for universal triggers, and
drawing is my first port of call when I have any idea;
it's a way to see what's in my head. I almost always
sketch an idea out before I fabricate anything.
I love things that describe feelings. And this always
starts with a drawing. I don't feel any difference
between a drawing made by me or made by assistants
as long as the drawing is 100% how I want it to be.

RG | For several groups of works, such as *The Secret
Gardens Paintings*, *Art & Artists*, and *Pipe Cleaner
Animals*, you have your assistants make highly
meticulous drawings in pencil or coloured pencil—
either alongside or even after the paintings and
sculptures. What is the idea behind this shift to a
different medium, this translation into another artistic
form?

DH | These works are kind of more photographic and
so what I want in the drawings is something fresh

dieser Verlagerung auf ein anderes Medium, dieser Übersetzung in eine andere künstlerische Form?

DH | Diese Werke sind eher fotografischer Natur, und deshalb möchte ich in den Zeichnungen etwas Frisches, das diese Art von Zeichnung widerspiegelt. Eine Aufzeichnung einer fertigen Skulptur ist allerdings etwas ganz anderes als die Skizze einer ersten Idee, die dann zu einer Skulptur wird. Oder sogar zu einem Gemälde. In meinem Werk hat das Zeichnen viele Funktionen: Ideen in dem Moment festhalten, in dem sie im Kopf entstehen, um die wesentlichen Aspekte nicht zu vergessen; eine Visualisierung erstellen, damit das Assistententeam und die Herstellung etwas danach anfertigen können; Dinge zeichnen, um räumliche Dimensionen kostengünstig zu prüfen, bevor sie tatsächlich umgesetzt werden; Ähnlichkeiten einfangen; Gefühle ausdrücken; fertige Kunstwerke zeichnen, um festzuhalten, wie diese im Vergleich zu den vorbereitenden Skizzen letztendlich aussehen; Zeichnungen um ihrer selbst willen anfertigen, etwa wie die Spin-Maschinen-Zeichnungen; ohne Worte ausdrücken, was man für Menschen, Dinge oder die Natur empfindet; etwas erschaffen, das zwischen Malerei und Druckgrafik liegt, mit oder ohne Handschrift des Künstlers, für den Markt oder unabhängig davon; Bücher und Objekte jemandem widmen und personalisieren; etwas auf Grundlage einer Malerei schaffen, das als Wandschmuck dient – mit einem niedrigeren Wert als eine Malerei, aber einem höheren als ein Druck.

RG | Du hast gerade die Spin Drawings erwähnt. Während deines DAAD-Stipendiums in Berlin im Jahr 1994 hast du bei Bruno Brunnet Fine Arts eine Maschine ausgestellt, die auch in unserer Ausstellung zu sehen sein wird. Mit dieser Maschine kann jede Besucherin oder jeder Besucher eine Zeichnung erstellen, wobei der einzige Unterschied zwischen diesen Zeichnungen und denen, die du mit der Maschine erstellst, deine Unterschrift ist. Wie ist diese Idee entstanden? Wie haben die Leute damals auf die Maschine reagiert?

that reflects that type of drawing. But a record of a finished sculpture is very different to a sketch of an initial idea that then becomes a sculpture. Or even a painting.

In my work, there are many functions to drawing. To draw ideas as they happen in your head and capture the important bits so that you don't forget them. To make a visualisation for assistants and fabricators to make things from. To draw things out to look at dimensions in space cheaply before actually making something. To capture likeness. To express your feelings. To draw completed artworks to keep a record of the way they looked when finished compared to the preparatory drawings. To make drawings for the sake of the process of drawing like the spin machine drawings. To communicate how you feel about people and things in the world or nature without using words. To make something in between a painting and a print that contains the hand of the artist/or not, for the market/or not. To dedicate and personalise books and objects. To make something based on a painting that can be hung on a wall for decoration like a painting but at a lower value than a painting and a higher value than a print.

RG | Speaking of the *Spin Drawings*, during your DAAD scholarship in Berlin in 1994, you exhibited a machine at Bruno Brunnet Fine Arts, which will also be featured in our exhibition. This machine allows every visitor to create a drawing, with the only difference between their drawings and those you make with the machine being your signature. How did this idea come about? How did people react to the machine at the time?

DH | The idea was I wanted to make a sculpture about the process of drawing. The process of drawing became a kind of sculptural thing, and I love that anyone can make those drawings if they could just believe in themselves. Nearly all children draw and paint, it's just that most stop to become pilots or bank managers or

DH | Die Idee war, dass ich eine Skulptur über den Prozess des Zeichnens machen wollte. Der Prozess des Zeichnens wurde zu einer Art skulpturaler Angelegenheit, und ich finde es toll, dass alle diese Zeichnungen anfertigen können, wenn sie nur an sich selbst glauben. Fast alle Kinder malen und zeichnen, nur hören die meisten auf, um Pilotinnen oder Bankmanager oder was auch immer zu werden, und ich möchte oft mein Publikum, das großteils aus Erwachsenen besteht, einbeziehen. Ich versuche allerdings auch etwas in den Prozess einzubringen, damit sie sich so fühlen wie damals, als sie noch Kinder waren. Viele meiner Arbeiten beschäftigen sich mit dieser Idee. In der Berliner Ausstellung habe ich den Leuten die Möglichkeit gegeben, meine Zeichnungen günstig zu kaufen oder kostenlos selbst welche herzustellen, und die meisten haben sich dann ihre eigenen kostenlos erstellt, das ist schon witzig.

RG | In deiner fiktiven Erzählung *Treasures from the Wreck of the Unbelievable* erzähltest du die Geschichte eines Schiffs des Kunstsammlers Cif Amotan II., das vor etwa 2 000 Jahren bei einem Sturm untergegangen ist. Die Ladung – bedeutende Kunstschätze – wurde in der Neuzeit entdeckt und aus dem Wrack geborgen. Interessanterweise gibt es eine Parallele zur Albertina und zu ihrem Gründer Albert von Sachsen-Teschen: 1792 ging ein Teil seiner Sammlung bei einem Sturm verloren, als sie auf dem Seeweg von Rotterdam nach Hamburg transportiert wurde, und ist bis heute verschollen. Laut deiner Erzählung wurden auch Zeichnungen für die Werke in der Sammlung von Cif Amotan II. angefertigt. Wie tragen diese Zeichnungen zu deiner Geschichte bei?

DH | Die Zeichnungen konnten sich natürlich nicht auf dem Schiff befinden, da sie nach all den Jahren im Meer verrottet wären. Also stellte ich mir eine Sammlung von Zeichnungen vor, die auf Augenzeugenberichten und Erinnerungen von Menschen basieren, die die Geschichte gehört oder die Schätze vor der Reise gesehen hatten, und dass die Existenz dieser Zeichnungen das Erste war, was die Fantasie der Schatzjäger beflügelte und die Entdeckung des Schiffswracks Wirklichkeit werden ließ.

whatever else and I often want to involve my audience who are mostly adults but I try to do something in the process to make them feel like they did when they were children. A lot of my work deals with this idea. In the Berlin show, I gave people the option to buy my drawings cheaply or make their own for free, and most people made their own for free, funny that.

RG | In your fictional narrative *Treasures from the Wreck of the Unbelievable*, you tell the story of a ship belonging to art collector Cif Amotan II, which sank around 2,000 years ago during a storm. The cargo— significant art treasures—was discovered and salvaged from the wreck in modern times. Interestingly, there is a parallel to the Albertina and its founder, Albert of Saxony-Teschen: in 1792, part of his collection was lost in a storm while being transported by sea from Rotterdam to Hamburg and remains missing to this day. According to your narrative, drawings were also created for the works in Cif Amotan II's collection. How do these drawings contribute to your story?

DH | Obviously the drawings couldn't have been on the ship as they would have perished in the sea after all those years. So, I imagined a collection of drawings created over time from eyewitness accounts and memories of people who had heard the story or seen the treasures before the voyage and that the existence of these drawings were the first things that captured the imagination of the salvage hunters and made the discovery of the shipwreck a reality.

„Die Idee ist wichtiger als
das Objekt."

'The idea is more important
than the object.'

Self-Portrait, 2020 | Bemaltes Kunstharz | Painted resin | 117 × 50 × 48 cm

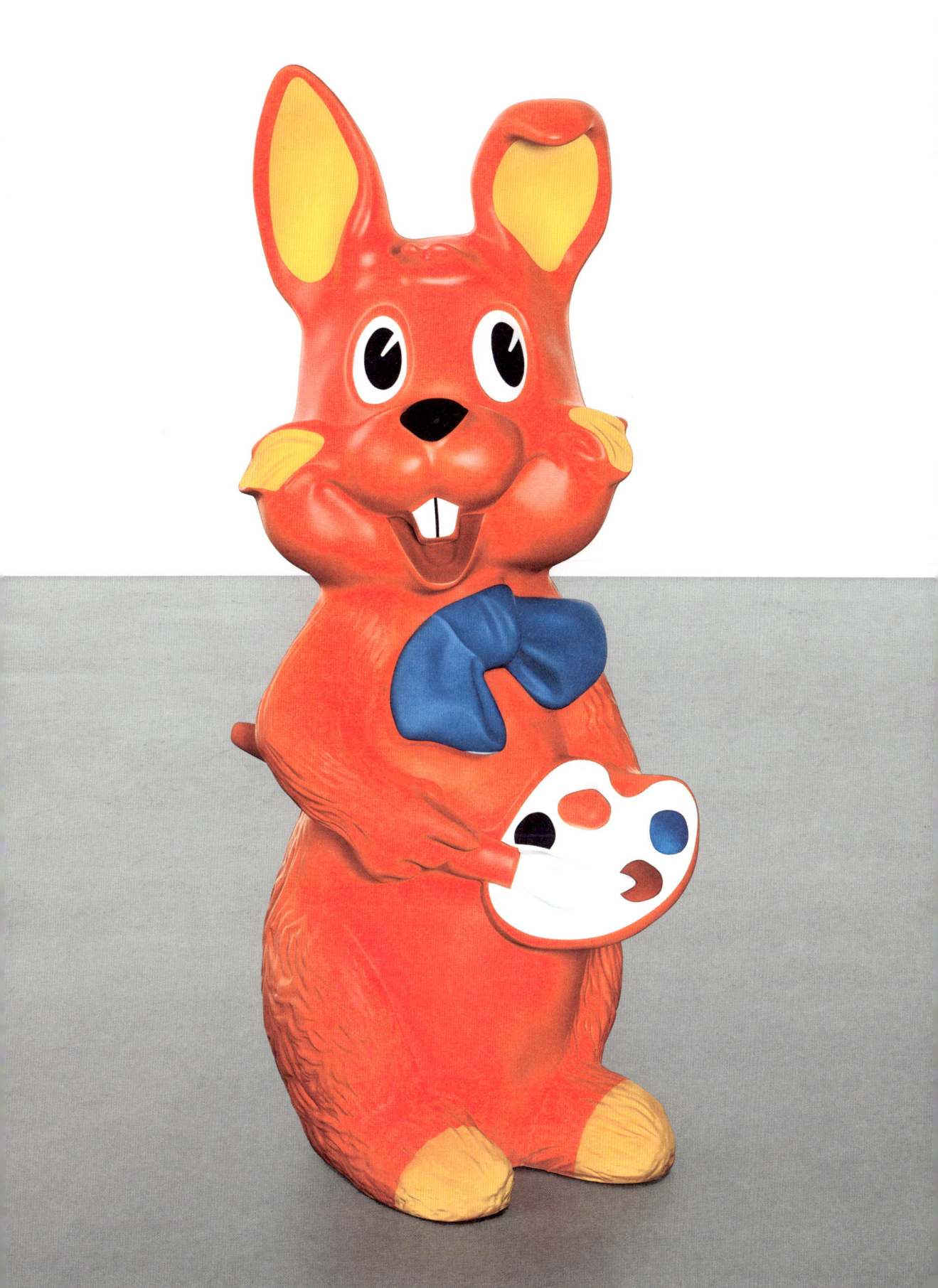

'Smurf Artists'

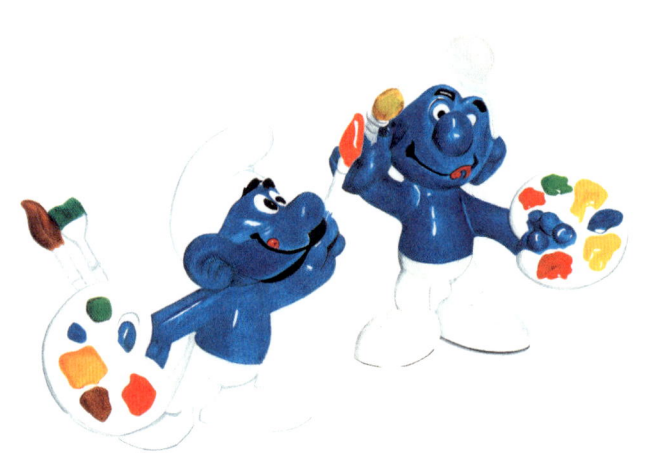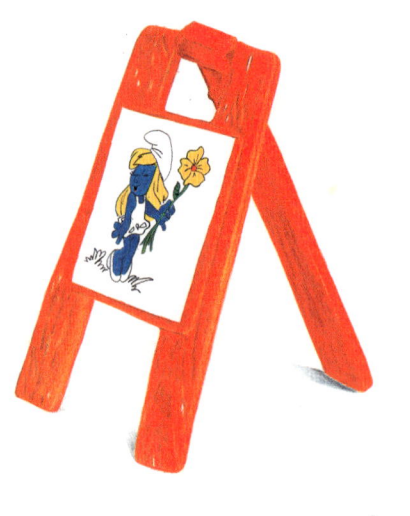

Smurf Artists, 2014 | Buntstift auf Papier | Coloured pencil on paper | 30 × 42 cm

'Hello Kitty Painter'

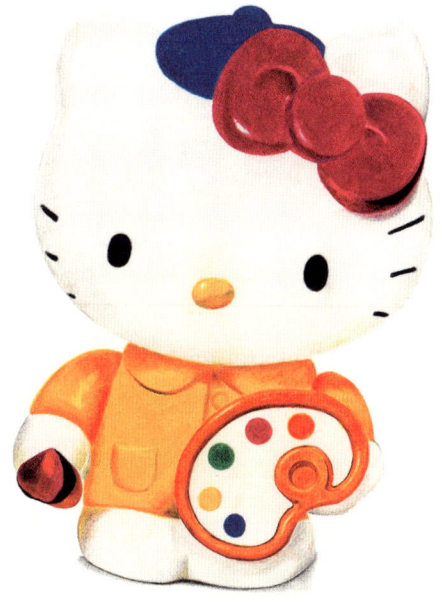

Hello Kitty Painter, 2014 | Buntstift auf Papier | Coloured pencil on paper | 42 × 30 cm

'The Skunk Paints'

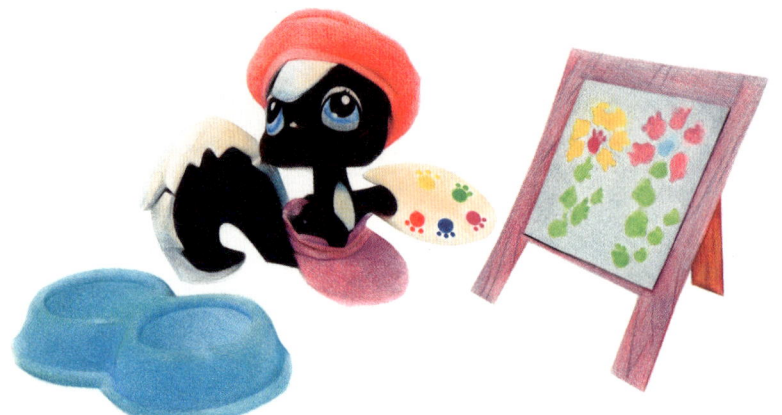

Painted Bronze

Art and Artists

The Skunk Paints, 2014 | Buntstift auf Papier | Coloured pencil on paper | 30 × 42 cm

' The Young Painter '

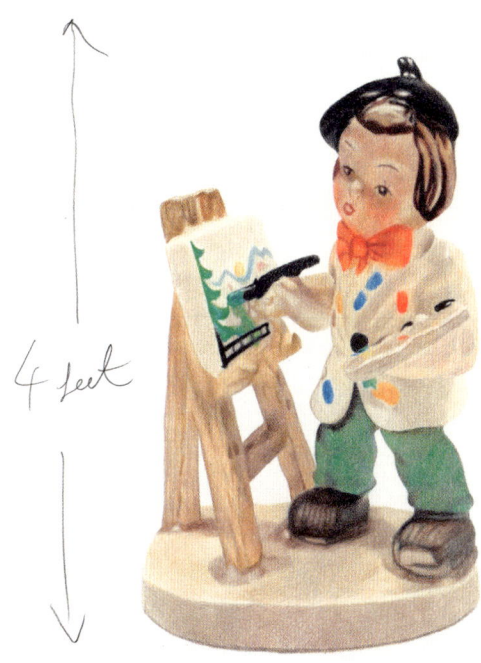

4 feet

Painted
Sculpture

Bronze or Marble

2015

Self Portrait

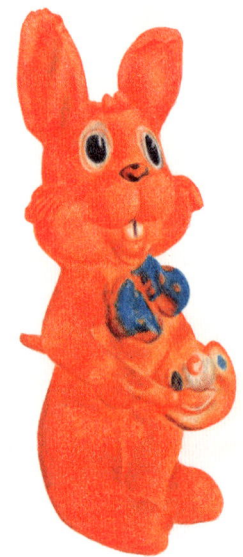

Self-Portrait, 2016 | Buntstift auf Papier | Coloured pencil on paper | 42 × 30 cm

'Paddington Painter'

Art and Artists

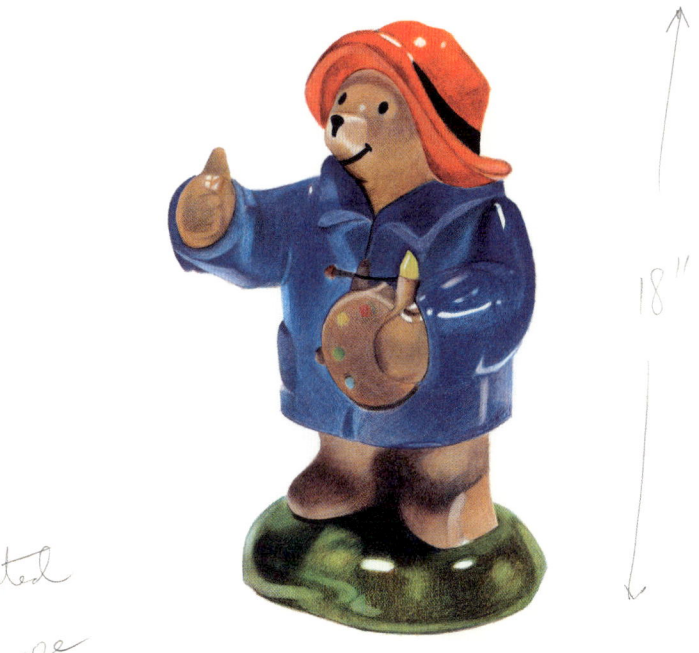

18"

painted
Bronze

„Die Schönheit des Lebens besteht darin, dass sie dir jeden Moment weggenommen werden kann. Die Schönheit einer Blume vergeht, sie verblüht. Vergänglichkeit hat mich schon immer fasziniert."

'The beauty of life is that it can be taken away from you at any moment. The beauty of a flower fades, it withers. Transience has always fascinated me.'

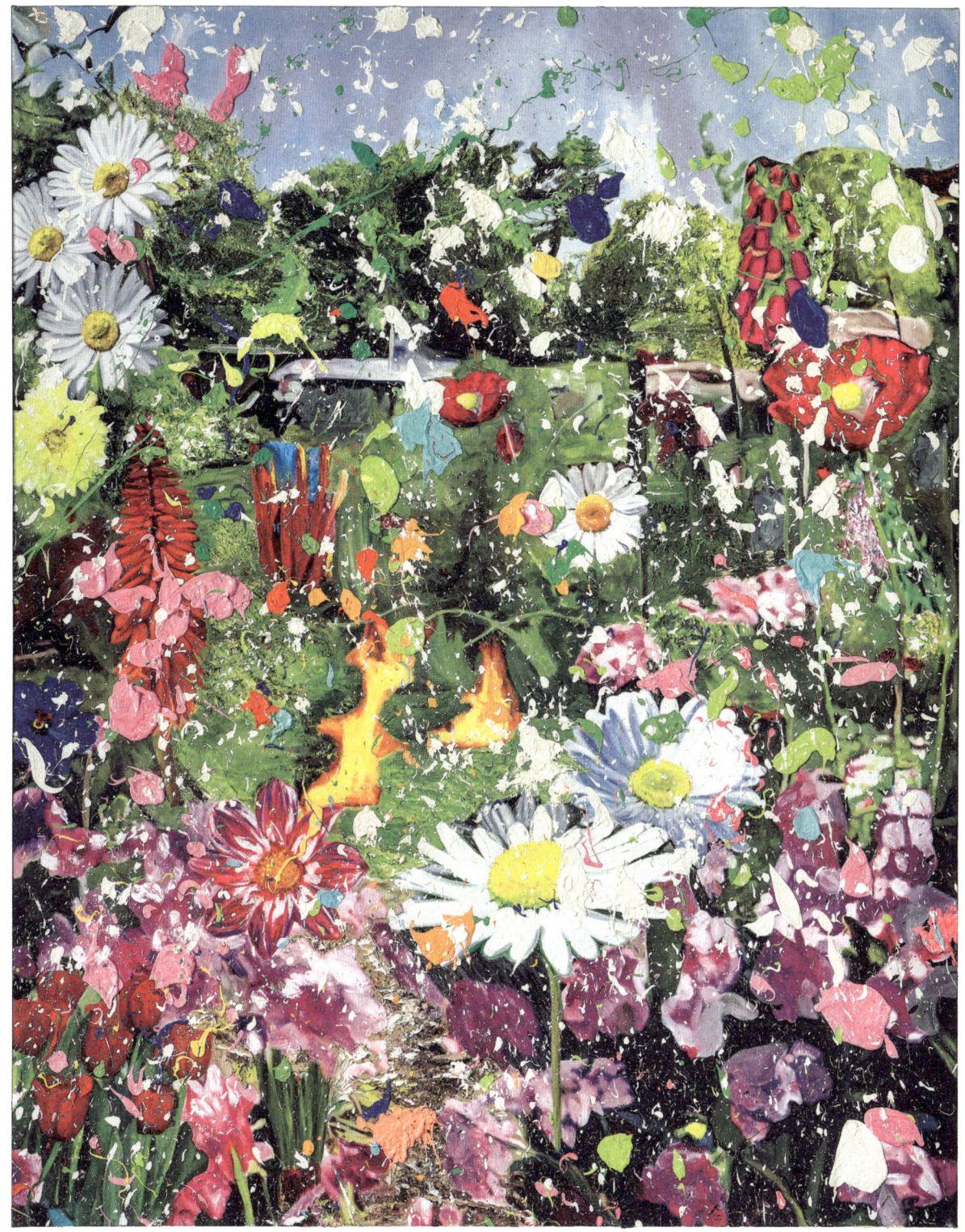

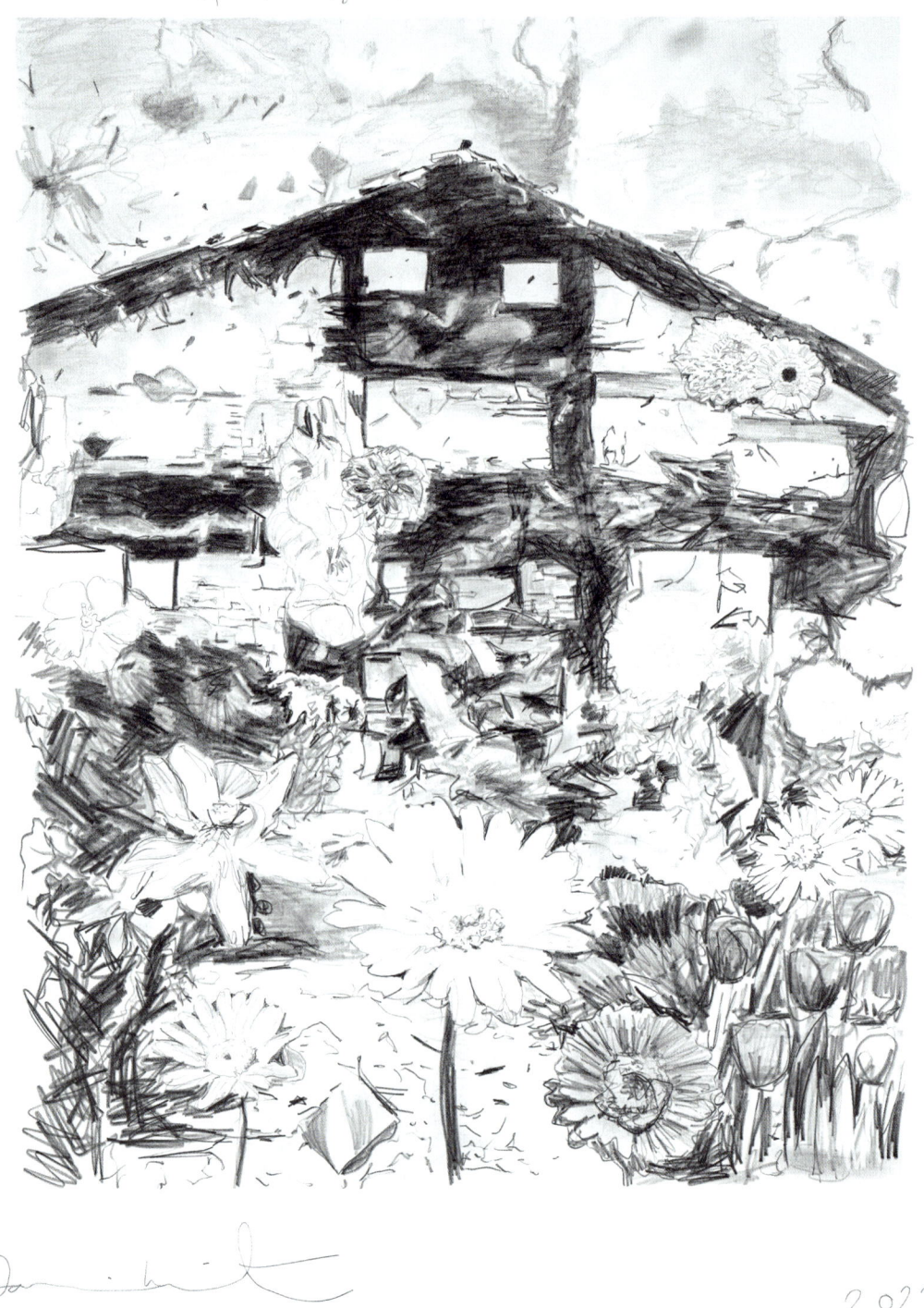

'Garden of Dreams 2'

2023

Garden of Dreams Drawing 2, 2023 | Bleistift auf Papier |
Pencil on paper | 100 × 70 cm

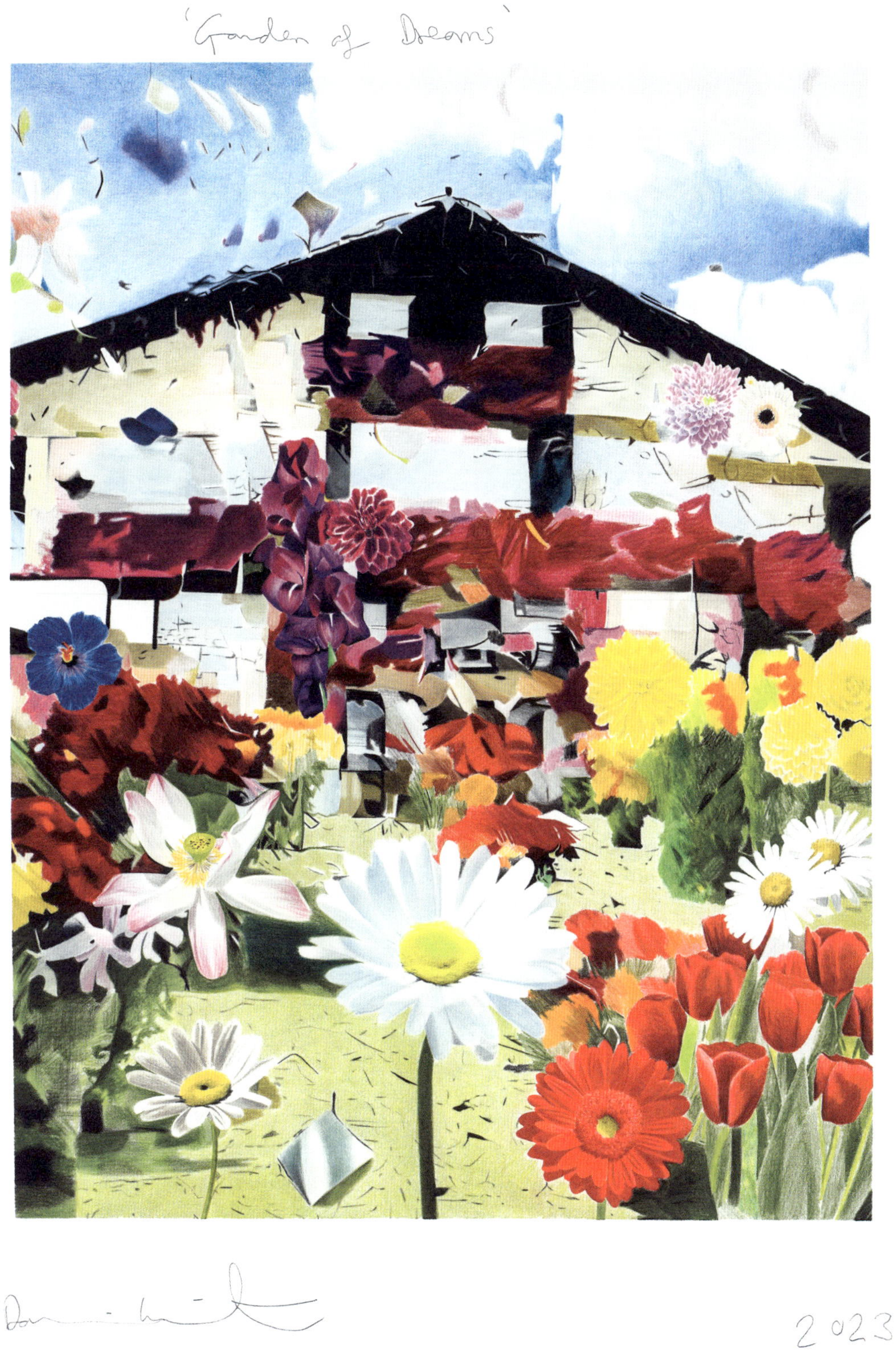

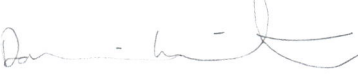

'Garden of Dreams'

2023

Garden of Dreams Drawing, 2023 | Buntstift auf Papier |
Coloured pencil on paper | 100 × 70 cm

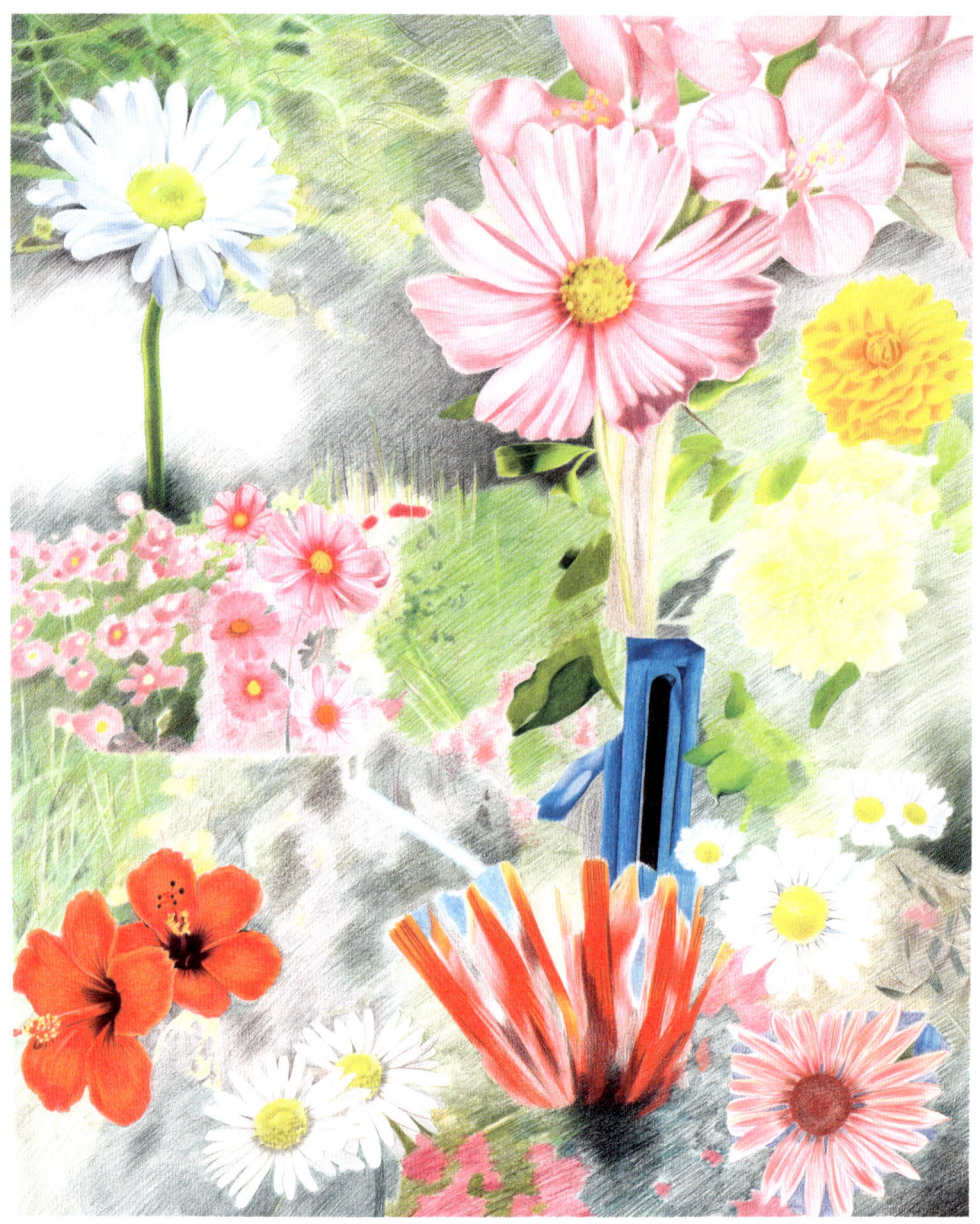

Playful Garden Drawing, 2023 | Buntstift auf Papier |
Coloured pencil on paper | 100 × 70 cm

'Playful Garden 2'

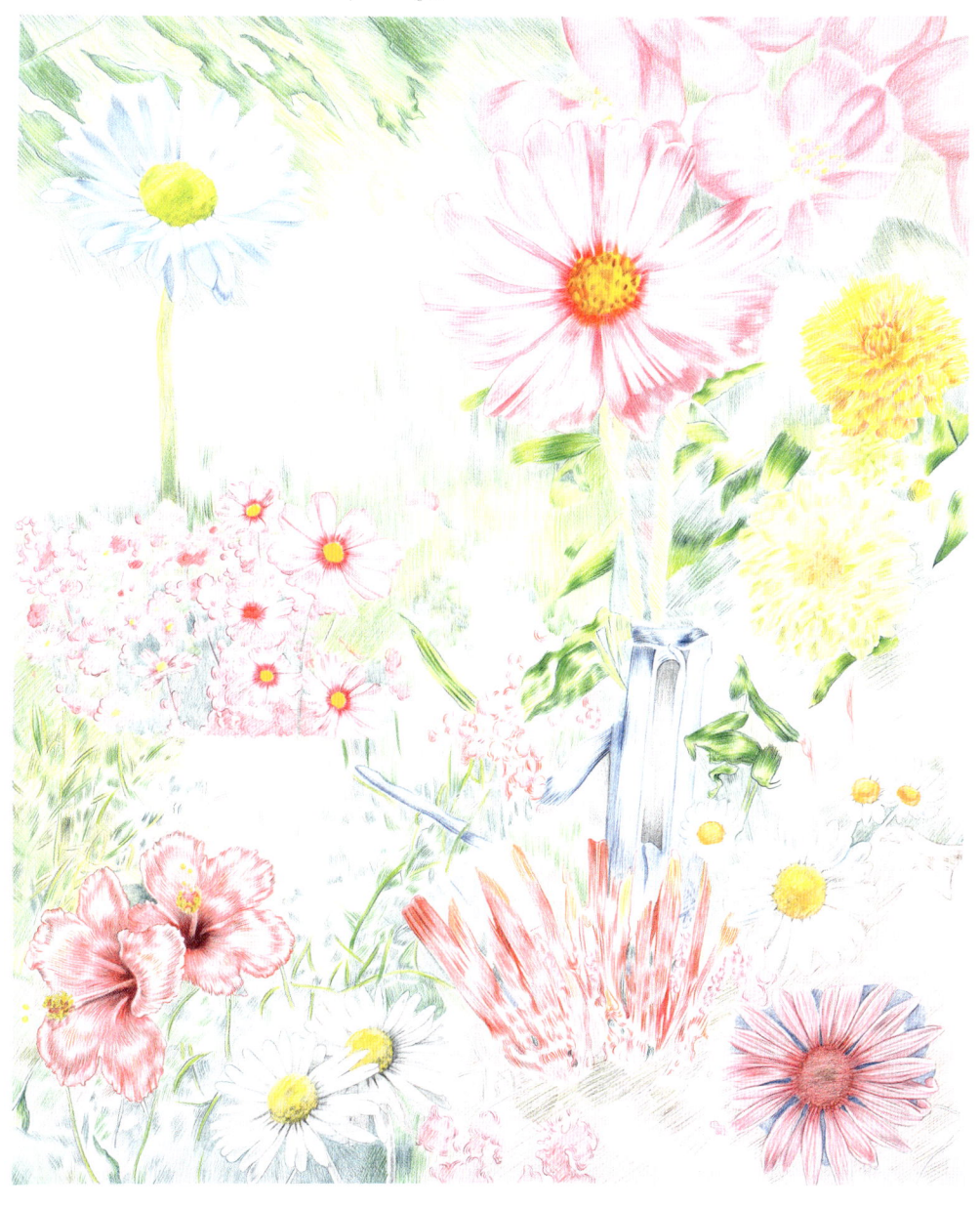

2023

Playful Garden Drawing 2, 2023 | Buntstift auf Papier |
Coloured pencil on paper | 100 × 70 cm

'Playful Garden 3'

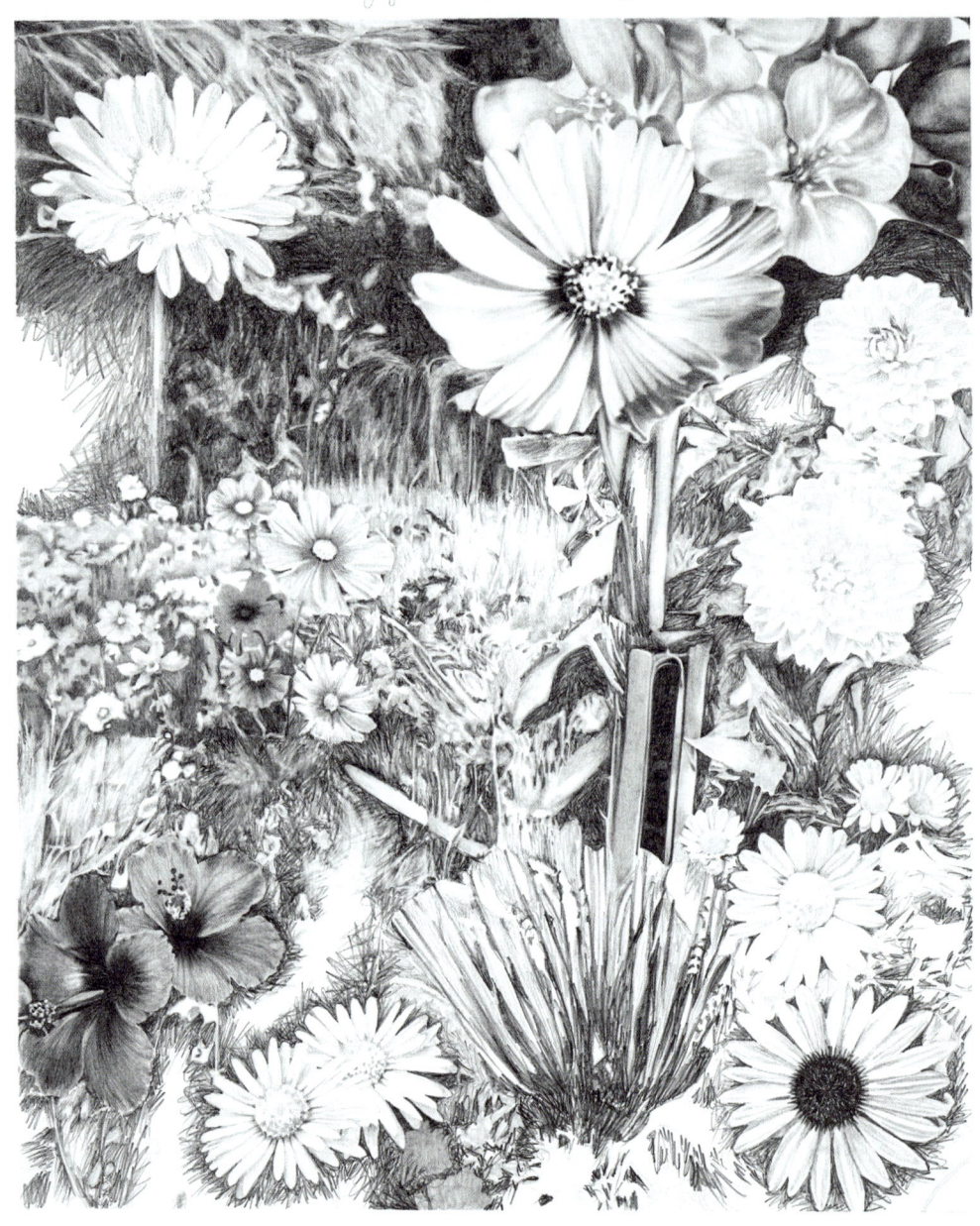

2023

Playful Garden Drawing 3, 2023 | Bleistift auf Papier |
Pencil on paper | 100 × 70 cm

'Playful Garden 4'

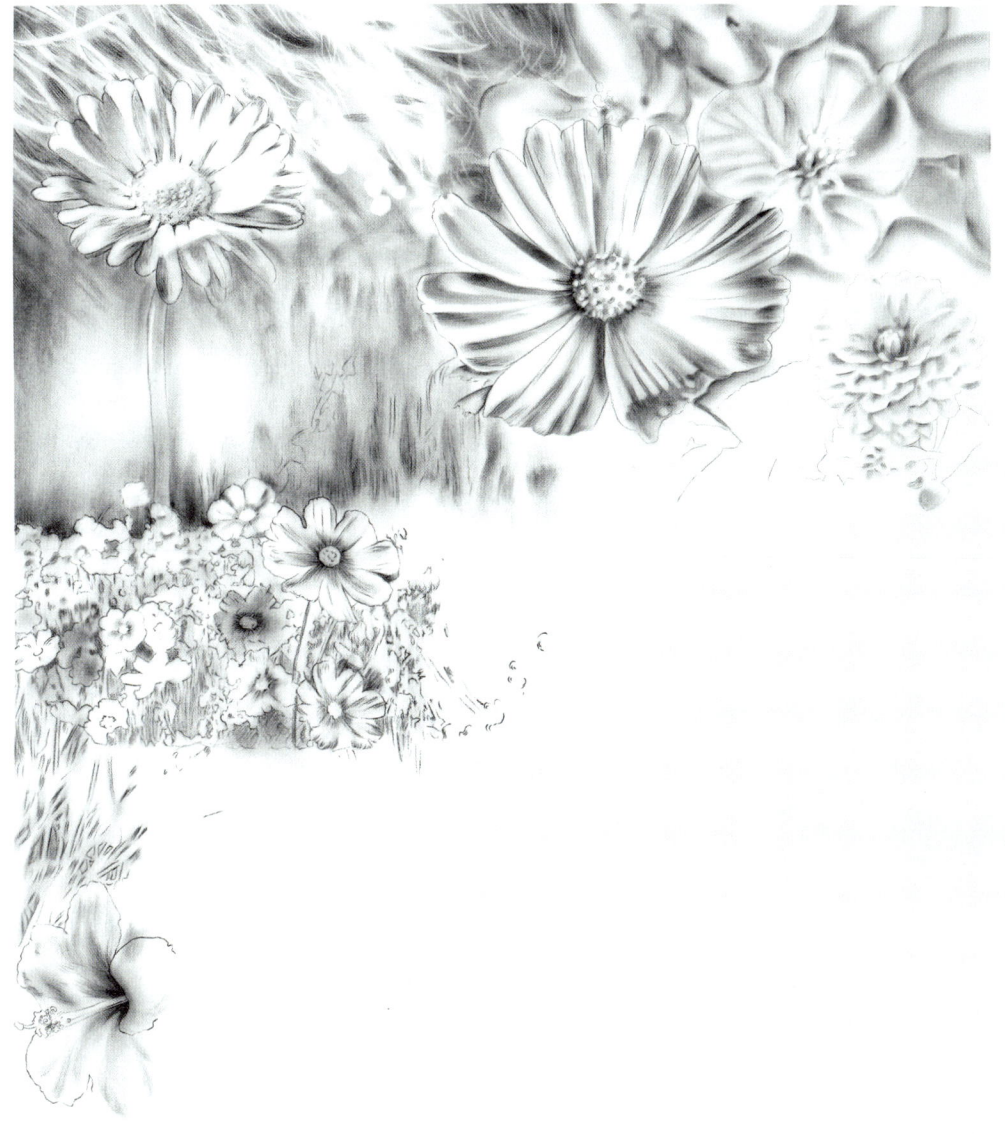

2023

Playful Garden Drawing 4, 2023 | Bleistift auf Papier |
Pencil on paper | 100 × 70 cm

'Allegorical Garden'

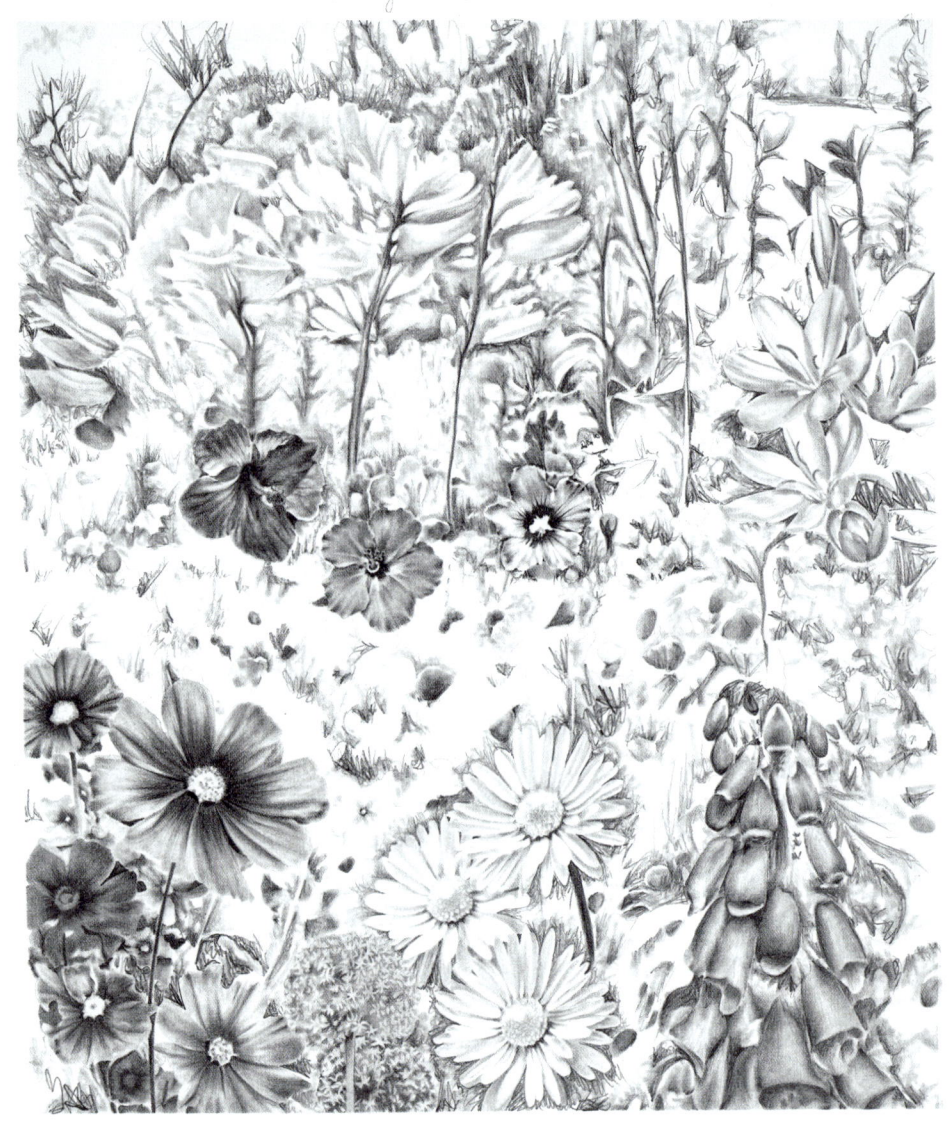

2023

Allegorical Garden Drawing, 2023 | Bleistift auf Papier |
Pencil on paper | 100 × 70 cm

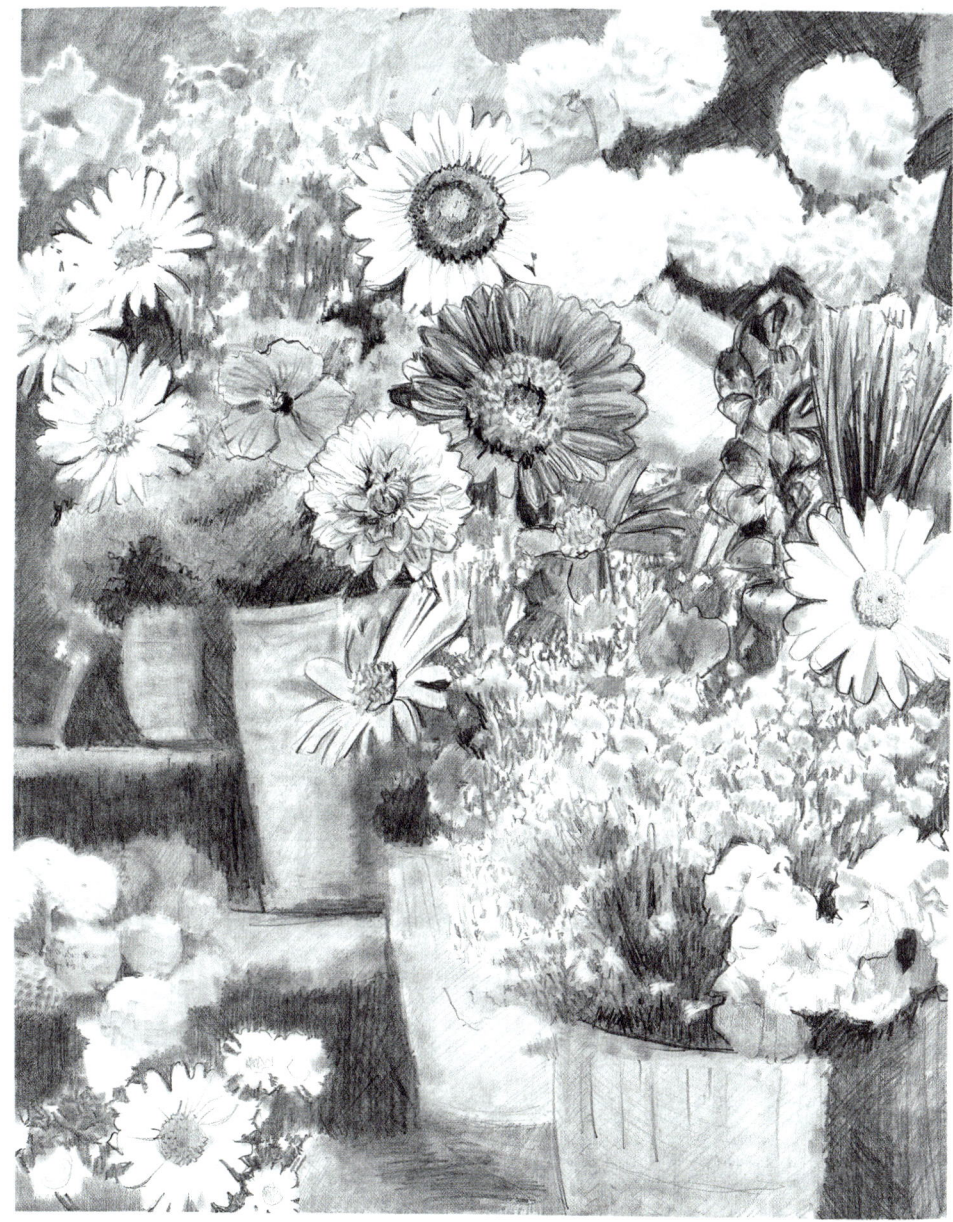

'Paradoxical Garden'

Paradoxical Garden Drawing, 2023 | Bleistift auf Papier |
Pencil on paper | 100 × 70 cm

„Mich interessiert die Verwirrung
zwischen Kunst und Leben, ich mag es,
wenn die Welt dazwischenfunkt."

'I'm interested in the confusion
between art and life, I like it when
the world gets in the way.'

Cat, 2018 | Stahl, Aluminium, Polypropylen, Acrylkleber, Epoxidharz, Nylon,
PETG, Acryl und Kupferdraht | Steel, aluminium, polypropylene, acrylic
adhesive, epoxy resin, nylon, PETG, acrylic, and copper wire | 77 × 62 × 56 cm

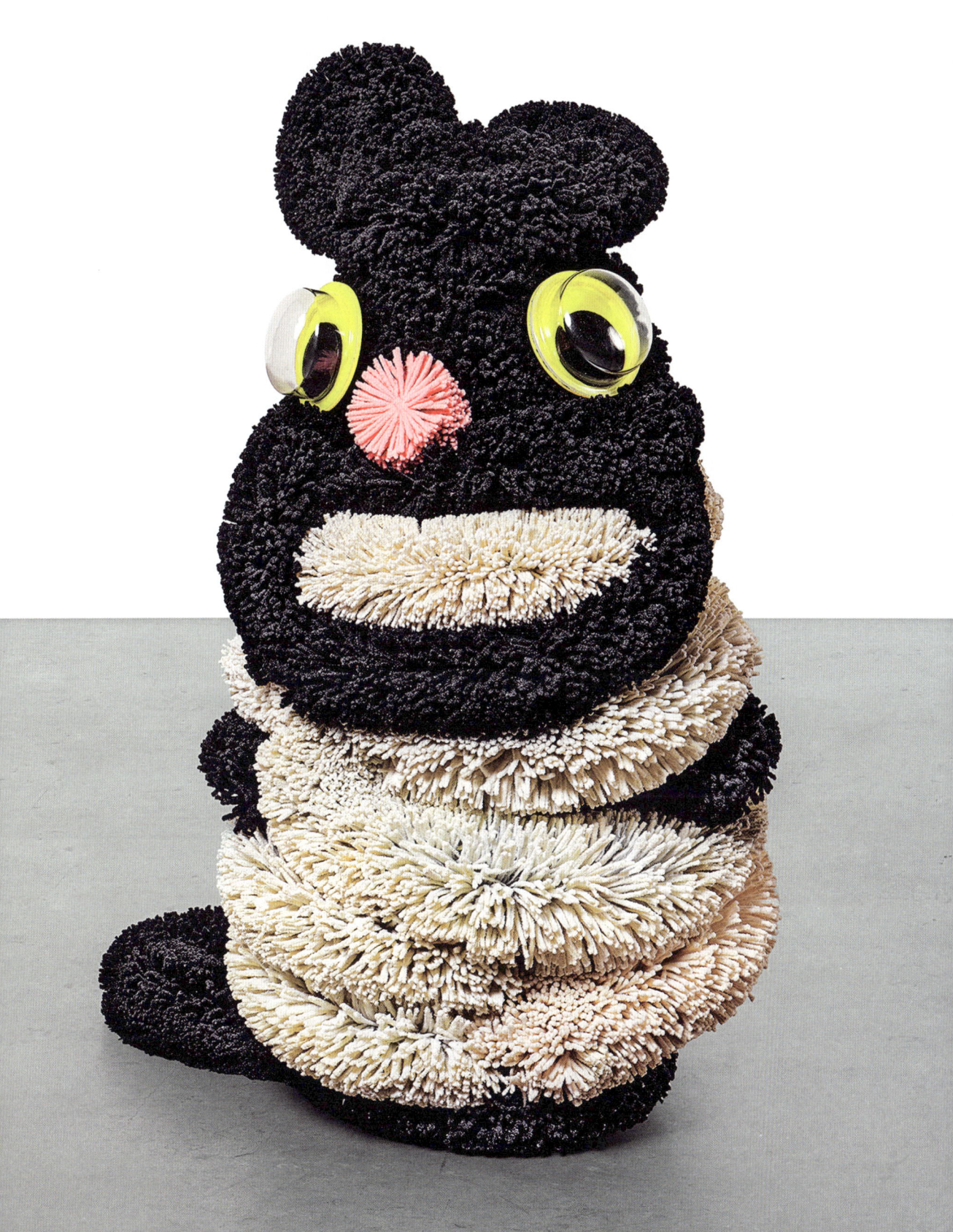

'Emu'

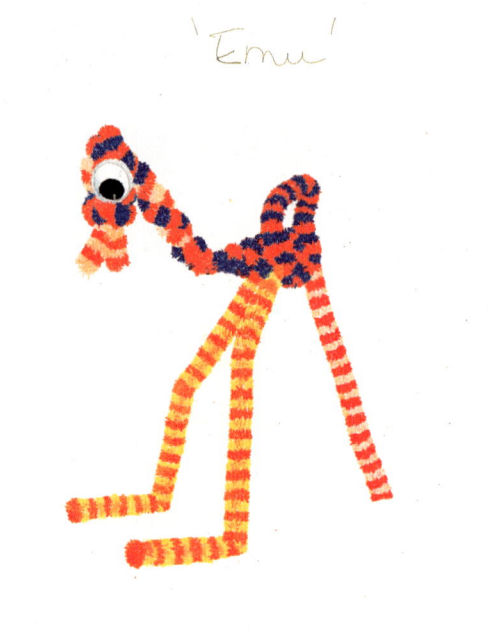

2024

Emu, 2024 | Wachsmalstift auf Papier | Crayon on paper | 59 × 84 cm

'Frog 2'

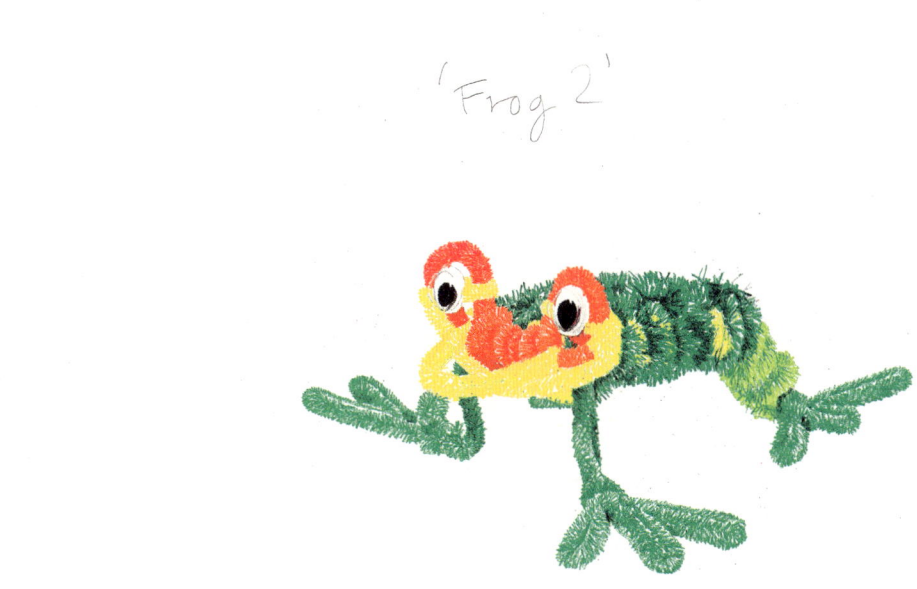

2024

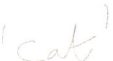

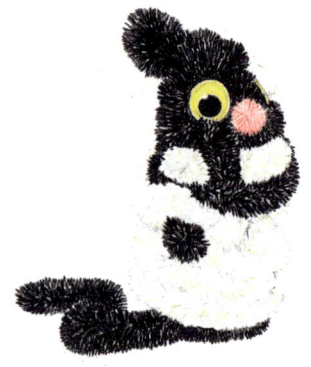

Cat, 2024 | Wachsmalstift auf Papier | Crayon on paper | 59 × 84 cm

'Butterfly on Flower'.

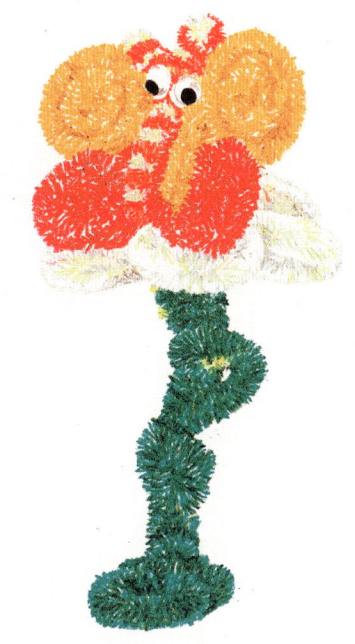

2024

'Thing'

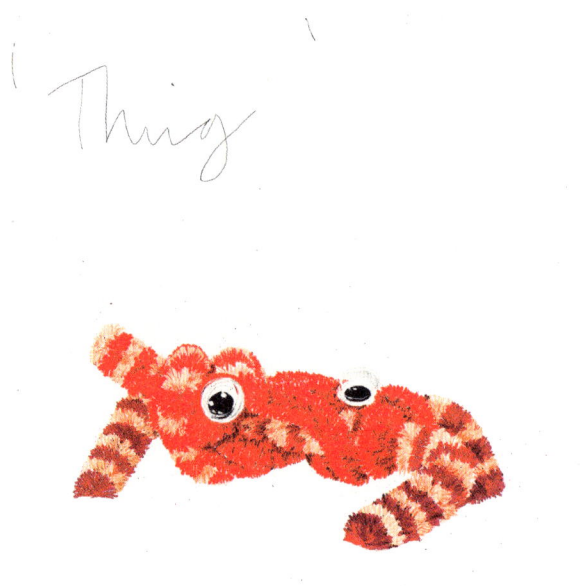

2024

'LIZARD'

2024

„Lass die Wahrheit niemals einer
guten Geschichte im Weg stehen."

'Never let the truth get in
the way of a good story.'

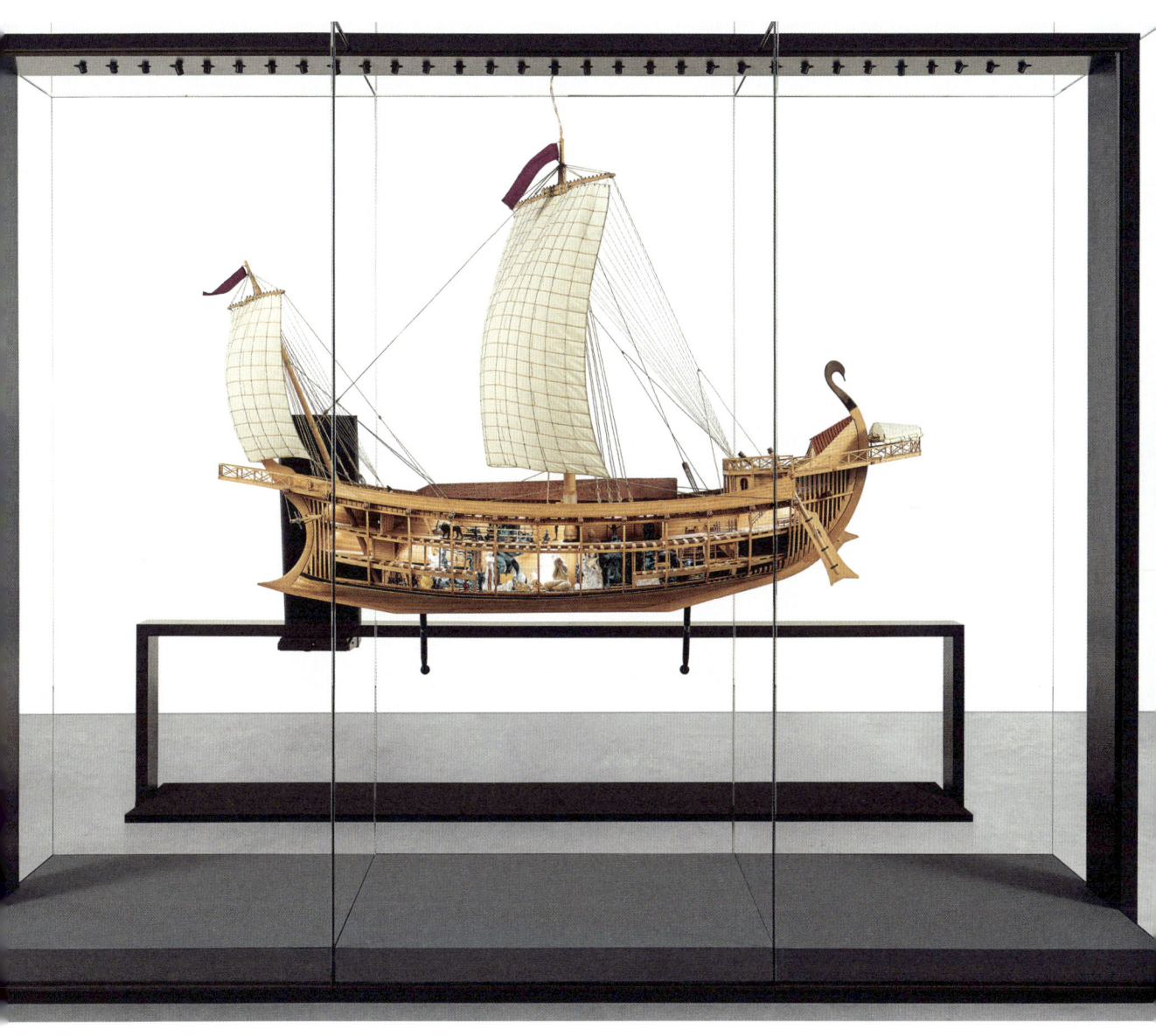

Scale model of the 'Unbelievable' with suggested cargo locations, 2015
(Maßstabsgetreues Modell der „Unbelievable" mit vorgeschlagenen Frachtpositionen)
Glas, pulverbeschichtetes Aluminium, lackiertes MDF, Silikon, LED-Licht, Edelstahl,
digitaler Bildschirm, Messschaltung, Mikrocontroller, PC, Rollschiene, Laserlicht, Kalk,
Aluminium, Leinen, Hanfschnur, lackierter Kunststoff und Harz | Glass, powder-coated
aluminium, painted MDF, silicone, LED lighting, stainless steel, digital screen, measuring
circuit, micro controller, PC, roller rail, laser light, lime, aluminium, linen, hemp cord,
painted plastic, and resin | 270 × 350 × 106 cm

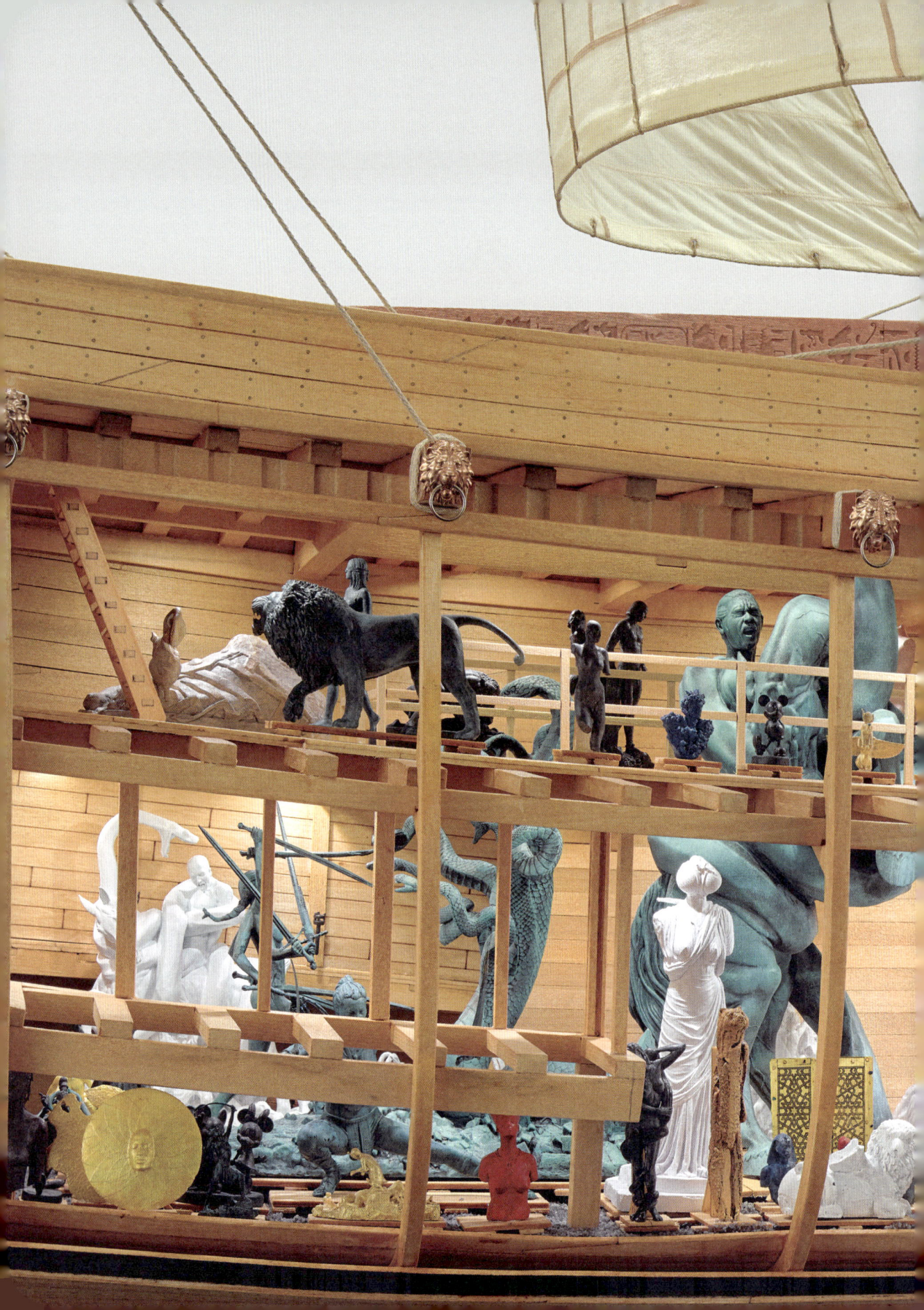

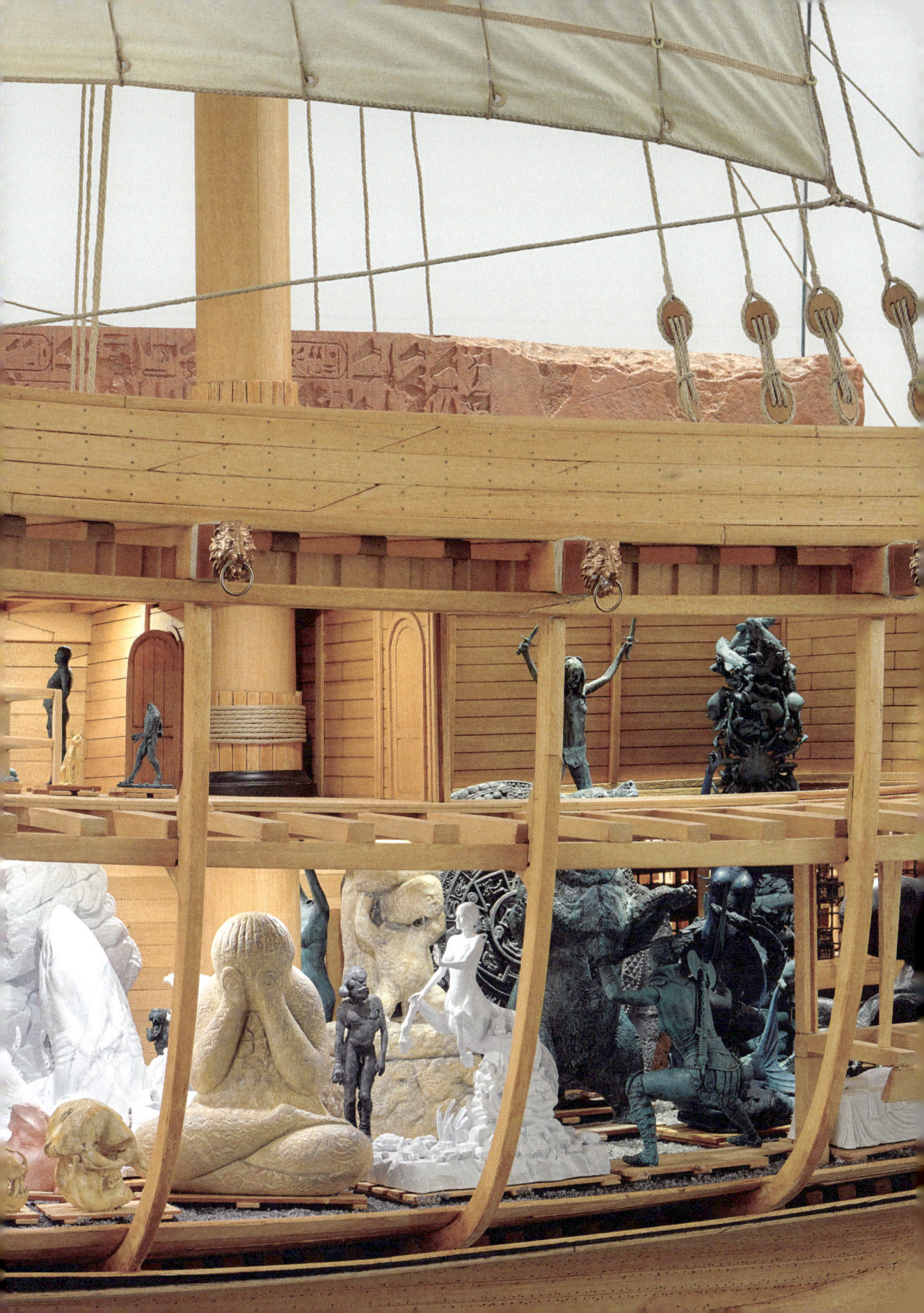

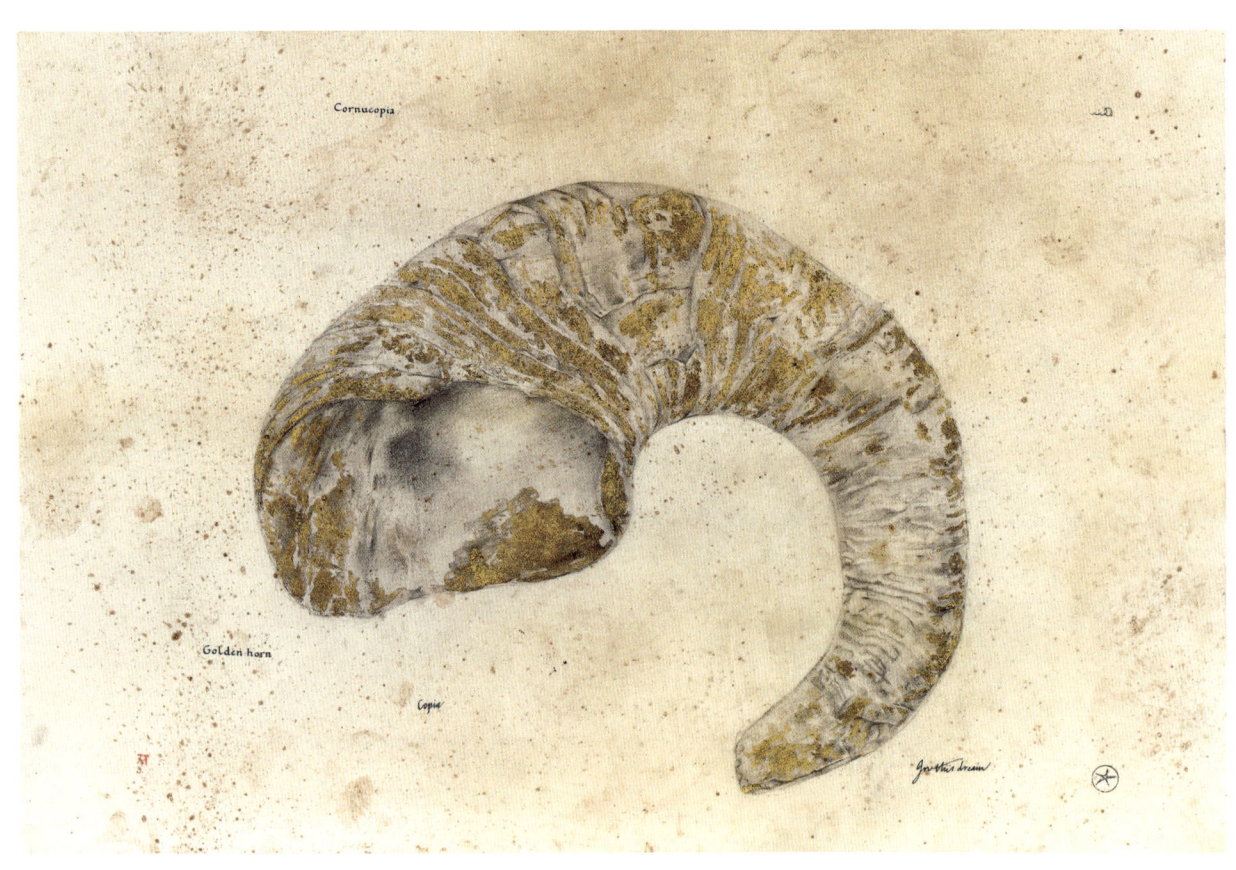

Copia (Gold), 2014 | Kohle, Graphit und Blattgold auf Pergament |
Charcoal, graphite, and gold leaf on vellum | 45 × 68 cm

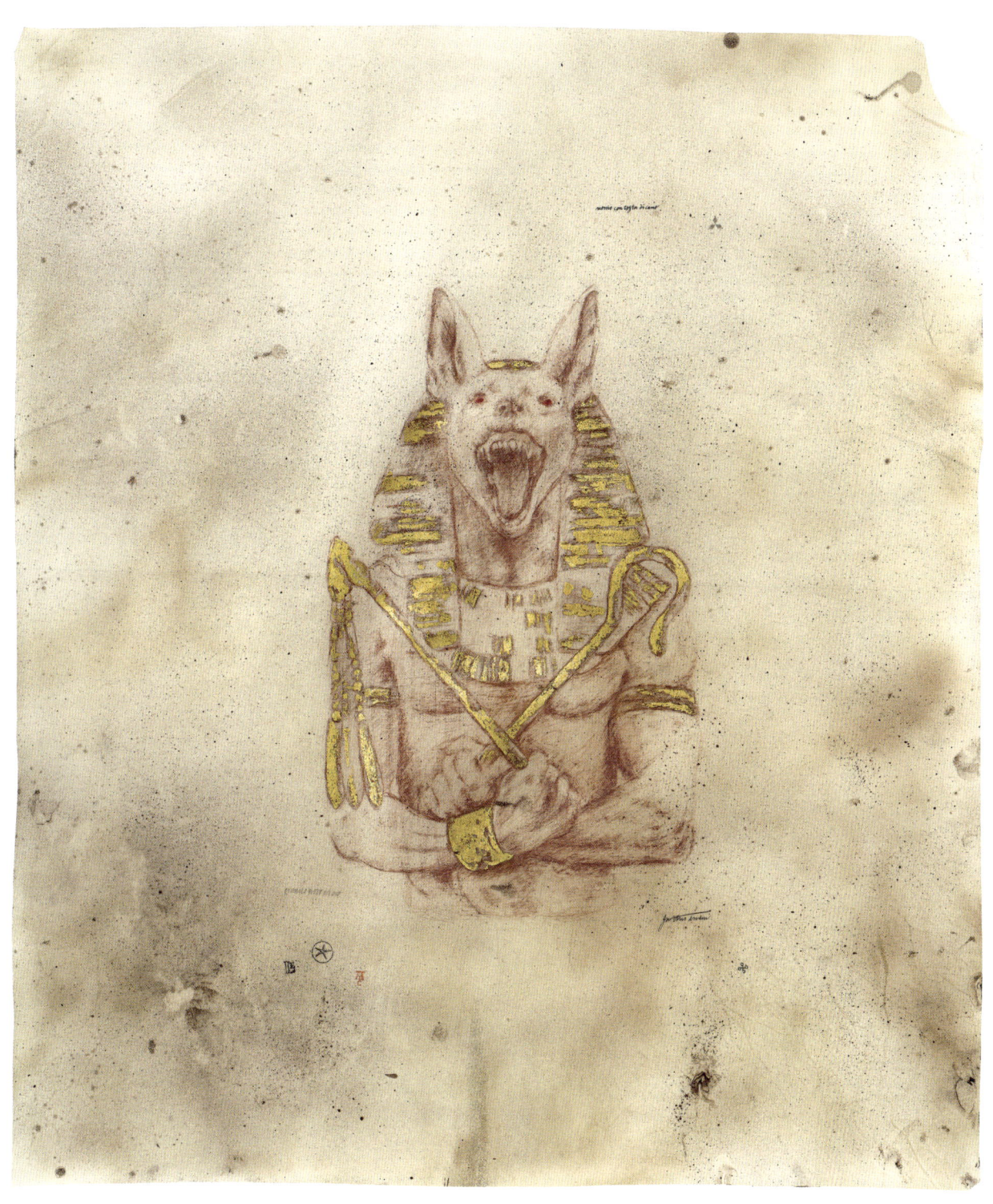

Anubis, 2016 | Bleistift, Tinte und Blattgold auf Pergament |
Pencil, ink, and gold leaf on vellum | 65 × 47 cm

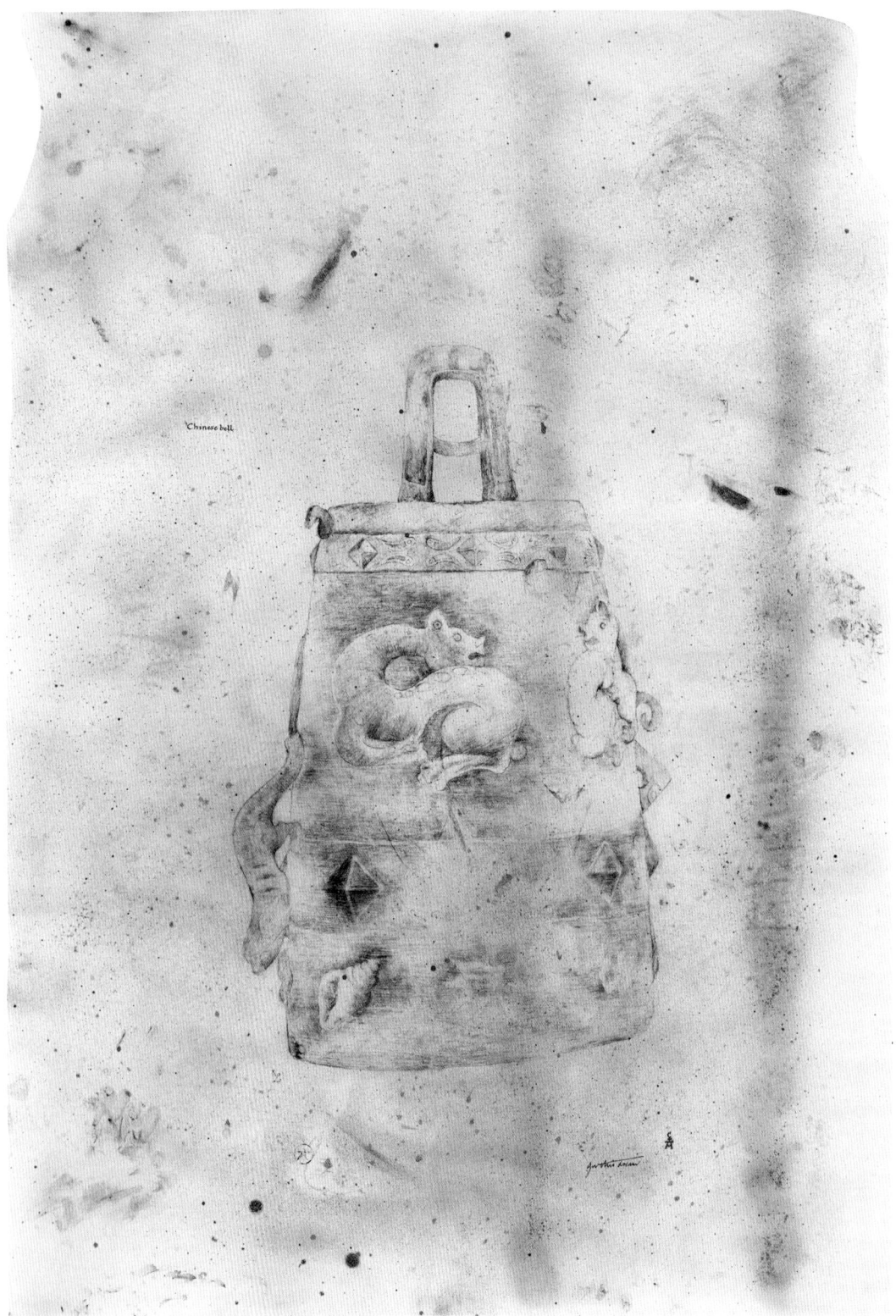

'Chinese bell'

Bell (Bo), Eastern Zhou Dynasty, 2014 | Kohle auf Pergament | Charcoal on vellum | 72 × 52 cm

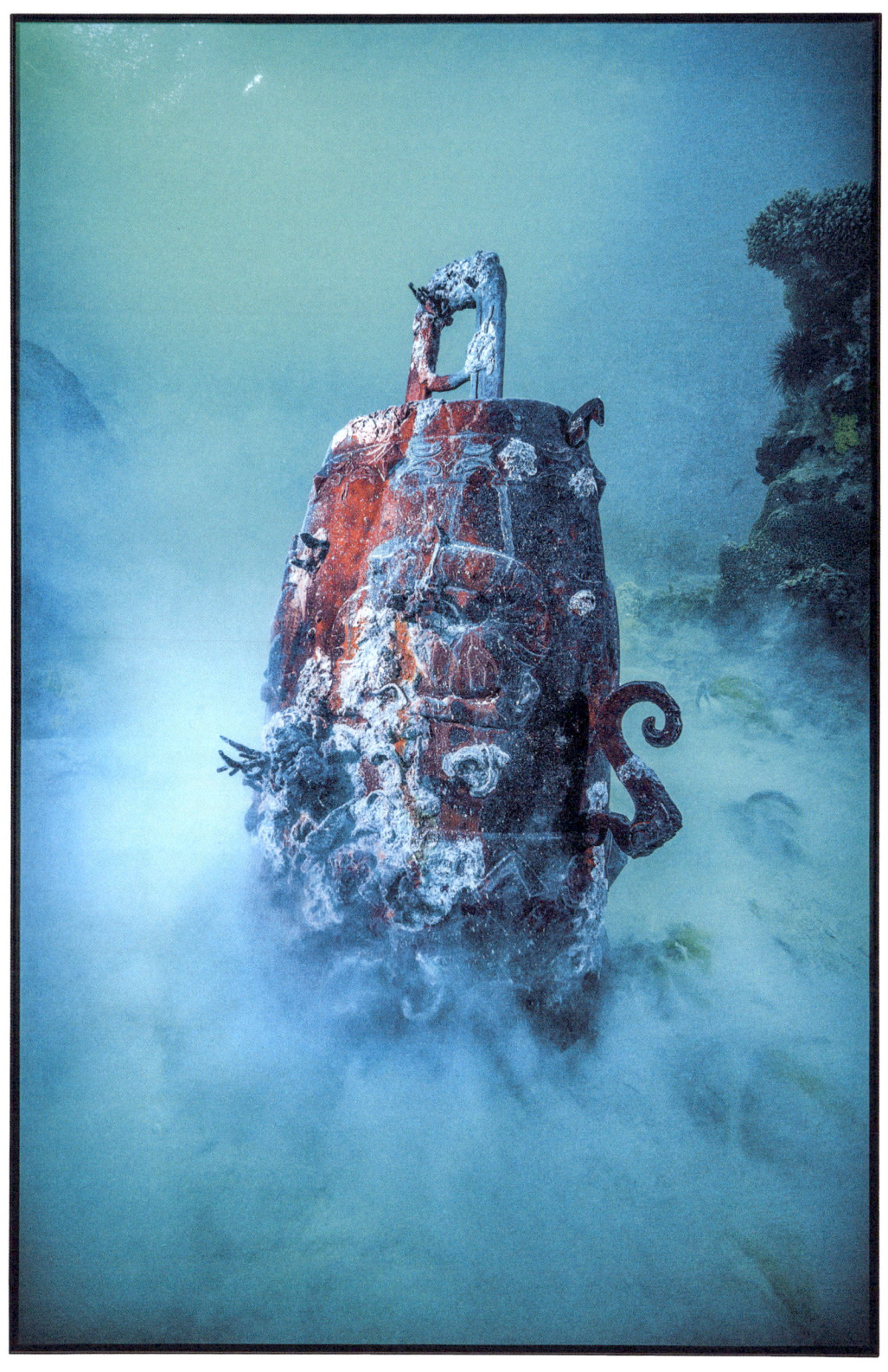

Bell (Bo) Under the Sea, 2015 | Pulverbeschichtetes Aluminium, bedruckter Polyester und Acryl-Leuchtkasten |
Powder-coated aluminium, printed polyester, and acrylic lightbox | 91 × 61 × 10 cm

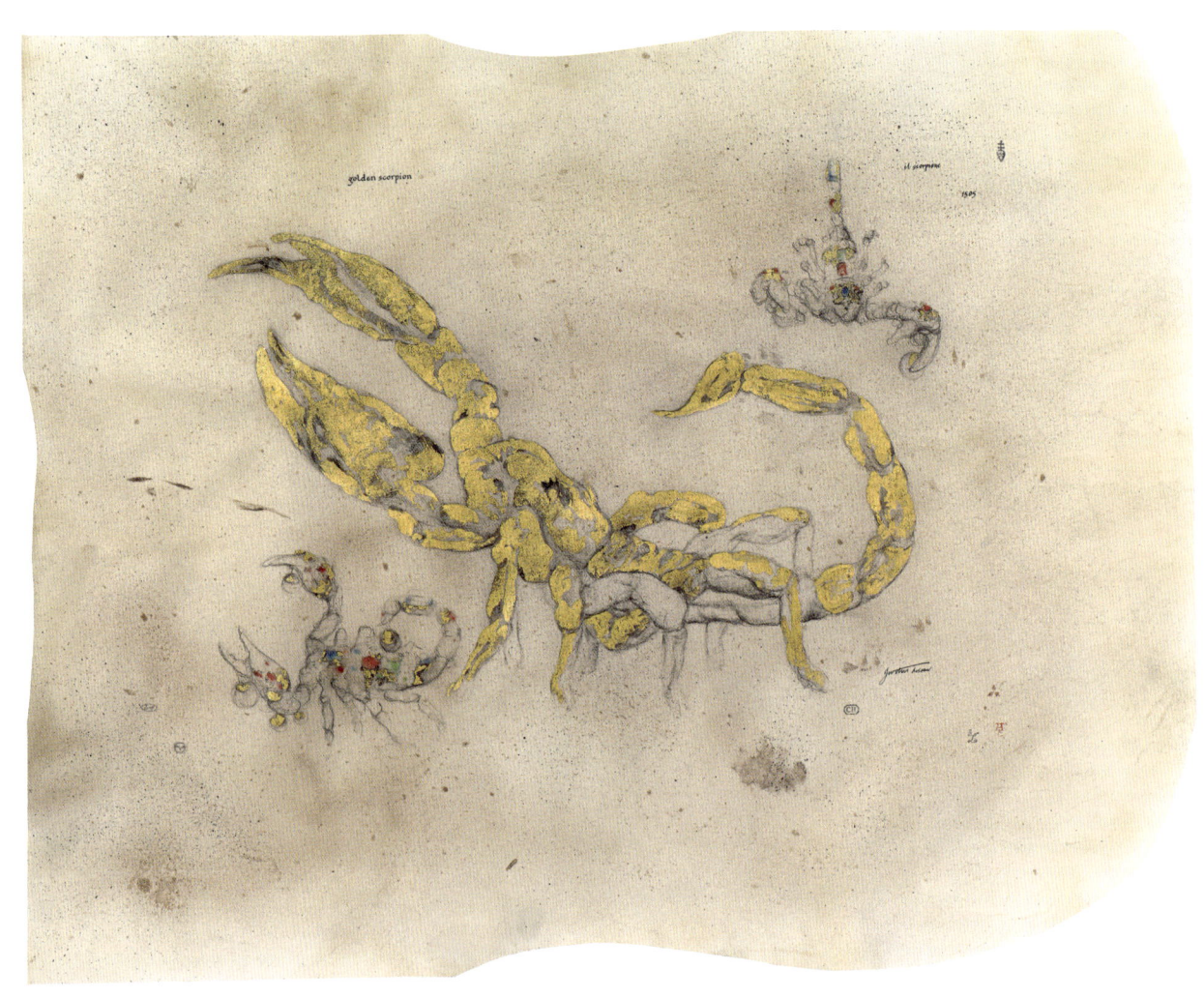

The Golden Scorpion, 1505, 2014 | Kohle, Tinte, Pastell und Blattgold auf
Pergament | Charcoal, ink, pastel, and gold leaf on vellum | 52 × 74 cm

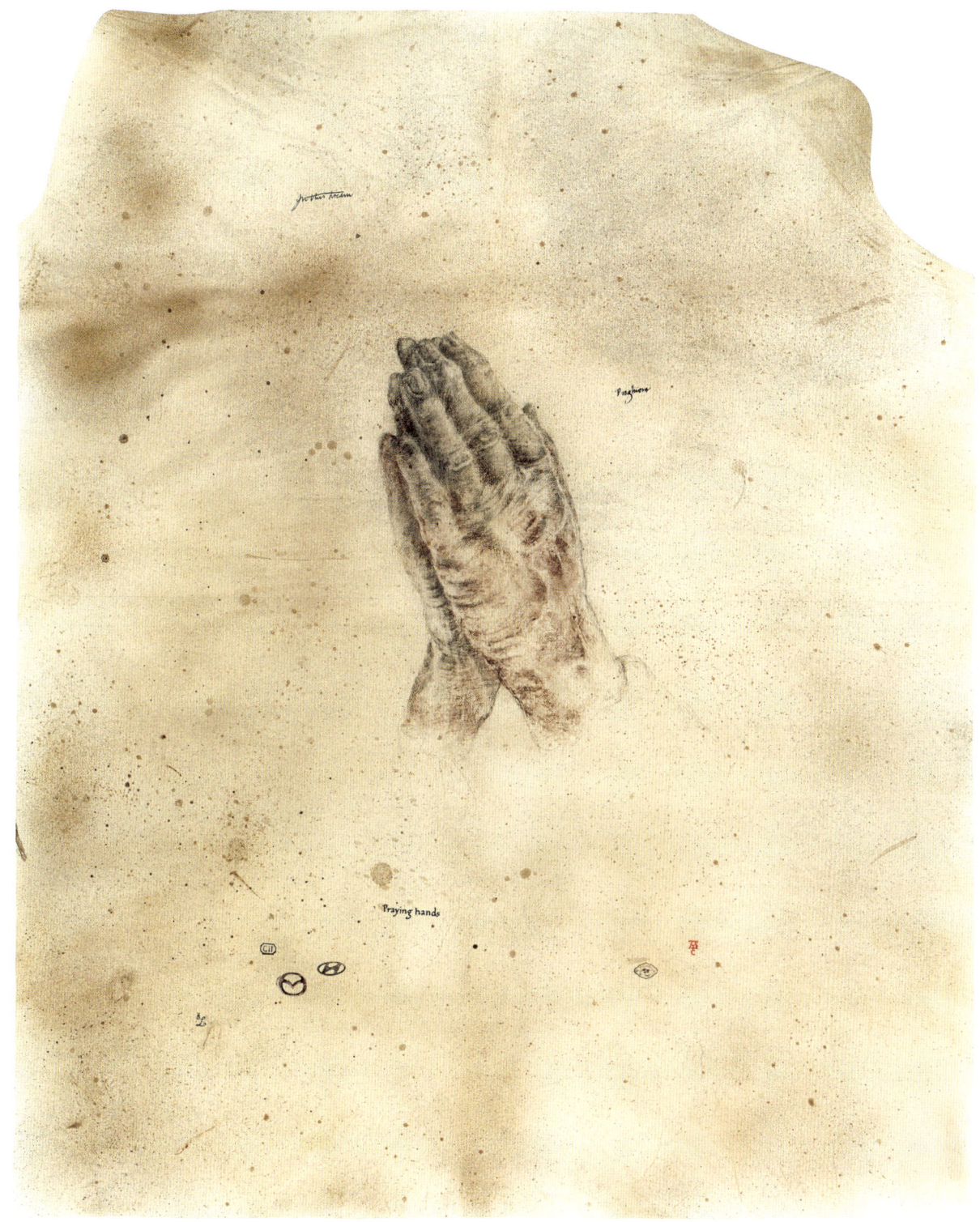

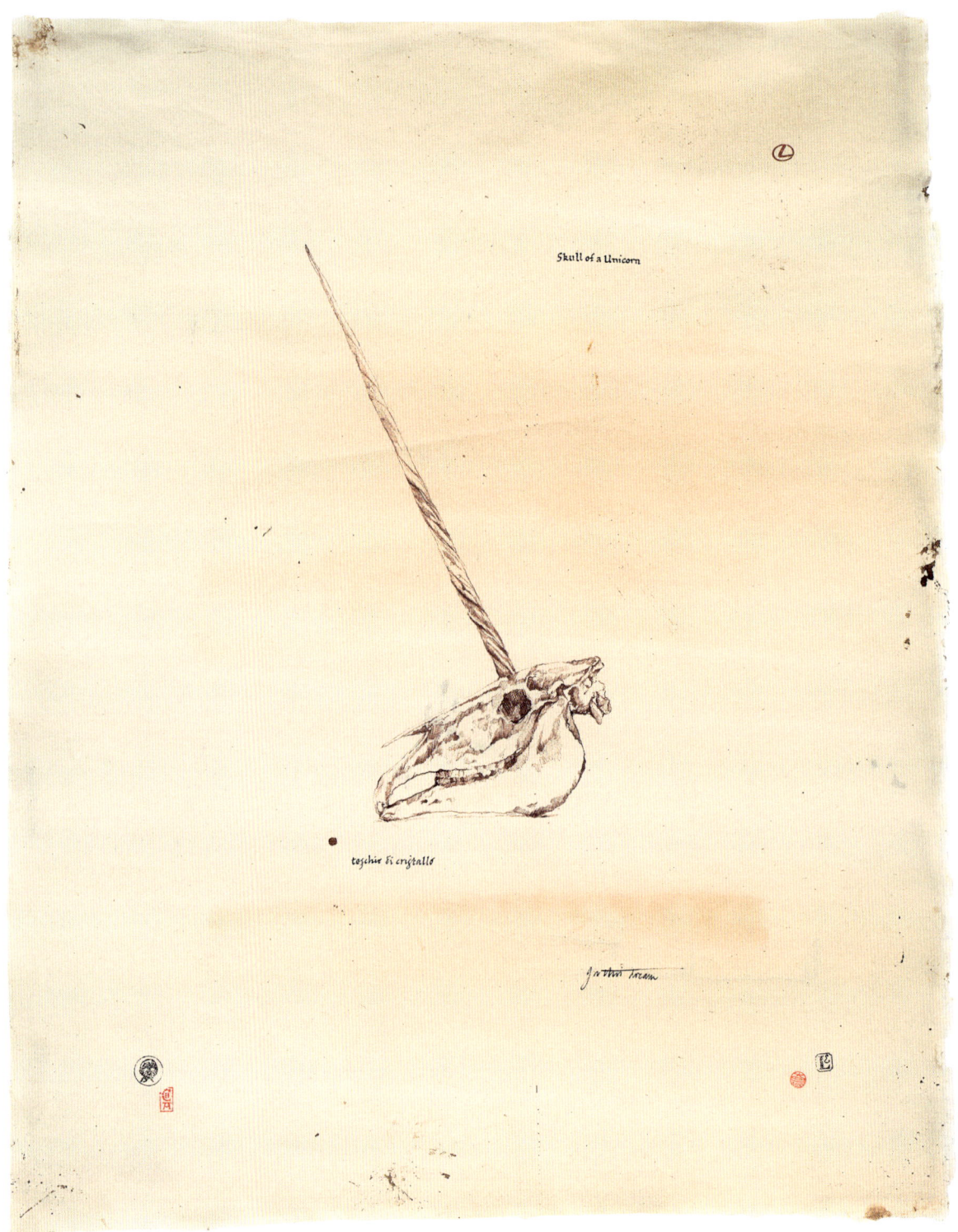

Skull of a Unicorn

teschio di cristallo

Skull of a Unicorn, 2014 | Tinte auf Papier | Ink on paper | 63 × 50 cm

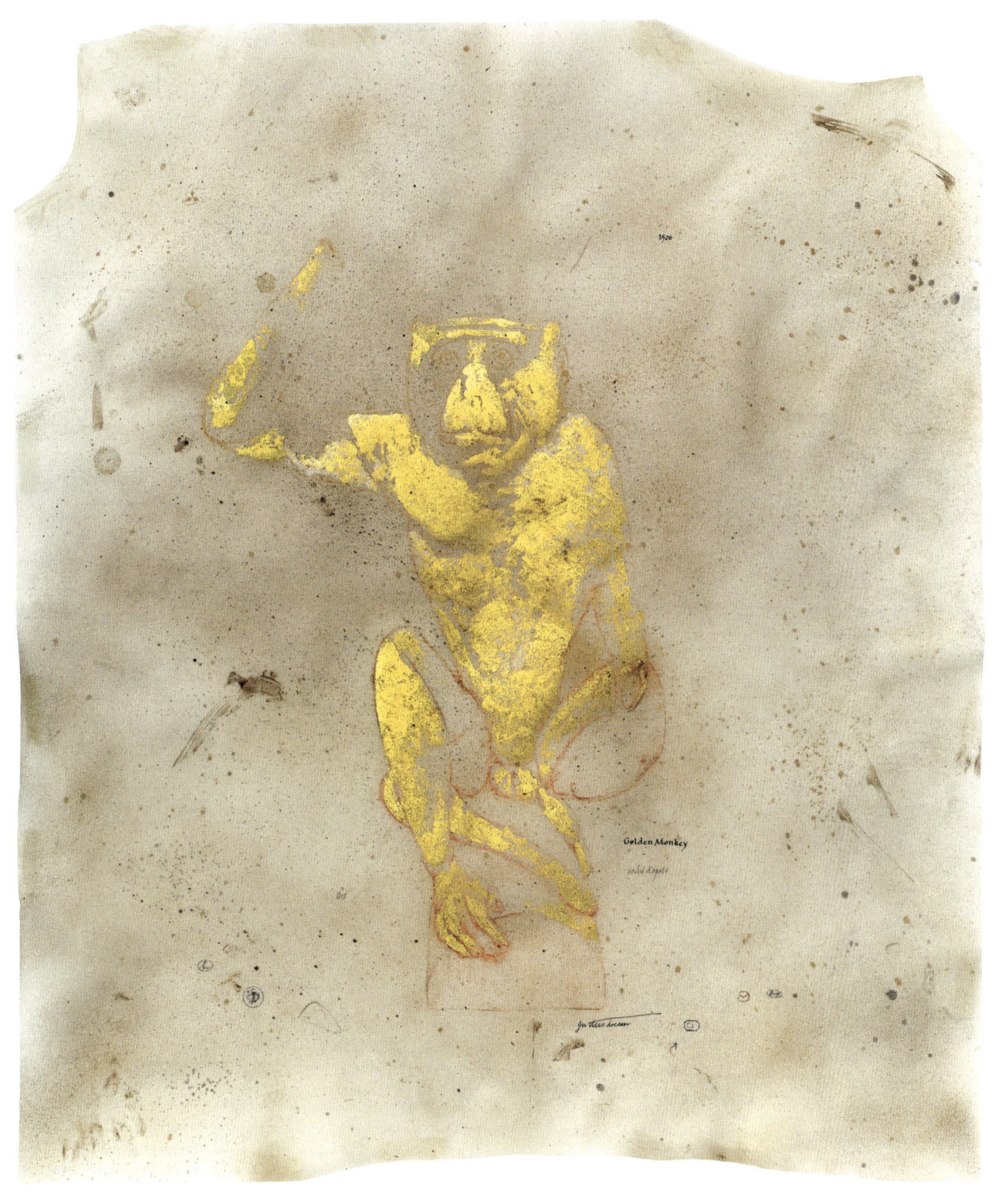

The Golden Monkey (with Opal Eyes), 1506, 2014 | Kohle, Bleistift und Blattgold
auf Pergament | Charcoal, pencil, and gold leaf on vellum | 65 × 47 cm

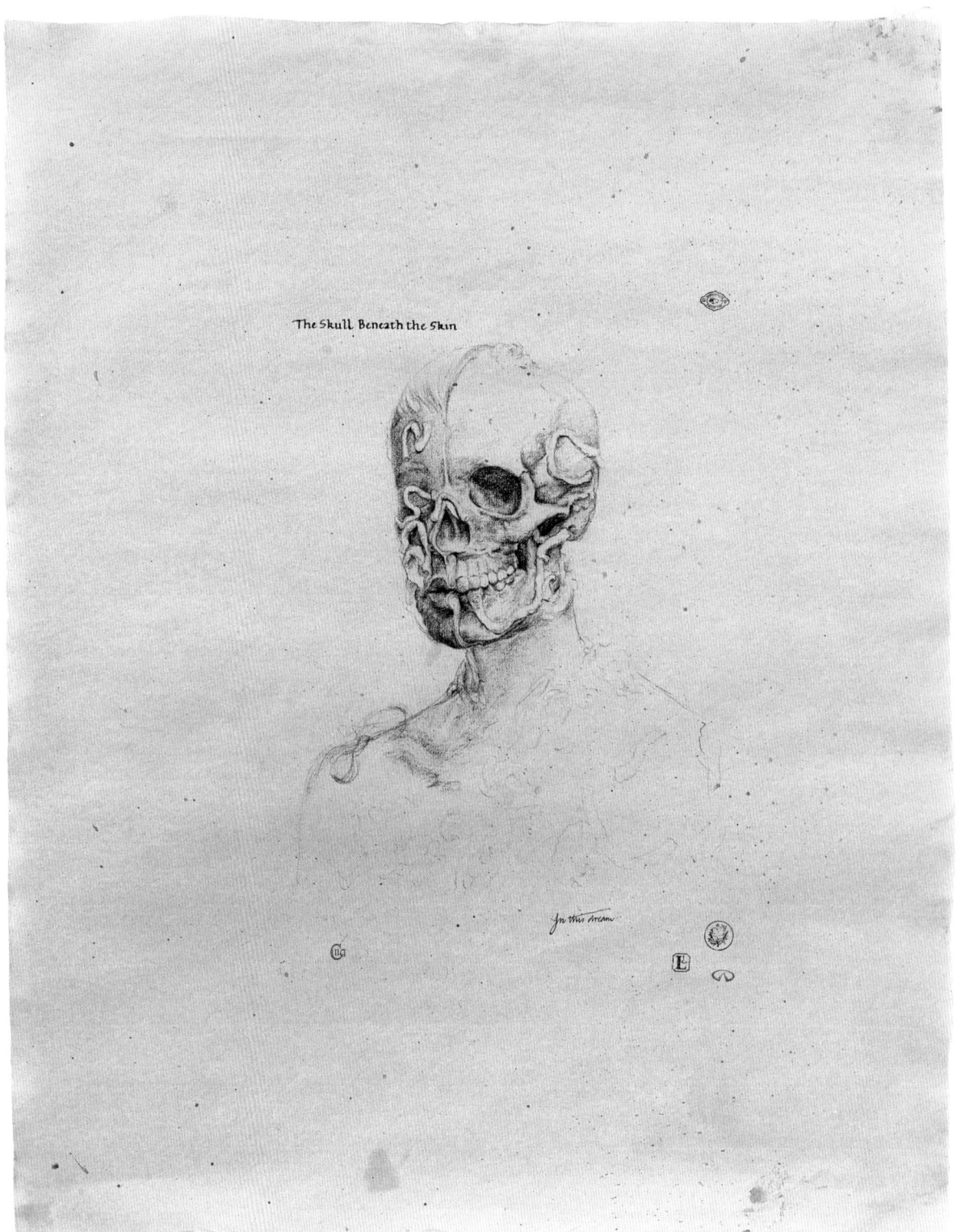

The Skull Beneath the Skin, Memento Mori, 2015 | Kohle auf Papier | Charcoal on paper | 62 × 50 cm

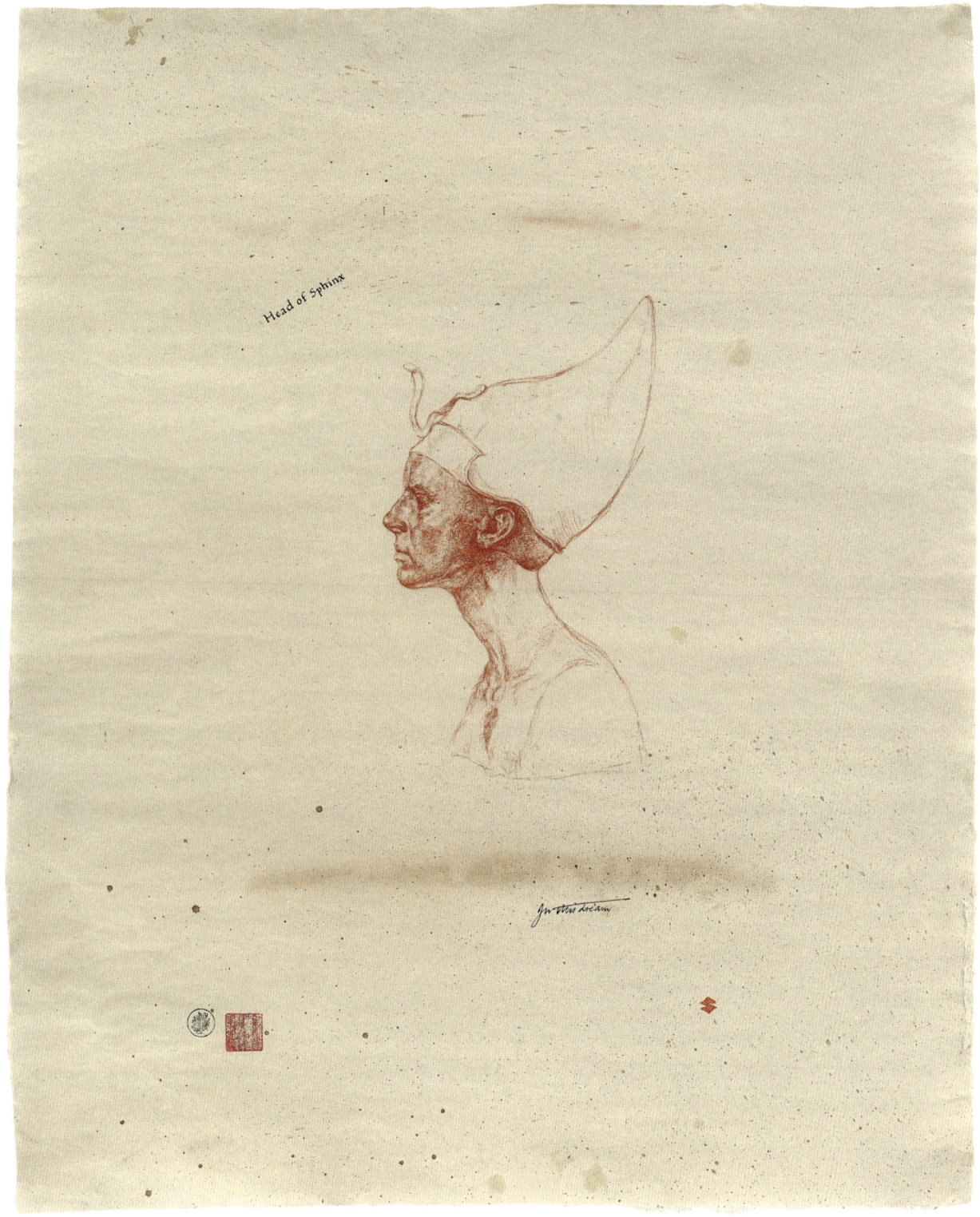

Head of Sphinx

Sphinx Head, 2015 | Bleistift auf Papier | Pencil on paper | 64 × 53 cm

Head of Sphinx, 2012 | Silber und Farbe | Silver and paint | 64 × 30 × 37 cm

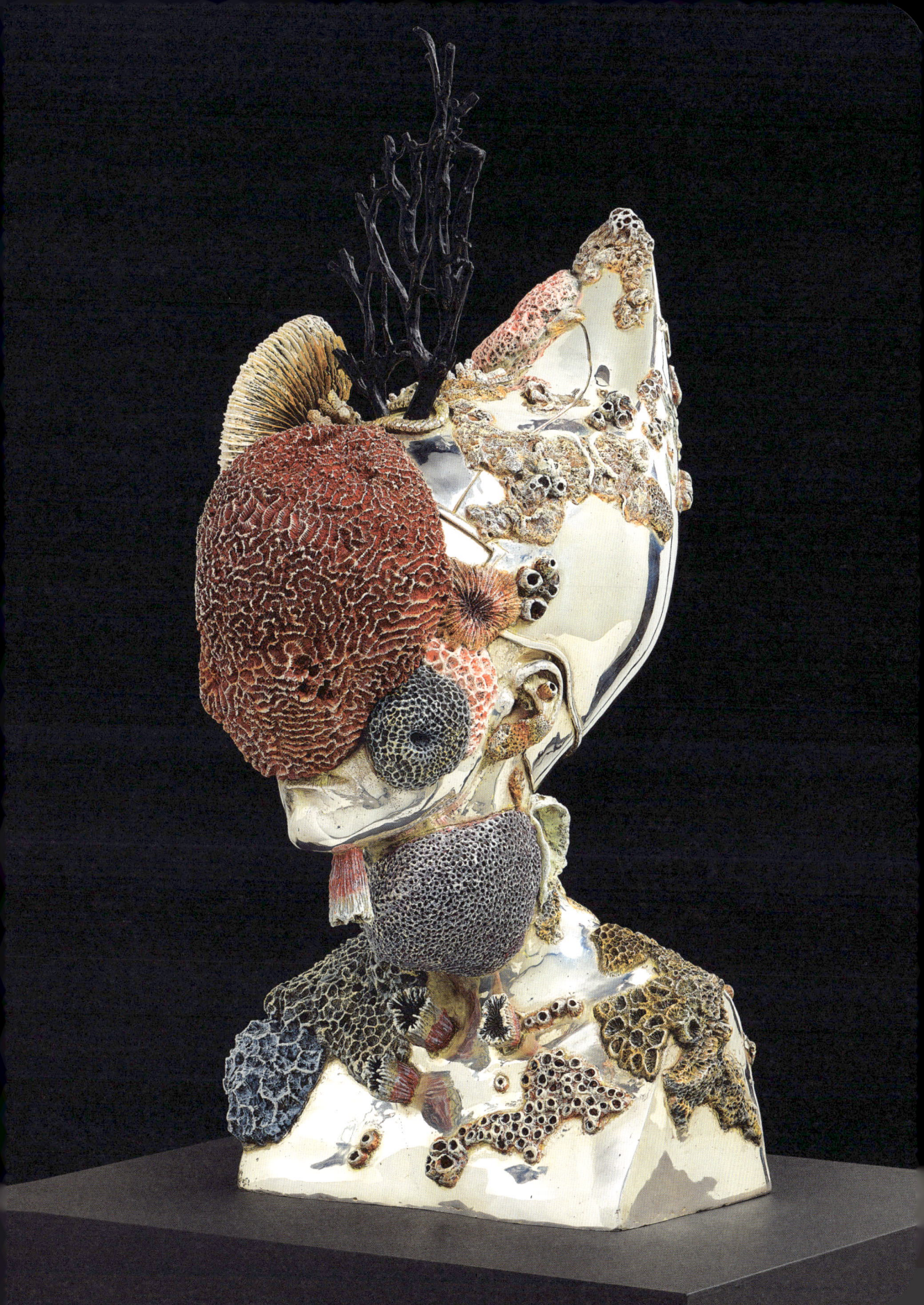

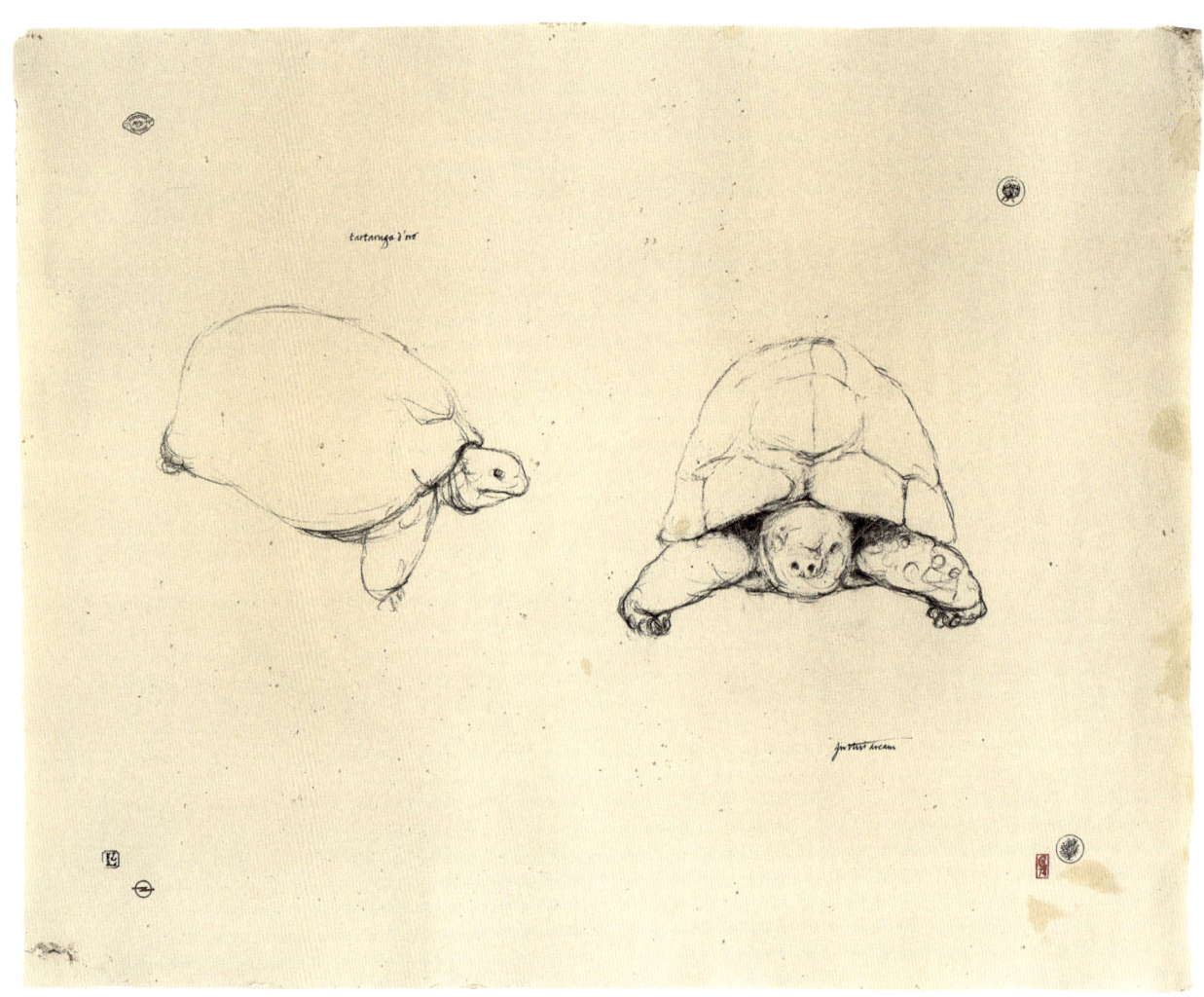

tartaruga d'oro

Golden Tortoise, Two Views, 2015 | Kohle auf Papier | Charcoal on paper | 51 × 63 cm

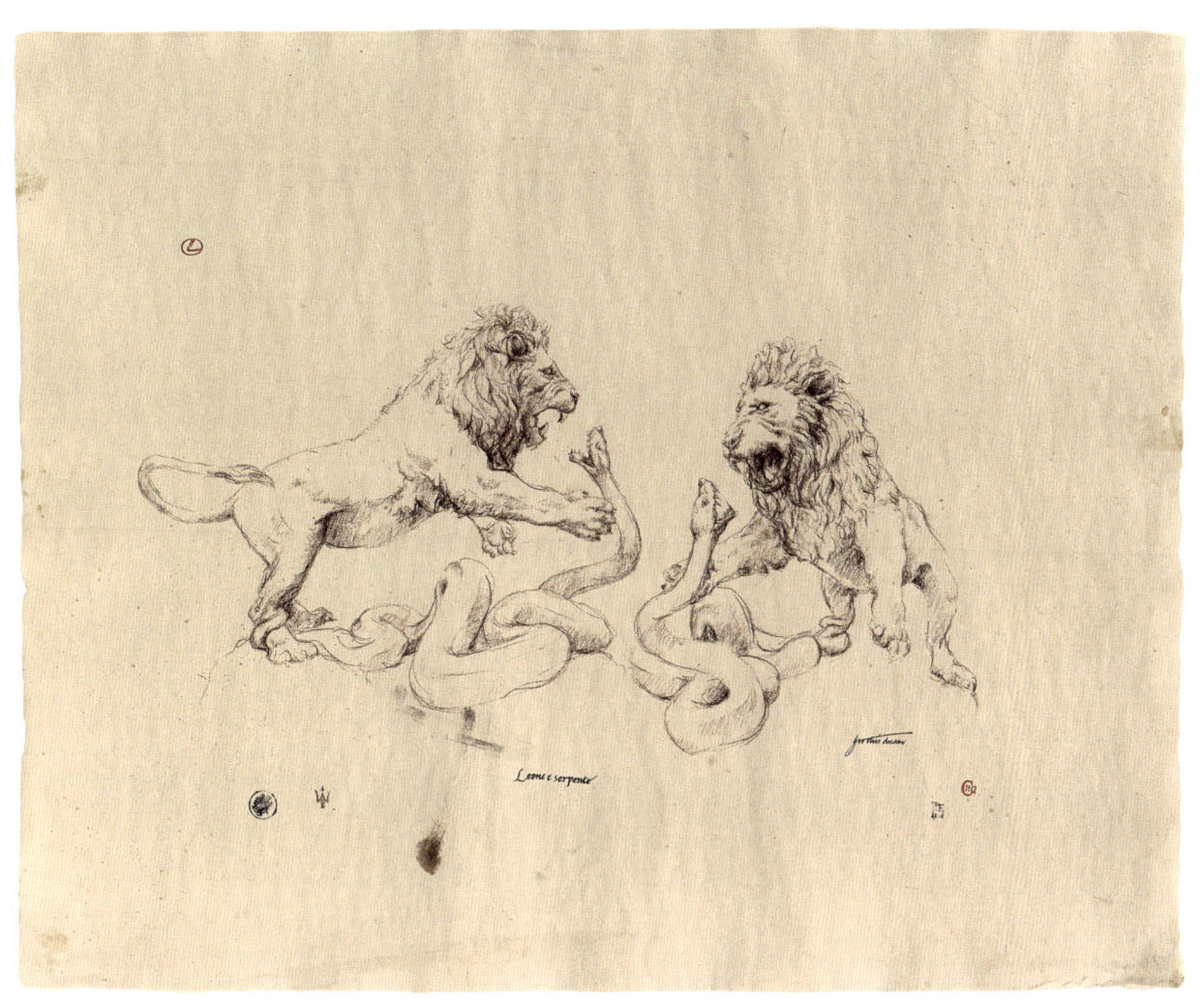

Leone e serpente

Leone e serpente (argento), 2016 | Bleistift auf Papier | Pencil on paper | 50 × 62 cm

Mickey, 2016 | Bronze | 91 × 71 × 61 cm

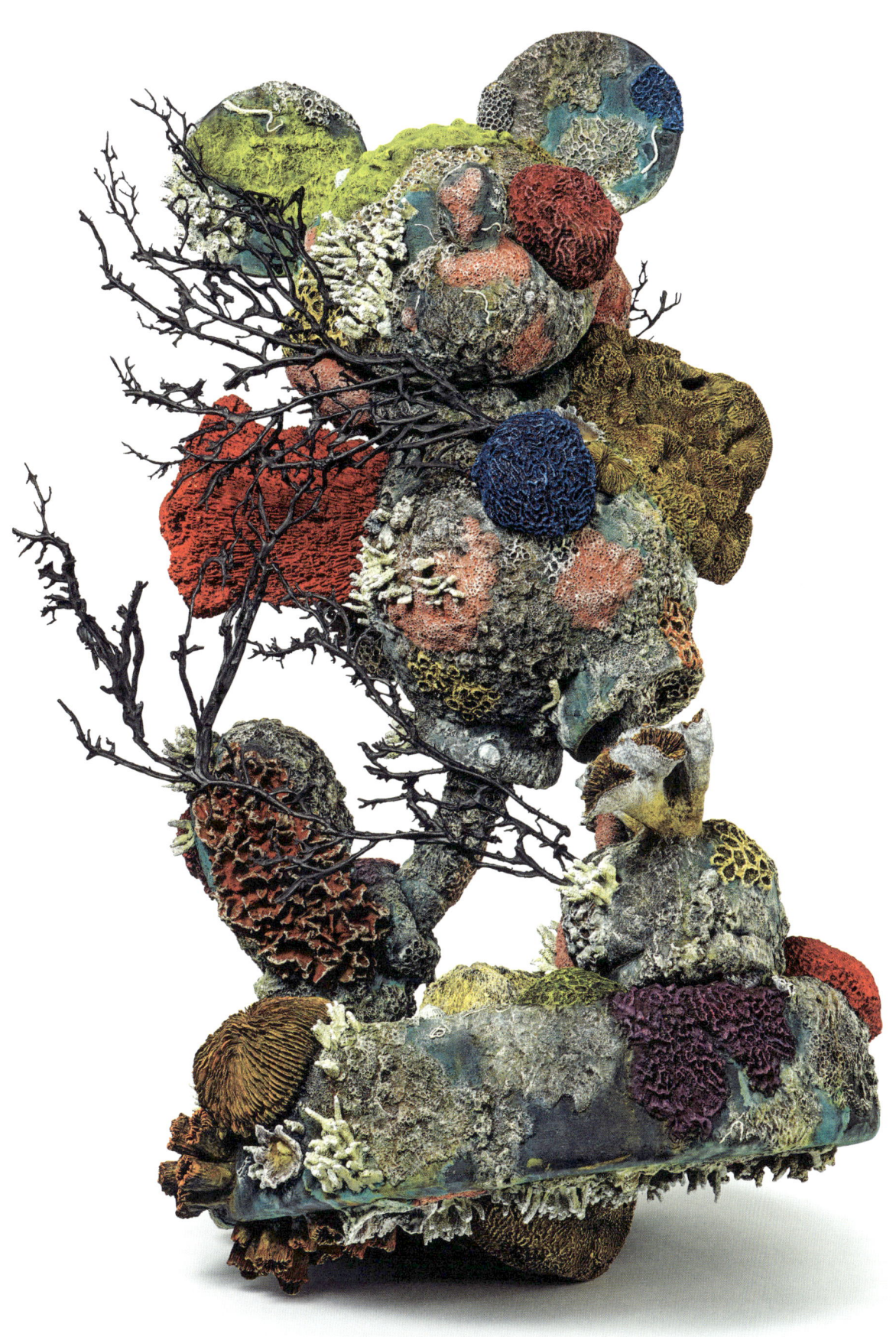

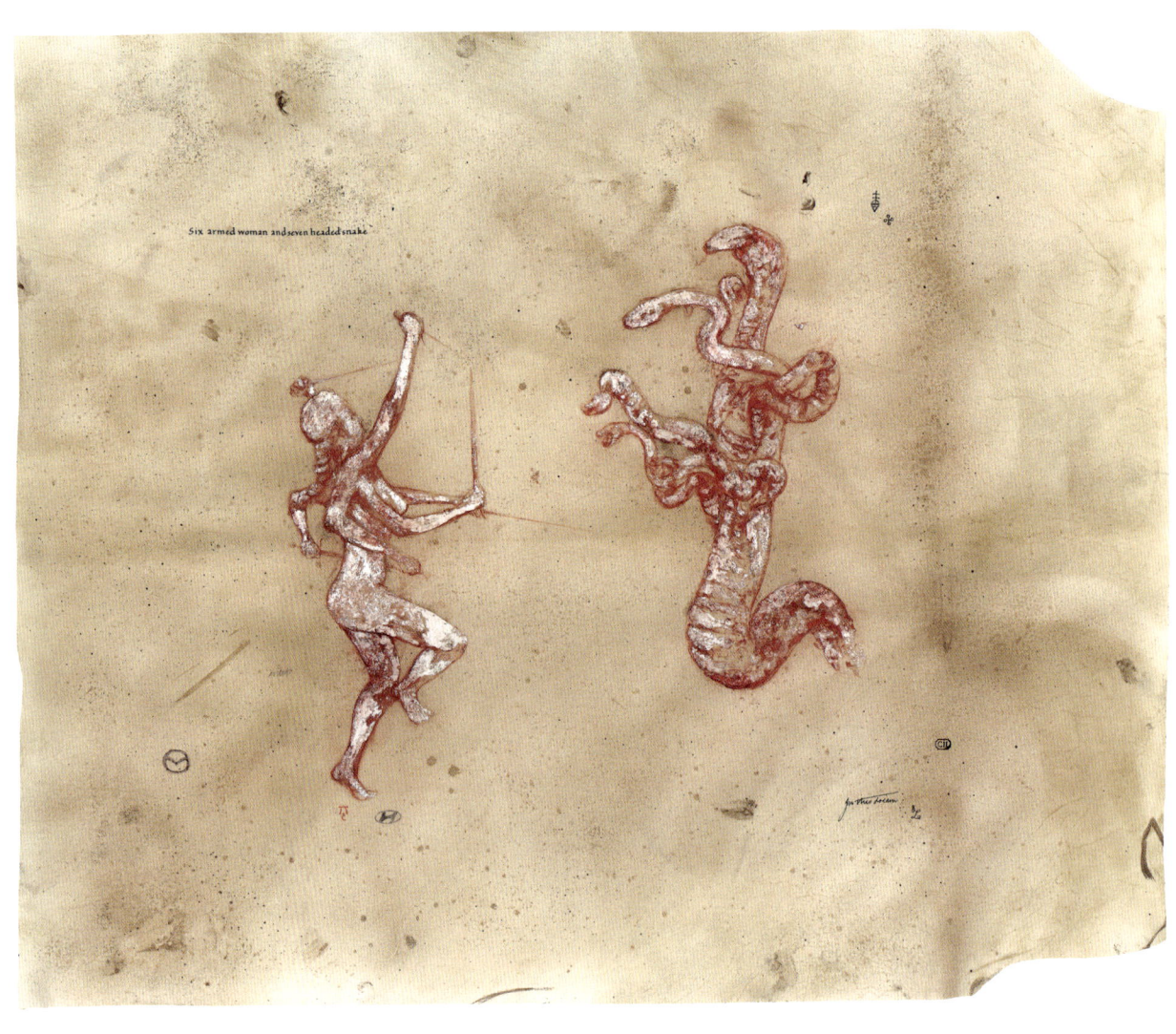

Six armed woman and seven headed snake

Kali Confronts Hydra, 2015 | Bleistift, Tinte und Blattsilber auf
Pergament | Pencil, ink, and silver leaf on vellum | 59 × 72 cm

Cerberus the Three-Headed Dog, 2014 | Bleistift auf Pergament | Pencil on vellum | 72 × 58 cm

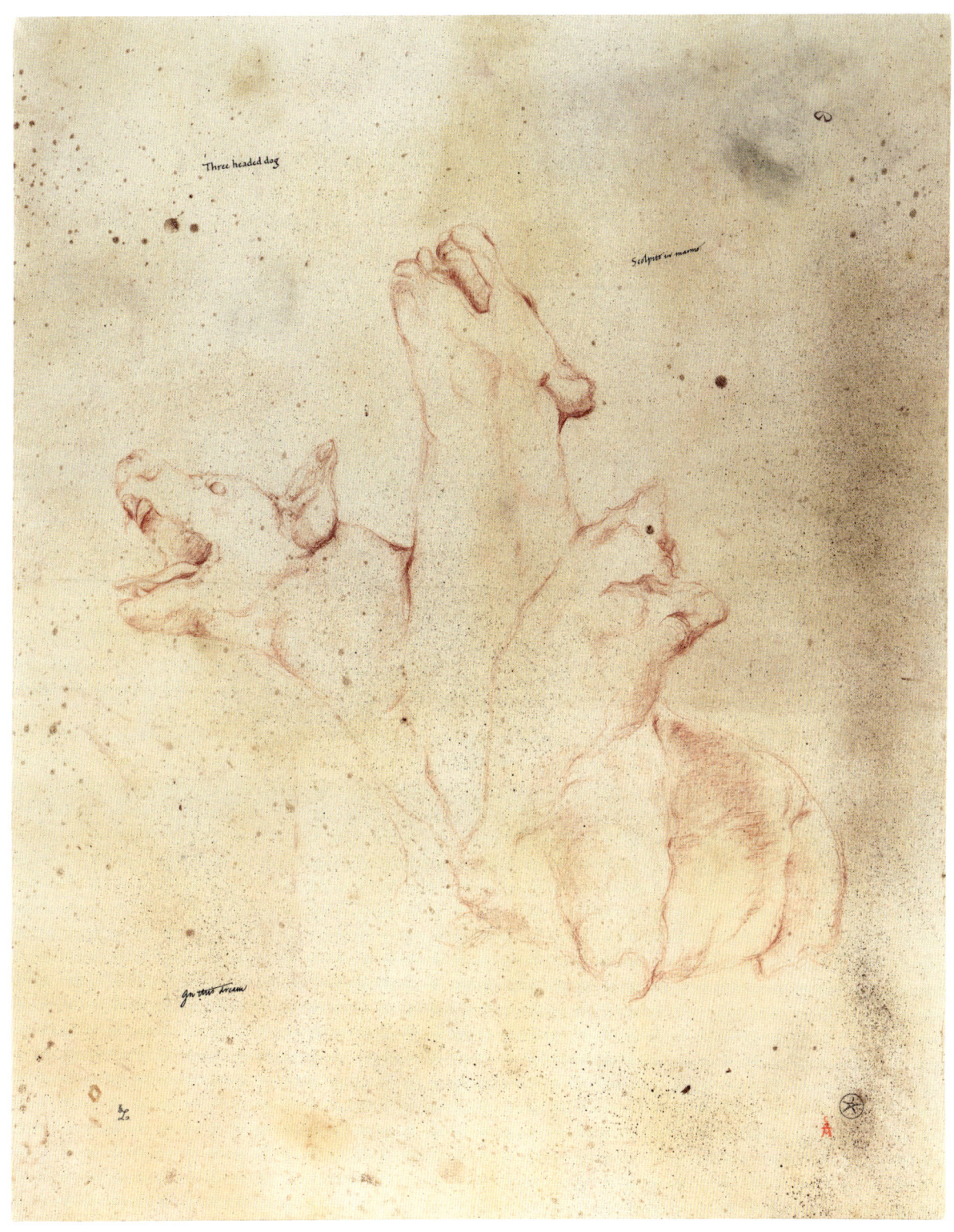

Three headed dog

Sculpes in marmo

gn tut trum

FOLGENDE SEITEN ¦ FOLLOWING PAGES: *Cerberus (Temple Ornament) on the Seabed,* 2015 ¦ Pulverbeschichtetes
Aluminium, bedruckter Polyester und Acryl-Leuchtkasten ¦ Powder-coated aluminium, printed polyester,
and acrylic lightbox ¦ 122 × 183 × 10 cm

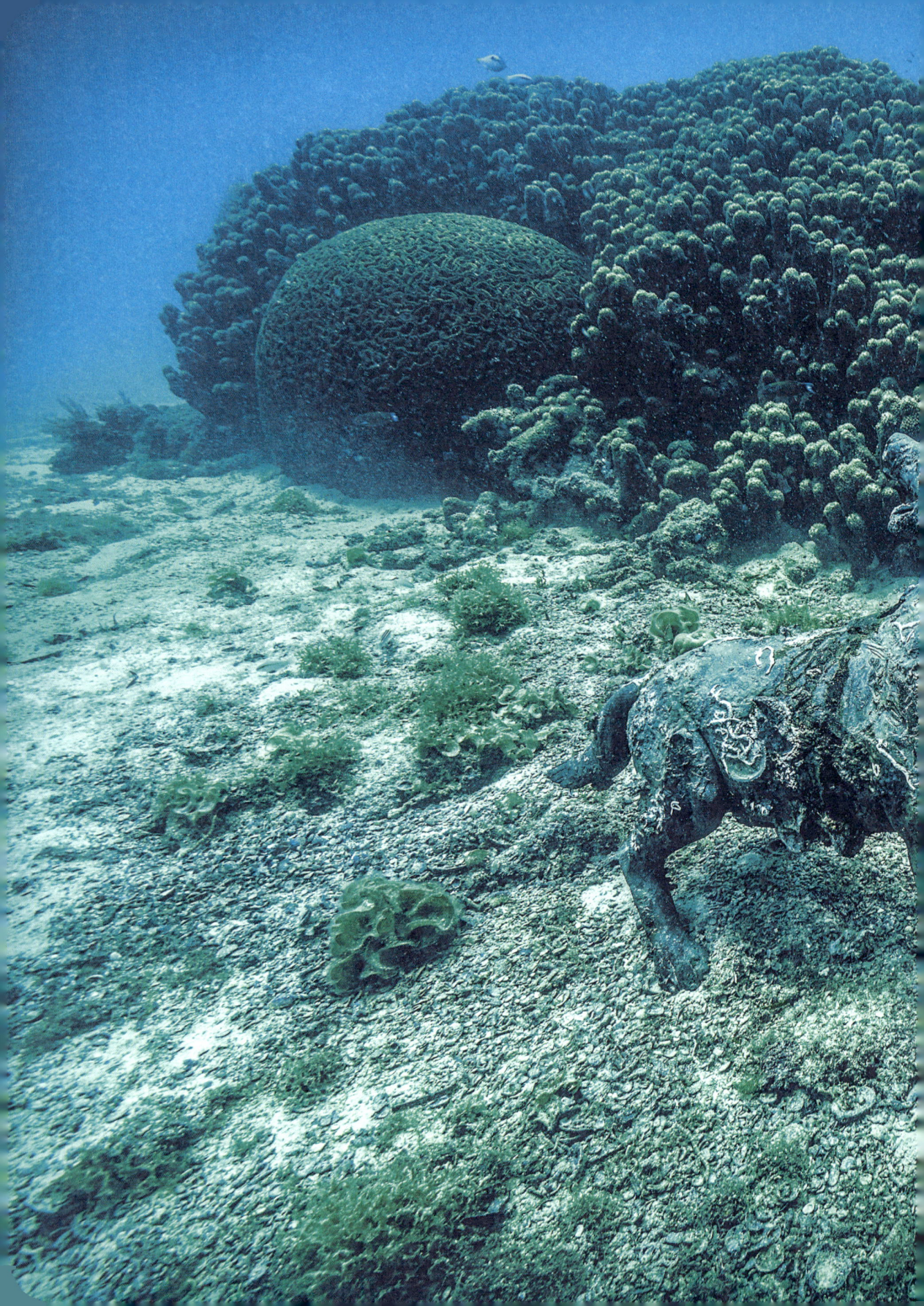

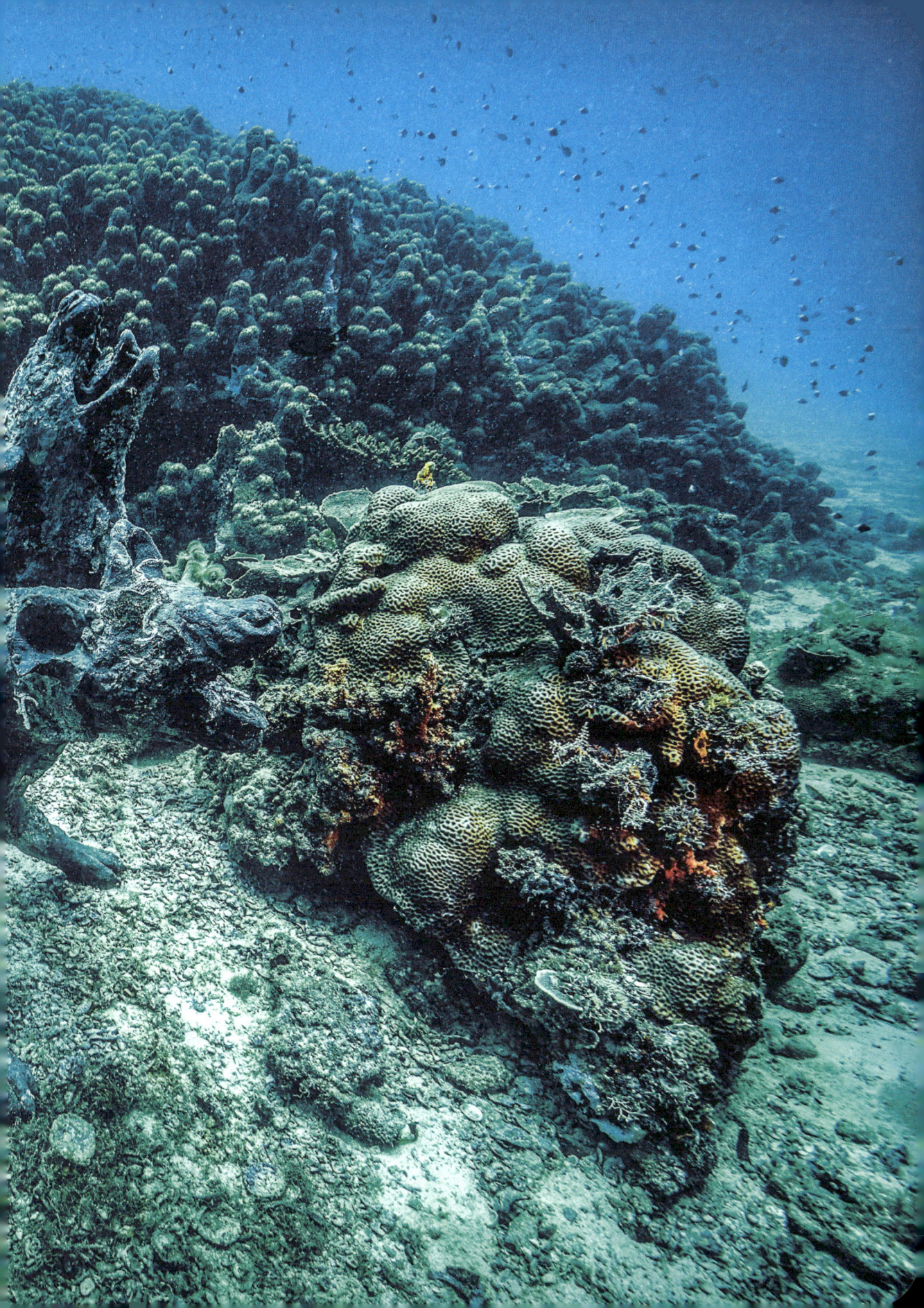

Notizen

Notizen

Notizen

Dank | Acknowledgements

Wir danken allen, die uns bei dieser Ausstellung unterstützt haben | We would like to thank everyone who supported this exhibition:

dem Künstler und allen bei Science | the artist and everybody at Science
Duerckheim Collection
Joe Hage
Marcus Harvey
Lonian Gallery LLC
Collection of Lisa and Steven Tananbaum sowie jenen Privatsammlerinnen und -sammlern, die ungenannt bleiben möchten | as well as those private collectors who wish to remain anonymous.

Leihgeber | Lenders

Duerckheim Collection: S. | pp. 23, 74, 79, 84, 90, 96, 98
Marcus Harvey: S. | p. 57
Lonian Gallery LLC: S. | p. 93
Private Collection, NY: S. | p. 99
Private Collection, UK: S. | p. 55
Collection of Lisa and Steven Tananbaum: S. | pp. 49, 72
Alle übrigen Werke | all other works:
Courtesy of the Artist und einiger privater Leihgeberinnen und Leihgeber | and several private lenders

Zitatnachweis | Quotation credits

S. | p. 20
Damien Hirst, Hirst-isms, hg. von | ed. by Larry Warsh, Princeton/Oxford 2022, S. | p. 53.

S. | p. 30
Damien Hirst, Hirst-isms, hg. von | ed. by Larry Warsh, Princeton/Oxford 2022, S. | p. 59.

S. | p. 44
Damien Hirst, von | by Adrian Dannatt, in: Flash Art, 02.12.2016, https://flash---art.com/article/damien-hirst-3/ [abgerufen am | accessed on 03.03.2025].

S. | p. 56
Damien Hirst, Hirst-isms, hg. von | ed. by Larry Warsh, Princeton/Oxford 2022, S. | p. 86.

S. | p. 100
Zit. nach | cited from Stefan Koldehoff, Der Künstler kauft sich selbst, in: Süddeutsche Zeitung, 16.12.2008, https://www.sueddeutsche.de/kultur/das-ende-des-kunstbooms-der-kuenstler-kauft-sich-selbst-1.773847 [abgerufen am | accessed on 03.03.2025].

S. | p. 108
Elena Cué, Interview with Damien Hirst, 08.11.2021, in: Alejandra de Argos, https://www.alejandradeargos.com/index.php/en/all-articles?start=7 [abgerufen am | accessed on 03.03.2025].

S. | p. 120
Damien Hirst, Making Beautiful Drawings (Ausst.-Kat.| exh. cat. Bruno Brunnet Fine Arts, Berlin), Berlin 1994, S. | p. 9.

S. | p. 144
Modern Painters, Sommer 1994, Bd. | vol. 7, Nr. | no. 2.

S. | p. 152
Damien Hirst, in: „Nüchtern ist alles besser", in: FOCUS Online, 19.11.2013, https://www.focus.de/kultur/kunst/vergaenglichkeit-fasziniert-skandalkuenstler-damien-hirst_id_1719903.html [abgerufen am | accessed on 03.03.2025].

S. | p. 162
Damien Hirst, Hirst-isms, hg. von | ed. by Larry Warsh, Princeton/Oxford 2022, S. | p. 10.

S. | p. 170
Damien Hirst, *Jesus of Nazareth King of the Jews*, 2004, Bleistift auf Papier | Pencil on paper

Jahrespartner der Albertina | Annual partners of the Albertina Museum

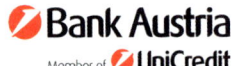 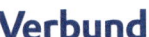

Partner der Albertina | Partner of the Albertina Museum

Diese Publikation erscheint anlässlich der Ausstellung | This catalogue is published in conjunction with the exhibition

Damien Hirst. DRAWINGS

Albertina modern, Wien | Vienna
7. Mai – 12. Oktober 2025 |
7 May – 12 October 2025

AUSSTELLUNG | EXHIBITION

Generaldirektor | Director General
Ralph Gleis

Kuratorin | Curator
Elsy Lahner

Assistenzkurator | Assistant Curator
Lorenz Ecker

Ausstellungsorganisation | Exhibition
Management
Barbara Buchbauer (Leitung | Head),
Christiane Steinbichler-Schranz

Restauratorische Betreuung | Restoration
and Conservation
Eva Glück (Leitung | Head), Hannah Backes,
Magdalena Duftner, Klaus Mohideen-Rubitzko,
Julia Wikarski

Grafische Gestaltung | Graphic Design
Mario Kiesenhofer (Leitung | Head),
Evelyn Leiter, Sarah Oos

KATALOG | CATALOGUE

Herausgegeben von | Edited by
Ralph Gleis und | and Elsy Lahner

Redaktion | Editing
Elsy Lahner, Lorenz Ecker, Paul Maercker

Produktionsleitung | Head of Production
Sandra Maria Rust

Projektmanagement | Project management
Hirmer
Karen Angne, Gunnar Musan

Lektorat Deutsch | German Copyediting
Iris Seemann, Essen

Lektorat Englisch | English Copyediting
James Copeland, Berlin

Übersetzungen | Translations
Gérard Goodrow, Köln | Cologne (Deutsch–
Englisch | German–English)
Nikolaus G. Schneider, Berlin (Englisch–
Deutsch | English–German)

Grafische Gestaltung | Graphic Design
Klaus E. Göltz, Halle a. d. Saale

Umschlaggestaltung | Cover Design
Unter Verwendung eines Entwurfs und der
Handschrift von Damien Hirst | Using a design
by and the original handwriting of Damien Hirst

Produktion | Production
Akademischer Verlagsservice Gunnar Musan

Lithografie | Prepress
Reproline mediateam, Unterföhring

Papier | Paper
Munken Lynx 120 g/m²

Schrift | Typeface
Officina

Druck und Bindung | Printing and Binding
Westermann Druck Zwickau GmbH

Printed in Germany

Dieser Katalog konnte realisiert werden mit
großzügiger Unterstützung von | This
catalogue was made possible with the
generous support of

Bibliografische Information der Deutschen
Nationalbibliothek: Die Deutsche
Nationalbibliothek verzeichnet diese
Publikation in der Deutschen Nationalbibliografie; detaillierte bibliografische Daten
sind im Internet über https://www.dnb.de
abrufbar.
Bibliographic information published by the
Deutsche Nationalbibliothek: The Deutsche
Nationalbibliothek lists this publication in
the Deutsche Nationalbibliografie; detailed
bibliographic data is available on the internet
at https://www.dnb.de.

© 2025 Albertina Museum, Wien, Hirmer
Verlag GmbH, München, und die Autor:innen |
The Albertina Museum, Vienna; Hirmer Verlag
GmbH, Munich, and the authors
© Damien Hirst and Science Ltd. All rights
reserved, DACS/Bildrecht 2025.

ISBN 978-3-7774-4612-7
(Buchhandelsausgabe | Trade edition)
ISBN 978-3-7774-4614-1
(Museumsausgabe | Museum edition)

HIRMER VERLAG
Geschäftsführerin | Managing Director
Kerstin Ludolph
Bayerstraße 57–59
D-80335 München | Munich
www.hirmerverlag.de
www.hirmerpublishers.com
www.hirmerpublishers.co.uk

www.albertina.at

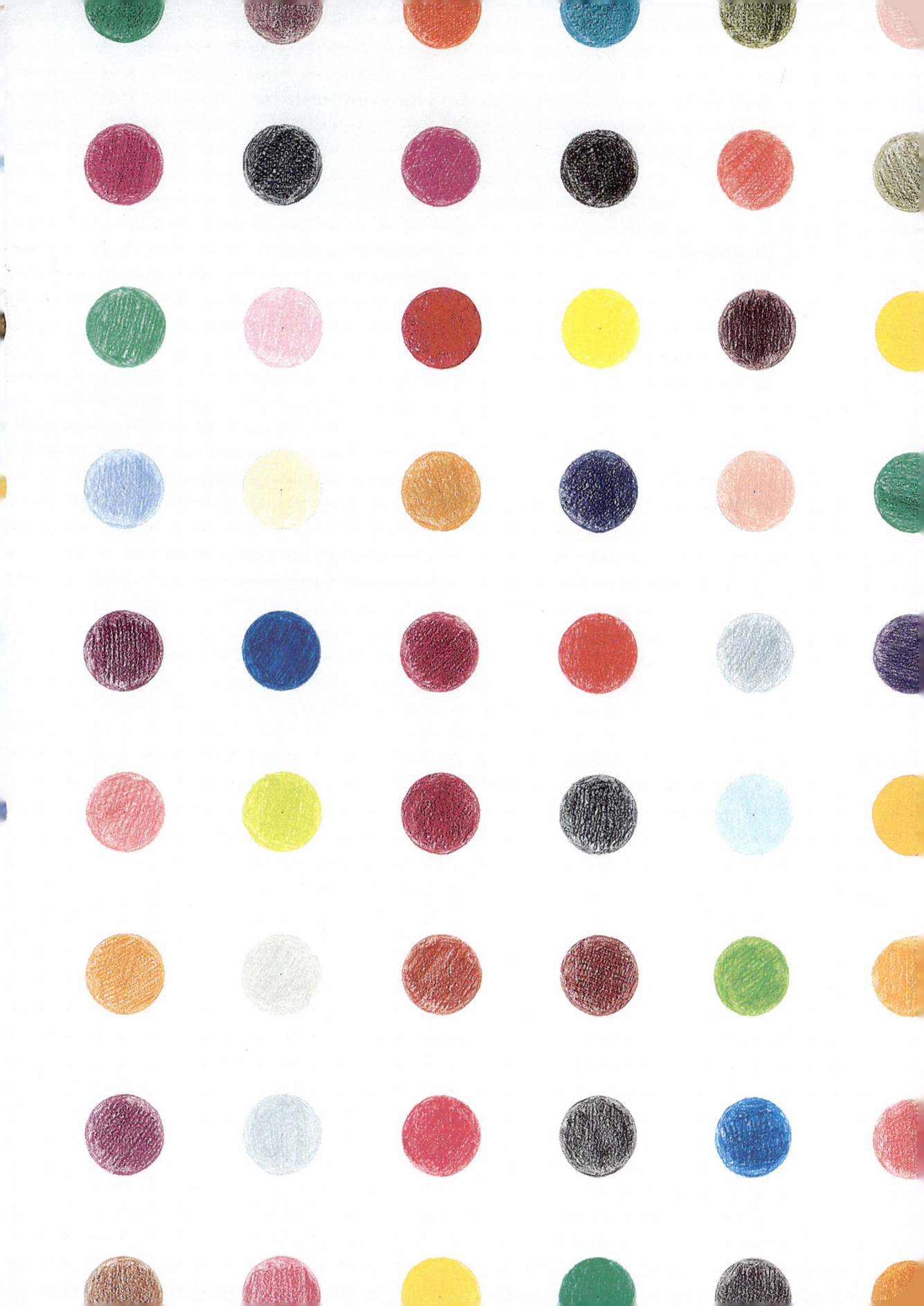

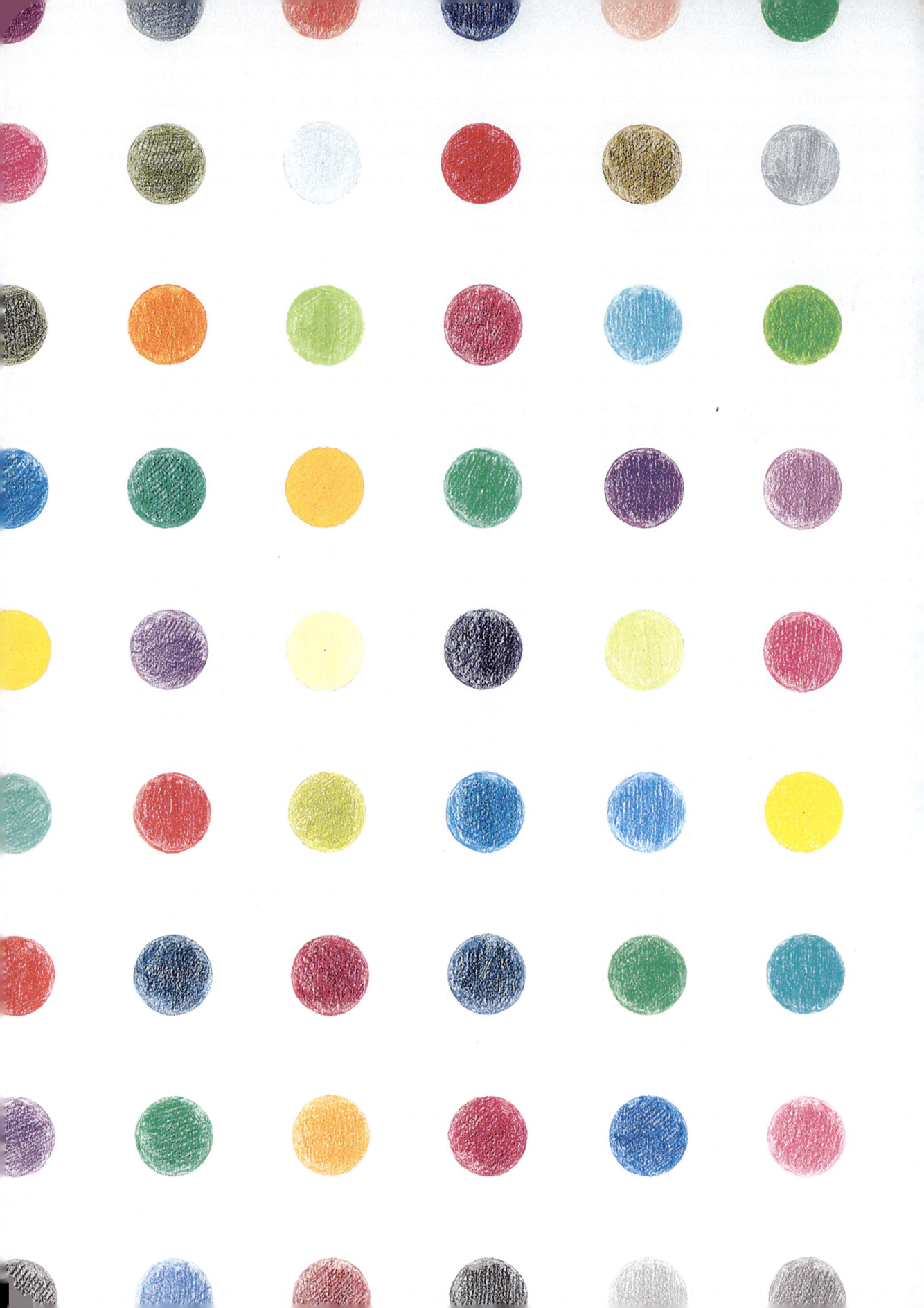